# EUROPE & CHINA

# EUROPE & CHINA

*A Survey of their Relations*
*from the earliest times to 1800*

BY

## G. F. HUDSON, M.A.

FELLOW OF ALL SOULS COLLEGE, OXFORD

WITH MAPS

BEACON PRESS   BOSTON

TO

STANLEY CASSON

# CONTENTS

# LIST OF MAPS

# INTRODUCTION

'OF our quality' (*di nostra qualità*) is the phrase used to describe the Chinese by Andrew Corsalis writing to the Duke Lorenzo de' Medici in the year 1515. The more superb Chinese repaid the compliment by a current proverb that they themselves alone possessed two eyes, that the Franks (i.e. Europeans) were one-eyed, and that all other inhabitants of the Earth were blind.

These two nations, Chinese and Europeans, had culturally grown up and come of age in geographical separation from each other, dwelling at opposite ends of the Old World, the one by the shores of the Pacific and the other by the Mediterranean and Atlantic. In the beginning neither had known of the other's existence; then came mutual perception through rumour and the passage of commodities in indirect commerce, then occasional communication by travel, and at last after the Portuguese capture of Malacca in 1511 direct intercourse and the contact of armed forces.

It may seem a misuse of language to speak of Europeans as a nation and to treat of relations between China and Europe in the singular, seeing that China to-day, whatever its divisions, ranks as a political and linguistic unit, whereas Europe is split up among a number of sovereign national states which it is a formidable task even to count. Yet a tide of events which hope would say is now ebbing has not rendered altogether ridiculous the title of a 'good European.' From history there remains a unity that is European and distinguished from all that is not European. It is also called Western, but with less force, for it is the geographical configuration of the continents which has in the long run determined the diffusion of cultures, while there is no particular significance in a quarter of the compass, nor has the adjective ' oriental ' ever been quite appropriate to the Moors living in the longitude of Killarney.

There is a hierarchy and ranking of nationalities in accordance with degrees of community or separateness in cultural inheritance. There is the supreme nationality which is mankind. Within this greatest whole are the few great unities formed by continuous dominant traditions of original civilization, and within these again are the many lesser groups, determined mainly by present spoken language, which are the only ' nations ' known in ordinary speech.

Europe and China are nations of the first division of mankind ; they are great continuities of historical development which may embrace many distinct languages and political units. Civilized Europe was one country under the Roman empire, while China has been divided between separate states through a great part of its history ; China no less than Europe has had its diversities of spoken language, and the unity bestowed by its common learned language has hardly been greater than that afforded by Latin in mediaeval Europe. The real unity in each case has been one of cultural tradition. European are all peoples and states deriving their dominant cultural form directly or indirectly from Hellenism, Chinese those deriving it from the ' Chinese ' empire of the Hoang-ho basin in the first millennium B.C. Each of these root cultures was entirely independent of the other ; they had no common heritage of literature or of institutions and ideas above the level of barbarism.

Only two other cultural traditions can compare with the Hellenic and the Chinese in degree of civilization, in independence and in strength and duration of influence. One is the West Asian, going back to Sumerian and Egyptian origins, and carried on and developed mainly by the Semitic and Iranian peoples ; the other is the Hindu with

Sanskrit as its classical language. These four, the Hellenic, the West Asian, the Hindu and the Chinese, are the four roots of civilization ; all else, with inconsiderable exceptions, is either barbaric [1] or has grown from one of the four roots. The number four appears to be irreducible. These great primary cultures have overlapped and deeply influenced one another, and in recent times the first has swallowed up the other three, yet no one of the four can be regarded as merely an offshoot of another. [2]

The Hellenic culture grew up in the peninsulas and islands of the narrow seas between Europe and Asia. To the east and south, in Asia and Africa, dwelt peoples too civilized in their own way, with cultures too fixed and stable and tenacious to yield easy converts to Hellenism. But to the west and north, in Europe, were races sufficiently advanced to make clever pupils yet sufficiently primitive to be culturally pliable. Thus it was that Europe and not Asia or Africa came to be the domain of Hellenism, in spite of the fact that its armed expansion under Alexander of Macedon was directed towards the east. In Western Asia and in India the Greeks profoundly influenced the already existing cultures but could not supersede them, and with the passage of time the native traditions recovered their ascendency. In Europe it was otherwise. Greek cities dotted the European coastline from the Rhone to the Crimea, and were the sole examples of civilization to the dwellers inland. Italy was permeated with Greek influences to an extent which has only recently been appreciated by historians. The culture of Rome from first to last was radically conditioned by contact with Hellenism, and the

[1] The minimum of civilization I take to be (1) settled life with intensive agriculture and fair-sized towns, and (2) writing.

[2] It may be claimed with considerable support from archaeology that Greek, Indian and Chinese cultures are all derived from the more ancient West Asian. Yet there was no literary inheritance, as far as can be ascertained, and it is the written word that is the decisive factor in conscious cultural tradition. The debt of the Greeks to Egypt and Babylonia, whatever it may have been, was thus different in kind from the debt of France or England to Greece and Rome.

Roman empire propagated its Helleno-Latin civilization through Europe to the Rhine and the Danube. Then, after Christianity had been adopted as the religion of the empire, it advanced from Rome and from Constantinople to the conquest of the further lands of Europe, to Germany and Scandinavia, to Poland and Russia. By A.D. 1000 all Europe except the wild Scythian steppe had received what may be called a ' Romanistic ' culture, and was rightful heir to the full classical legacy of Miletus, Athens and Rome.

Europeans were not indeed at that time actually in possession of any great part of their heritage. It was not that an older native civilization had revolted and cast out an alien ascendency as in Persia, Syria or Egypt ; in Europe there had been no original civilization except the Greek. But the Christian Roman civilization which Europe had received was so strongly flavoured with the spirit of West Asian culture that the tradition of Hellenism had been in many ways almost obliterated. Christianity had brought with it from Asia an order of ideas and a priestly regulation of society alien to Hellenism, had brought also a new art developed mainly from Syrian and Mesopotamian origins. For at least the five centuries 600–1100 the classical tradition of Europe was in eclipse, and a critic has not altogether without justice described the Middle Age as the triumph of the Orient over Rome. Nevertheless, Europe remained a world apart from Asia ; it was, as it were, reserved for Hellenism whenever the latter should reassert itself. It did reassert itself in Latin Christendom in the late Middle Age, and with the Renaissance restored the classical heritage to Western Europe. Subsequently it advanced to reclaim the lands of Eastern Orthodoxy which had not only continued in Byzantine mediaevalism, but had also received fresh infusions of the West Asian tradition through Tatar and Turkish conquests. Russia above all had seemed lost to Europe ; Moscow in the seventeenth century had more in common with Samarkand than with Paris, and the reforms carried out by Peter the Great were in a sense the first example of 'westernization,' anticipating later revolutions in Japan and China, Turkey and Persia. Nevertheless, even here there was really more of restoration than of transfer to an alien tradition ; Russia belonged historically to the Romanistic company of nations, and long before Peter clipped the beards of his nobles Moscow had claimed to be the 'Third Rome.'

The tale of Chinese culture in its extensions and vicissitudes of contest with influences from without shows many points of similarity to that of the Helleno-Roman. The congeries of petty states under the nominal suzerainty of the Chou dynasty which composed China in the time of Confucius (551–479 B.C.) only occupied a fraction of present-day China. It was only in the last two and a quarter centuries B.C. that the Chinese advanced south of the Yangtse to the South China Sea conquering and absorbing the old non-Chinese kingdom of Yüeh and various half-savage tribes. Korea was overrun during the same period, while to the north-west Chinese power was extended ihto Mongolia and Kashgaria and even beyond the Pamir watershed into Ferghana. The great Ts'in and Han dynasties (246 B.C.–A.D. 220) under which these advances were made were contemporary with Rome from the First Punic War to the Emperor Elagabalus. In the late Han period and in the time of disunion which followed, while Christianity was advancing to supremacy in the Roman empire, China was invaded by Buddhism, a religion of Indian origin propagated by way of Kashgaria. Buddhism bore much the same relation to the prevailing mental outlook of China as did Christianity to that of Rome, but whereas Christianity became in time the official religion of the Roman empire and of Europe, Buddhism, in spite of great gains in all classes of society, never succeeded in overthrowing the Confucian 'paganism,' and had to be content to be merely one of 'the three doctrines,' i.e. Confucianism, Buddhism and Taoism. As a carrier of Chinese civilization in a modified shape, however, Buddhism performed a function similar to that carried out by the Church in contemporary Europe. Just as Germany and Scandinavia, never subdued by the Roman legions, were won by Roman Christianity, so insular Japan, secure from Chinese arms, was conquered by Chinese Buddhism.[1] As finally established, the domain of Chinese culture included China itself, Korea, Japan and Annam. Burma, Siam, Tibet and Mongolia also received Chinese influence, but drew their main cultural inspiration through Buddhism directly from India.

When we begin to compare in character the Chinese and Hellenic cultures we come at once to the fundamental difference which separates the European from all that is not European. The China of Confucius was a swarm of feudal principalities ; contemporary Hellas was a world of city-states.

All the Asiatic cultures were based upon a land-revenue economy. The surplus value of agriculture in fertile plains and river valleys went as taxes and rents to support an upper class of state officials and private or semi-private landlords. There was often an extensive commerce, but it was subsidiary to agriculture and its local marketing. The form of government was normally monarchy with variations from feudal to absolute ; occasionally in the earlier stages of development it was a republic of landed gentry.[2] The great peasant masses which were the base of the social pyramid gave to culture a massive stability and permanence in spite of all wars and rebellions that might shake it, but they rendered it also immobile and

[1] Although Japan is part of China in the wider sense, I have for convenience excluded European-Japanese relations from the scope of this book.

[2] Such were the Indian republics of the time of the Buddha, the Sākiyas, Bulis, Kālāmas, Mallas, etc. All these disappeared later. Of the same type in reality were the inland Greek city-states of the Peloponnese and Thessaly ; the fact that they were formally cities must be attributed to the prestige given to the *polis* by the successful maritime states. Sparta and the Thessalian ' cities ' were made by groups of landed proprietors with peasant serfs, not by genuine urban agglomerations.

tenaciously conservative. The whole organization of such a society tended towards fixity and routine ; the value of land once brought under cultivation changed little, and revenue could only be increased by the acquisition of new territories.

The country-state of land-revenue economy represents the normal line of human progress after the invention of agriculture, and everywhere it shows similar features ; it is true to type in China as in Egypt, and in the isolation of America we find it again in the culture of the Peruvian Incas. But the republican city-state is an exceptional variation in history. It was brought to birth in the Aegean, and it does not seem to have been independently originated anywhere else.[1] It arose from a unique set of conditions, the chief of which appear to have been : a region of small islands, peninsulas and mountain valleys opening on the sea, an excellent climate, a juxtaposition of a vigorous maritime barbarism and centres of ancient civilization, great commercial opportunities, and an advance of the art of fortification far beyond that of siegecraft.

The typical Hellenic city-state was a walled town on the seashore with a minute land territory around it, but communicating to great distances by sea. On the amazing smallness of these states as contrasted with the range of their activities Professor F. E. Adcock writes [2] : ' Compared with the thousand square miles of Attica, the territory controlled by any other Greek city-state was very small. . . . Corinth [governs] 350, the eight cities of Euboea on an average 180, even islands with a single city like Chios little more than 300, and this island is the greatest. In Ceos, which is less than half the size of the county of Rutland,

---

[1] A stray exception is the Japanese city of Sakai in the sixteenth century ; its constitution was compared to that of Venice by an early European observer. But the period of Sakai's independence was brief. The Phoenician cities only became republics at dates later than the rise of the Greek city-states, and Greek influence in their case cannot be ruled out, though as city-kingdoms devoted to commerce they had something of the city-state character from the beginning.

[2] *Cambridge Ancient History*, Vol. III, Ch. XXVI p. 698.

there were in the sixth century four independent cities and three independent currencies.'

In these free cities of Hellas the commercial-industrial interest, the *bourgeoisie*, first attained to a share in political power and developed social institutions and ideas suitable to itself. It was not that the commerce carried on by the city-states was greater in volume than that done by Asiatic merchants, but that the social and political importance of the merchant and artisan was so much greater in the city republic than it could ever be in the most prosperous of the Asiatic empires. Until quite recently economic conditions have always been such that over a large area there must be a preponderance of the rural over the urban, of agriculture over commerce and industry, and therefore it was only in the independent town that the townsman could come into his own. In the land-revenue country-states the trader, though he might acquire great wealth, was politically impotent and socially inferior ; laws were designed not so much for his benefit as to humiliate him and restrict his activity. The dominant classes, courtiers and bureaucrats, military nobles and priests, everywhere regarded him with a mixture of contempt and jealousy ; the most he could do was to obtain monopolies by well-placed bribes, and such monopolies only led to economic stagnation. Mentally he accepted in essentials the outlook and values of his superiors. But in the city-state commerce had free rein ; in public life the mercantile reached at least to an equality with the landed interest, and there was no bureaucracy. And the shifting of the centre of gravity in social formation reacted upon thought. The Hellenic city-state produced as its proper ideology an individualist jurisprudence suited to capitalist enterprise and the intellectual mood which brought forth Hellenic mathematical and natural science.[1]

[1] According to M. Meynial (Chap. VI, iii, in *The Legacy of the Middle Ages*, ed. C. G. Crump and E. F. Jacob) ' the formulation of Roman Law was the greatest triumph of the ancient world.' But in the full perspective of human history the claim of Greek mathematics to that eminence is perhaps a stronger one.

It may perhaps be objected that the city-state, brilliant though its achievements were, has been only a passing phase of European history, that even greater advances in civilization have been made by European nations which never were city-states, and that therefore the free city is to be regarded rather as an incidental manifestation of the European genius than as the foundation of all European culture. It may be pointed out that the Greek city-states were swallowed up in the Macedonian and Roman empires, and that European progress from the sixteenth century onwards has been the work not of cities but of national states. Yet on investigation it turns out that it is precisely the city-state which has given their specifically European quality to these larger societies.

Rome was herself a city-state and her empire was based on a league of cities ; these, after they had been stripped of sovereignty, retained domestic autonomy as *municipia*. It was only when with the economic crisis of the third century A.D. the central government took over the administration of the *municipia*, and municipal office became a burden instead of a privilege, that the distinctive urban life of the Helleno-Roman world was destroyed, and it was then that European culture began to undergo its Byzantine transformation, ' the triumph of the Orient over Rome.' In modern times, on the other hand, the transition from the age of the free cities to that of national states avoided in its main line of evolution the tendencies which led the Roman empire away from commercialism to predominant land-revenue economy and bureaucratic absolutism. Seventeenth-century Europe achieved, though only in certain countries, what the Roman empire had not ; it effected a real synthesis of large-scale territorial sovereignty and *bourgeois* political power. The synthesis was attained by means of two instruments : parliamentary representation and the joint-stock chartered company.

Parliamentarism was not in itself favourable to the mercantile interest ; where, as in Poland and Hungary, the diets were controlled by the feudal nobility, it was more adverse than royal absolutism to *bourgeois* power. But in England the landed gentry other than peers joined with the burgesses to form the Commons instead of combining with the magnates to form an order of nobility, and this rendered the free city superfluous, inasmuch as the mercantile interest could express itself through effective national representation and did not have to isolate itself in order to survive. Thus while the city-states and communes were being overwhelmed by the march of events in France, Germany and Italy, the *bourgeois* in England steadily increased his power.

The joint-stock chartered company gave an even greater degree of autonomy to the mercantile interest. It was indeed until the rise of the new industrialism in the nineteenth century the chief residuary legatee of the city-state political inheritance. With their large-scale organization, their courts of directors and their financial system attracting investment by persons other than merchants, the great trading companies had almost the character of states, and could wage war on their own. Between 1610 and 1717 the Dutch East India Company annexed territories several times larger than Holland and paid an average annual dividend of just under 26 per cent. on its capital. The chartered companies set the pace in the struggle for world-trade in the seventeenth and eighteenth centuries. The English and Dutch, who had led the way in developing the new economic form, were the most successful. France, where the joint-stock companies were the creatures of the bureaucracy, fell behind in spite of her greater population and her military strength. In Spain Castilian officialdom had strangled the commercialism of the Portuguese and Andalusian ports, and the joint-stock principle could not emerge ; Spain was driven right out of the commercial arena. And where Spain was inadequate, no Asiatic power could hope to compete at all.

Before the end of our survey we shall see the East India Companies of the various European nations trying to force open the gates of China for the expansion of their trade.

They are genuine offspring of the earlier urban liberties of Europe,[1] and rightful heirs of the spirit of mercantilism which sent Genoese merchants to China in the early fourteenth century under the *Pax Tatarica*. But between the epoch of those Genoese and the arrival of the East India Companies the decisive move, the opening of the all-sea route round Africa to India and China, is made by the Portuguese, and this may seem at first sight to be incompatible with the importance we have assigned to the city-state as the dominant factor in European history. For the Portuguese adventurers represented neither a city-state nor a joint-stock company but a national state and a royal monopoly. Yet here also the inspiration of a city-state is found, for the Portuguese sea-power turns out to have been the creation of Genoa.

The revival of the city-state in mediaeval Europe begins with Venice and Amalfi in the ninth and tenth centuries.[2] Once grown strong the impulse gradually spreads by a sort of infection through the Latin world until at last it reaches the North Sea and the Baltic. The movement reaches its climax at the beginning of the fourteenth century, and at this time Genoa leads in range of commercial activity. The Venetians perhaps conducted a more lucrative commerce, but the Genoese traversed the Old World from end

[1] Professor G. N. Clark in *The Seventeenth Century* (p. 34) declares that 'it was in England that the joint-stock principle first definitely emerged, with the foundation of the Russian Company in 1553 and the first African Company in the same year.' Before 1553 the greatest organization of mercantile interests in Northern Europe had been the Hanseatic League. This was now in decay, and the early joint-stock companies in England were essentially efforts to attain by new methods a power and efficiency such as had formerly belonged to the Hansa. The Hansa was thus really the starting-point of the new movement.

[2] The mediaeval city-state may claim descent from the ancient through three channels : (1) the actual survivals of the old municipal life in Italy right through the Dark Age ; (2) the diocesan organization of the Church which was based on the *municipia* and tended to separate the towns from rural feudalism ; and (3) Roman public and private law which transmitted the republican-capitalist ideology of the mature city-state culture.

to end with a vigour that is almost incredible. From Tana, Trebizond and Lajazzo the Genoese merchants penetrated to India and China, from the Black Sea also they made their way into Russia, they crossed the Sahara to the Sudan [1] and they sailed round Spain to the ports of Flanders. By the last of these lines of their activity the Genoese established themselves in Lisbon, and King Diniz enlisted them in his service to provide Portugal with a navy and teach the Portuguese the arts of shipbuilding and navigation. Thus was forged the instrument with which Henry the Navigator and his successors found the way by sea to the Indies and drove the Arabs from the Indian Ocean.

The Portuguese learned well the lessons taught by Genoa ; they combined the Italian commercialism and new naval technique with a fervent crusading enthusiasm all their own, and they became in the fifteenth century the boldest and most skilful seamen in the world. Cadamosto, himself a Venetian, says that in his day the Portuguese caravels were the best sailing ships afloat. Admiral G. A. Ballard,[2] who writes as an expert, declares that Vasco da Gama's direct voyage to the Cape in 1497 ' has a strong claim to rank as the finest feat of pure navigation ever accomplished.' If it has a rival, it is surely the voyage of Magellan, who was likewise a Portuguese. By these expeditions and by that of the Genoese Columbus the seas of the world were conquered for Europe, and all coasts made accessible to European enterprise.

The naval technique by which so prodigious an expansion was brought about was a new thing in the fifteenth century. It was the product of two factors : commercialism and the invention of cannon. Without the driving power and incessant application of commercial enterprise guns did not by themselves make sea-power, as many episodes of history were to prove. But without the use of cannon the maritime city-states had never been led to develop sea-power as something quite different from land-power. Hitherto the

---

[1] See M. Ch. de la Roncière, *La découverte de l'Afrique au Moyen Age.*
[2] *Rulers of the Indian Ocean*, p. 29.

evolution of the ship and of naval tactics had been checked
by the fact that a sea-battle could nearly always be turned
into a land-battle by grappling and boarding ; this cancelled
all superiority of manœuvre and made the fighting qualities
of men at close quarters the deciding factor in naval warfare.
The Athenians in antiquity had acquired a naval superiority
by manœuvre and the use of the ram, but later the Romans,
a people unused to the sea, had more or less superseded
ramming tactics by the invention of a very effective grappling device (the *corvus*), and not even the use of great
catapults or of Greek fire restored the decision to manœuvre.
With the appearance of cannon, however, during the
fourteenth century all this was changed. It now became
possible to disable a ship at long range, and power of
manœuvre at once became all-important. Such power
depended partly on the build of the ship and partly on
seamanship. This gave a new impetus to shipbuilding,
and new types of vessel were evolved, especially of sailing
ship ; all improvements necessarily had reference to fighting
capacity, for every merchantman at that time had to be
also a warship. There was likewise a rapid advance in
seamanship and tactics, as sea-captains sought how to make
best use of their gunnery. With the new nautical science
the Portuguese were enabled not only to find the all-sea
route to the Indies but also to destroy the more numerous
Arab fleets that opposed them and to obtain undisputed
mastery of the Indian Ocean. The decisive battle off the
Malabar coast in 1502 was won by the same tactics which
the English later used against the Spanish Armada, by
keeping to windward and fighting at long range.

The completeness of the European ascendency on the
sea from the beginning of the sixteenth century onwards has
led many historians to an undue depreciation of the maritime achievements of non-European peoples and to an
assumption that superior seamanship is somehow innate
in persons inhabiting the littoral of Europe or perhaps in
the conformation of Nordic skulls. But the fact is that if
we go back to mediaeval and ancient times the superiority

is not evident. The Greeks were good sailors, yet the greatest voyage of antiquity, the circumnavigation of Africa, was the achievement of the Phoenicians.[1] The Vikings dared greatly on the sea, yet if we are to award the palm for long-distance, open-sea voyages before Columbus, we must give it rather to the intrepid mariners of the Pacific, the Polynesians. The Greeks of Egypt in the first two centuries A.D. sailed to India, and a few even reached Tongking, but the Arab and Indian [2] maritime enterprise of the same period was quite comparable to theirs. In the days of Islam the Arabs held for a while a naval supremacy in the Mediterranean, while on the other side of the Isthmus of Suez their range extended to China and Java in the east and to Madagascar in the south. The Chinese have traded to India by sea at several periods of their history, and in the early fifteenth century the Ming ' tribute-collecting ' fleets not only carried out a successful invasion of Ceylon, but even sailed as far as East Africa. The Japanese and Malays also produced bold seamen.

Altogether, Asia has no mean record to show in maritime achievement, and this makes it all the more remarkable that the Asiatic powers so easily yielded command of the sea to the Europeans. But the Asiatics, although they had developed a sea-going commerce of great dimensions in Indian and Pacific waters, could not contend with the newcomers for sea-power ; there was behind their enterprise no driving force of politically powerful commercialism, no persistent state support for overseas expansion, no active naval ambition to promote innovations in shipbuilding and tactics. The Asiatic monarchies rooted in their land-revenue economy viewed the sea with indifference, and strove as far

[1] Assuming the authenticity of this voyage. None of the attempts to demolish the testimony of Herodotus seem to me convincing.

[2] Hindu settlements were made by sea in Malaya, Java, Borneo and Cambodia. Cf. *Milindapañha*, 359 : ' As a shipowner who has become wealthy by constantly levying freight in some seaport town will be able to traverse the sea and go to Vanga or Takkola or China or Sovira or Surat or Alexandria or the Koromandel Coast or Further India or any other place where ships congregate.'

as possible to seclude themselves from it; the junk and the dhow remained what they had been, while European vessels underwent continual improvement. For a moment, at the beginning of the seventeenth century, it seemed as if Japan were about to enter the race and become a great naval and colonizing power; but the Yedo government chose instead to abolish its own mercantile marine and seclude the country from all contact with the outer world except the Chinese and Dutch trade at Nagasaki.

Thus the ocean ways were left to European supremacy. In the seventeenth century 'the westerners were masters of all the seas of the world.'[1] The command of the sea was disputed between various European nations, but never seriously, from the battle of Lepanto in 1571 to the Russo-Japanese War of 1904, between Europeans and Asiatics. Through sea-power the European colonial system was established, bringing about a continual flow of wealth into Europe, increasing accumulations of capital, incessant progress in financial technique and ever greater self-confidence and independence of outlook in the commercial class. Or as J. A. Hobson[2] more bluntly puts it : ' The exploitation of other portions of the world through military plunder, unequal trade and forced labour has been one great indispensable condition of the growth of European capitalism.'

In the late eighteenth century and in the nineteenth European capitalism aided by European science applied steam power and machinery to manufacture and to transport by land and sea, thus effecting the greatest transformation in the fundamental conditions of human life since the invention of agriculture. By their new economic power and efficiency the Europeans in the nineteenth century overwhelmed Asia, not only in the military sense, but also culturally. By abandoning the sea and withdrawing to the land, where they were stronger, the greater powers of Asia had put off the evil day and preserved their independence for a while with-

[1] G. N. Clark, *The Seventeenth Century*, p. 191.
[2] *The Evolution of Modern Capitalism*, p. 10.

out modifying their traditional modes of life and thought ;
even regions which had been long under European domination, such as Ceylon and Java, had remained in essentials as
impervious to European cultural penetration as had Persia
and Syria to the Hellenic two thousand years previously.
But with the new economy all this was changed.   The divine
right of trade was not to be denied, all barred gates were
forcibly burst open, and the engines of economic change
assaulted the inmost strongholds of the mind.   And Asia
yielded to ' westernization.'   Let not this process of our
time be misunderstood ;   its decisive forces have been
neither the big gun nor the Christian missionary nor the
appeal of pure science, but the railway and the factory
and the dynamo.   These have transformed life radically in
the East as in the West.   Indeed the latest age may claim
to be so great a variation as to supersede all former divisions
of culture, to be developing a new culture of its own totally
different from all that has gone before whether in West
or East.   This new world of machine industrialism, radio,
automobiles, democracy, feminism and bourgeois-prole-
tarian politics seems almost as alien to the world of Bourbon
Versailles and ' Alt-Wien ' as to that of the old Forbidden
City of Peking, almost as remote from the age of the
Spanish galleons as from that of the ' great ships of Zayton.'
Nevertheless, the new world is European in its ancestry ;
the great banks and the stock exchanges and the machines
are ultimately products of the city-state and the commercialism and scientific bias of its ideology.

  If then the whole Earth is ' westernized,' does it not follow
that the old Asiatic cultures are without significance for
a good European apart from their interest for comparative
anthropology, that they are blind alleys of history, altogether alien to our life and thought and now brought to
an end ?   Not at all.   They have left behind great monu-
ments of art which are, or should be, the heritage of all
civilized men.   They still affect the development of civilization in half the population of the globe, for the character
of revolutions is determined by that which they destroy.

And, not least, they have entered into the making of the European tradition itself. For if Hellas has determined the form and direction of European culture, Asiatic elements are inseparably fused with Hellenism in the total result. Some of these elements have been so thoroughly assimilated that their Asiatic origin has been forgotten, nor can it easily be rediscovered by European historians who know nothing of Asia and do not wish to. But in fact Asia before the nineteenth century influenced Europe far more deeply than ever Europe influenced Asia, and this must be attributed to the greater instability of the social order in Europe and the more radical changes it has undergone. It has been in periods of doubt and uncertainty consequent on the sense of social crisis that the European mind has been most plastic and susceptible to exotic influences. One such period was that which saw the wrecking of the social fabric of Helleno-Roman antiquity after the age of the Antonines; another was that which led up to the French Revolution. In the first period Europe accepted from West Asia the Christian religion and much of the quality of Byzantine art, from India, *pace* Dean Inge, the seed of the Neoplatonist philosophy. In the eighteenth century it was China that fascinated.

Through imports into Europe of Chinese painted silks, porcelain, lacquer, screens and fans the principles of Chinese decorative design and the peculiar artistic vision of the Far East were made familiar in Europe and especially in France; thus Chinese influences helped to form the Rococo style, and make themselves felt in the work of two European painters of the first rank, namely Watteau and Cozens. At the same time literary accounts of Chinese institutions and translations of the Chinese classics affected several thinkers of the French Enlightenment, notably Quesnay.

The eighteenth century concludes our survey of European-Chinese relations in the following pages. It closes the period during which the two worlds of culture confront each other intact and on approximately equal terms. We shall not

follow the story into the nineteenth century. We take
leave of our subject in 1800 with Napoleon First Consul
in France and the Ch'ing dynasty at Peking just entering
on the long road of decline that was to end in the abdica-
tion of 1912.

# CHAPTER I

## *Beyond the North Wind*

IT is generally held [1] that the earliest references to China
in European literature occur just before the beginning
of the Christian era, after the opening of the silk trade over
the Pamirs in the first century B.C. But there is reason to
believe that a definite knowledge of China, obtained by
way of a trade-route across Central Asia, was an ingredient
in the *Arimaspea* of Aristeas of Proconnesus, dating from
either the sixth or the seventh century B.C.

Apart from a fragment preserved by Tzetzes the *Arimaspea*
is a lost work ; it seems indeed to have disappeared already
in late classical times. But a portion of it has been sum-
marized for us by Herodotus [2] in connection with his study
on the origin of the Scythians, the horde of waggon-dwell-
ing, mare-milking nomads who in his time held an empire
over the steppes from the Don to the Carpathians and were
neighbours to the Greek cities on the northern shores of
the Black Sea. Herodotus considers four different accounts
of their origin. The first two do not concern us ; they
clearly refer to the agricultural tribes in the region of the
lower Dnieper, who had been conquered by the Scythians
and were commonly confused with them by the Greeks.
The third account does refer to the true, i.e. the nomad,
Scythians, and appears to have been their own tradition ;
according to it, ' the nomad Scythians who dwelt in Asia,

---

[1] As by Yule, *Cathay and the Way Thither* (and edition revised by
Cordier, 1915), and by G. Coedès, *Textes d'auteurs grecs et latins relatifs
à l'Extrême Orient*. Coedès includes the reference to the Seres in Ctesias,
but is inclined to regard it as an interpolation—which it certainly is.

[2] Herodotus, IV, 13.

27

being harassed in war by the Massagetae, crossed the river Araxes,[1] and entered the land of the Cimmerians ; for the country the Scythians now inhabit is said to have belonged formerly to the Cimmerians.'

The fourth version is that given in the *Arimaspea*, which is summed up as follows : ' Aristeas, son of Caystrobius, a native of Proconnesus, declares in his hexameter poem, that he journeyed to the Issedones by the inspiration of Apollo ; that beyond the Issedones dwell the Arimaspi, a one-eyed people, beyond them the gold-guarding griffins, and beyond them the Hyperboreans who reach to the sea [κατήκοντας ἐπὶ θάλασσαν] ; that each of these nations except the Hyperboreans encroached on its neighbour, the Arimaspi giving the initial impulse [ἀρξάντων 'Αριμασπῶν] ; that the Issedones were driven from their country by the Arimaspi, the Scythians by the Issedones, and that the Cimmerians, who lived by the southern sea, were pressed by the Scythians and abandoned their territory.'

On the face of it this passage with its mention of one-eyed men and griffins is so fantastic that the great majority of the modern commentators on Herodotus have declined to take it seriously, and have endorsed the unfavourable verdict which Herodotus himself passed on Aristeas and his Hyperboreans. But if the passage be examined in the light of all the relevant evidence, including not only classical but also Chinese sources, archaeological clues and, last but not least, geography, the result will be, as I believe, in favour of the supposition that Aristeas, in spite of a mixture of the fabulous, possessed real knowledge of the events which led to the Scythian migration and of the people whom he called Hyperboreans.

In the time of Herodotus, about the middle of the fifth century B.C., there was a trade-route leading from the north-east corner of the Sea of Azov to a people called the Argippaei who were contiguous with the Issedones. Six

---

[1] Here presumably the Volga (called Rha in Ptolemy). Herodotus apparently uses the name Araxes for three different rivers—the Aras, the Oxus, and the Volga.

peoples including the Argippaei are mentioned by Herodotus as then intervening between the Scythians of the Don-Carpathians area and the Issedones; they form a continuous series along the trade-route, except for a desert between two of them, and the route itself is described. As the Argippaei are contiguous with the Issedones, the series along the Argippaean trade-route joins on to the series Issedones—Arimaspi—Hyperboreans given by Aristeas, and we have a series of nine peoples, or counting in the desert as a term, of ten regions, extending from the Sea of Azov to the sea of the Hyperboreans. The full list is as follows :

1. The Sauromatae.
2. The Budini.
3. A desert.
4. The Thyssagetae.
5. The Iurcae.
6. A detached horde of Scythians.
7. The Argippaei.
8. The Issedones.
9. The Arimaspi.
10. The Hyperboreans.

Before attempting to plot this series on the map it may be well to quote the actual words of Herodotus indicating his sources of information other than Aristeas. He says :[1] ' As far as these bald people [i.e. the Argippaei] the country and the nations that inhabit it are well known [πολλὴ περιφάνεια τῆς χώρης ἐστὶ καὶ τῶν ἔμπροσθε ἐθνέων], for there are Scythians who journey to them, and it is not difficult to obtain information from these or from Greeks of the mart on the Borysthenes and the other Pontic marts. The Scythians who make the journey do business through seven interpreters in seven languages. . . . The country to the east of the bald men is known for certain [γινώσκεται ἀτρεκέως] to be inhabited by the Issedones, but the region beyond towards the north both of the bald men and of the Issedones is unknown, except for such stories as these peoples tell of it. . . . There is

[1] Herodotus, IV, 24–7 and 32.

a report from the Issedones that in the land beyond them are the one-eyed men and the gold-guarding griffins ; the Scythians have passed on this tale, and we have it from them together with the Scythian name, Arimaspi, for *arima* in Scythian means " one " and *spou* " eye ". . . . As for the Hyperboreans, neither the Sycthians nor any other people in that quarter give any account of them, unless it be the Issedones [εἰ μὴ ἄρα ᾽Ισσηδόνες].¹ For my part I do not believe that even the Issedones tell of them, for if they did, the Scythians would speak of them as they do of the one-eyed men.'

It should be clear from the above quotations that Herodotus considered himself to have very good information with regard to this part of the world  He is perfectly frank in admitting the limits of his knowledge, but such candour only renders more impressive the statement that the lands as far as the Argippaei are ' well known,' and we are entitled to assume that these chapters of his work are founded on something better than vague rumour.  On the other hand the very fact that Herodotus relies on contemporary testimony, whereas the *Arimaspea* is at least a century, and perhaps two centuries,² earlier in date, leaves the negative finding of the former inconclusive against the positive assertions of the latter.  The memories of primitive tribes without writing are notoriously short and uncertain, the tale of more recent events tends to blot out that of the more remote, and Aristeas may well have learnt from traditions that had perished or lost their shape by the time of Herodotus.  The entry of the Scythians into Europe can hardly be put later than 700 B.C., or a quarter of a millennium before Herodotus compiled his work, and it is only necessary to consider how

¹ According to Herodotus, IV, 16, Aristeas said that he obtained his information on the ' parts beyond ' (ie. of the Arimaspi and Hyperboreans) from the Issedones.

² Herodotus (IV, 15) assigns Aristeas to the first half of the seventh century, but Suidas makes him a contemporary of Croesus. The mention of the Issedones and of the Rhipaean mountains by Alcman is in favour of the earlier date.  But for the argument of this chapter it is not necessary to press the point.

obscure remain the wanderings of the Teutonic peoples on the very threshold of their recorded history in order to appreciate the importance of the time factor in this connec-

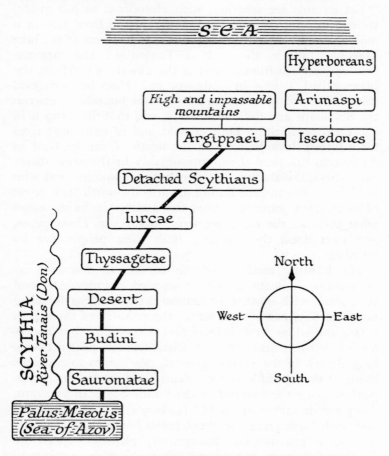

DIAGRAM ILLUSTRATING THE REGIONS FROM THE SEA OF AZOV TO THE HYPERBOREANS, AS CONCEIVED BY HERODOTUS

tion. If then we find that what Aristeas says about the Hyperboreans and the disturbance that led to the Scythian migration tallies with what we otherwise know of the

geographical and historical facts, the case is not lost
because Herodotus failed to obtain confirmation in his
day of his predecessor's statements.

Let us now see whether, with Herodotus as our guide,
we can find our way to the country of the Issedones on a
modern map. Our starting-point is the ' recess of the lake
Maeotis,' that is, the Gulf of Taganrog ; the caravans
probably set out from a mart at the mouth of the Don, the
place called Tanais in antiquity and Tana in mediaeval
times. We are told that the Don was the boundary between
the Scythians and the Sauromatae, and that the latter held
a ' territory destitute both of wild and of cultivated trees
for a fifteen days' journey to the north ' from the Gulf of
Taganrog. Beyond them (presumably in the same direction) dwell the Budini, whose country is wooded and who
sell furs. ' Beyond the Budini towards the north ' is a desert
of seven days' journey. After the desert, ' inclining somewhat towards the east,' we come upon the Thyssagetae,
and next upon the Iurcae ; both these people live by
hunting.

The hunting methods of the Iurcae, as described by
Herodotus, indicate a lightly wooded country. Beyond
the Iurcae, with another inclination to the east, is a detached
horde of Scythians. ' As far as the country of these Scythians the whole land is level and deep-soiled, but henceforth it is stony and rugged ; when one has passed over a
long stretch of the rugged ground, one comes to a people
living at the foot of lofty mountains.' These are the Argippaei, who are the terminus of the Pontic Scythian caravans.
They are described as ' bald ' ($\varphi\alpha\lambda\alpha\varkappa\rho o\iota$), flat-nosed ($\sigma\iota\mu o\iota$)
and with large chins (or cheek-bones ?—$\gamma\acute{e}\nu\varepsilon\iota\alpha$) ; certainly
a tribe of pronounced ' mongoloid ' physical type. ' So
far then is known, but no one can speak with certainty of
what is beyond the bald men, for high and impassable
mountains form their boundary, and no one ever crosses
them ; but the bald men say, though I do not believe it,
that men with goats' feet inhabit the mountains, and that
on the other side of them are men who sleep six months in

the year. All this I do not accept. But the country to the east of the bald men is known for certain to be inhabited by the Issedones.'

There are in this itinerary three definite, determining landmarks. The first is the river Don, the second is the desert of seven days' journey between the Budini and the Thyssagetae, and the third is the range of high and impassable mountains which bounds the territory of the Argippaei.

A glance at the map on page 37 shows that the Don after its great bend near Stalingrad (former Tsaritsyn), where it approaches to within 48 miles of the contrary bend of the Volga, flows to the Sea of Azov from the north-east, and rather more from the east than from the north. This point is of crucial importance. For if the Don was the frontier between the Scythians and the Sauromatae, and the Sauromatae lived on the left bank, their country could not have extended *to the north* from the Gulf of Taganrog. We have here one of those errors of direction which are so familiar to the student of ancient geography, and in this case the initial error involves all the subsequent notes of direction along the route. Herodotus was ignorant of the great eastward bends of both the Dnieper and the Don ; he imagined both rivers as flowing more or less straight from north to south. Hence we have a trade-route, starting from the Gulf of Taganrog and running on the left bank of the Don, conceived as leading first to north and later on inclining towards the east. But it is clear that the direction of the initial fifteen days' journey through the Sauromatae was roughly north-east ; if the two subsequent inclinations to the east are added to this instead of to the initial north supposed by Herodotus, we may well get an ultimate direction somewhat to the south of due east. Unfortunately Herodotus does not give us any idea of the angle of these inclinations nor any notes of distance with the exception of the figures in days for the Sauromatae and the desert beyond the Budini ; we cannot therefore plot the route from notes of direction alone. But we now have as a premiss that the initial direction was north-east, and as we are told that the route curved to the ' east,' or as we may say, with less ambiguity, to the right, the *net* direction must have been at any rate east of north-east, and may have been due east, or even south of east.

If we keep close to the Don and pass through the Stalingrad ' isthmus ' between the Don and the Volga, holding on towards the north-east, our fifteen days' journey over the steppes of the Sauromatae brings us somewhere near Kamishin on the Volga.   Here, according to Herodotus, the treeless steppe ends and the timber zone begins ; which is a fact—for the right bank of the Volga.   The great river flows along the edge of the low plateau of the Central Russian Uplands ; on the right bank is rising ground, cut up with small streams and patched with woodland, but the left bank south of Samara is flat and treeless, and south of the Great Irgiz river is saline and barren, and a great part of it sheer desert.   In the succession of treeless steppe (of the Sauromatae), wooded country (of the Budini), and desert, which we find in Herodotus, we have just the sequence which would be encountered to-day, making of course due allowance for modern deforestation in the second stage, on a journey from Rostov to Orenburg, crossing the Volga [1] obliquely between Kamishin and Saratov and inclining towards the right shortly before reaching Orenburg (the first inclination to the east in Herodotus).

We are not told the distance through the Budini, so we are entitled to suppose what is required by such a route, namely that only the south-eastern corner of the land of the Budini was traversed ; or perhaps there was a detour in order to visit the half-Greek, wooden town of Gelonus [2] described by Herodotus (IV, 108).   However this may be,

[1] Apparently the Oaros in Herodotus, IV, 123, where Darius is supposed to have reached this region and to have stopped short on the Oaros at the beginning of the desert.   The Volga is called Rha by Ptolemy.

[2] Since Herodotus in IV, 123, makes Darius continue his march to the Oaros (Volga) after burning Gelonus, it seems that Gelonus was not on the Volga, but to the west of it.

there can really be very little doubt as to the identification of the desert of seven days' journey beyond the Budini. So that there shall be no mistake about it, Herodotus explicitly says that the desert is uninhabited (ἡ δὲ ἔρημος αὕτη ὑπὸ οὐδαμῶν νέμεται ἀνδρῶν). It is true that Herodotus uses the term ' desert ' for the uninhabited forests north of Scythia, but that cannot be meant here ; that kind of ' desert ' would be impassable for a caravan, and along a frequented trade-route in a habitable country there would be some population however sparse. ' Desert ' must signify what we usually mean by the word—a stretch of utterly barren land. Such a region is the northward extension of the Ural Desert towards the Great Irgiz, the Obschiy Syrt country. But no real desert tract of the required size is to be found further north than the Great Irgiz, and this fact is fatal to theories which would take the route to the north, whether to or across the Ural Mountains.

This brings us to the question of the ' high and impassable ' mountains which tower above the Argippaei. Westburg,[1] followed by How and Wells [2] and others, identifies these with the Urals. The principal objection to this view is that by no stretch of imagination can the Urals be called either high or impassable. Both adjectives, on the other hand, are appropriate to the great ranges of the Altai system far to the east. The highest point of the Urals is only 5,535 feet above sea level, and the chain is crossed by many low and easy passes ; it has never constituted an effective barrier to anyone. The southern Urals do not reach the limit of perpetual snow. In contrast to this the Altai attains to an altitude of 14,890 feet (Bielukha peak), bears perpetual snows and numerous glaciers, and with its branch ranges interposes a most formidable division between Dzungaria on the one side and central Siberia and the Kobdo basin on the other. To quote a geographical authority,[3] ' the Ek-tagh Altai is a true border-

---

[1] *Klio*, IV, 183 *seq.*
[2] *A Commentary on Herodotus.* Note on IV, 21–5.
[3] Article on the Altai in the *Encyclopaedia Britannica* (14th ed.).

range in that it rises in a steep and lofty escarpment from the Dzungarian depression, but descends on the north by a relatively short slope to the plateau of north-western Mongolia. . . . The north-western and northern slopes of the Sailughem mountains (north-west of the Ek-tagh) are extremely steep and very difficult of access.'

The identification of the Argippaean mountains with the Altai, required by the description of them, is confirmed by our identification of the desert beyond the Budini ; for since the desert is south of the Great Irgiz and we incline to the right after crossing it, we do not strike the Urals at all, but pass to the south of them, and go roughly due east over the plain of Kazakstan with a slight curve to the north to skirt the ' tree steppe ' of the Iurcae on the Tobol and Ishim. Before reaching the Irtysh we again incline to the right and find the detached Scythians near the modern Semipalatinsk ; soon we leave the ' level and deep-soiled ' country for the ' stony and rugged ' tract formed by the outlying spurs of the Altai-Tarbagatai mountain system. Finally we reach the Argippaei, who may be located on the upper Irtysh round Lake Zaisan-nor with the main mass of the Altai just to the north-east of them.

Zaisan-nor is in almost just the same latitude as the Gulf of Taganrog ; the net direction of the trade-route is therefore virtually due east. The long curve to the north, which probably, however, did not reach the fifty-third parallel,[1] must have been due, partly to an endeavour to

---

[1] E. H. Minns (*Scythians and Greeks*, 1913), following Tomaschek, identifies the Argippaean mountains with the Altai, but takes the route far to the north, up to the Kama and across the Urals. This interpretation has not only to meet the difficulty of finding an adequate desert far enough to the north, but also appears incompatible with the statement that the country is level as far as the detached Scythians. Minns says (p. 107) that ' the incline of the Urals is so gentle that they do not strike a traveller as mountains.' Perhaps not as ' mountains,' certainly not as ' high and impassable,' but surely not quite as ' level.'

In contrast to this northern plotting of the route other scholars

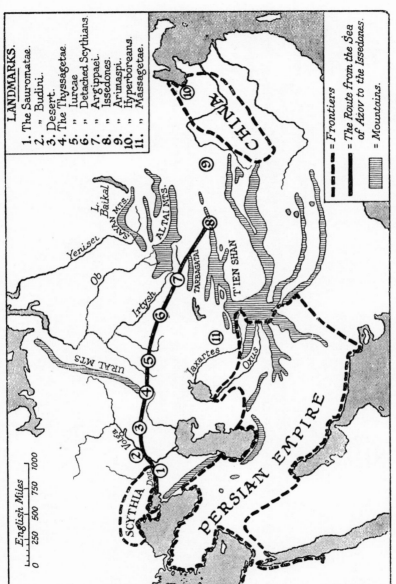

LANDMARKS.

1. The Sauromatae.
2. " Budini.
3. Desert.
4. The Thyssagetae.
5. " Iurcae
6. " Detached Scythians.
7. " Argippaei.
8. " Issedones.
9. " Arimaspi.
10. " Hyperboreans.
11. " Massagetae.

▬ ▬ ▬ = Frontiers
▬▬▬ = The Route from the Sea
of Azov to the Issedones.
▥ = Mountains.

TRADE ROUTE FROM THE SEA OF AZOV TO THE ISSEDONES IN THE TIME OF HERODOTUS

avoid as far as possible the deserts on the direct line, and partly to the desire for trade in furs with tribes in the northern forests.

The axis of the Altai lies north-west and south-east, and the mountains bound the upper Irtysh valley on the north-east. But to the south-east the plain of Dzungaria lies open, and in this direction we may expect to find the Issedones who dwell to the ' east ' of the Argippaei. We shall look for them in south-eastern Dzungaria and around the eastern end of the T'ien-shan mountains near modern Chensi and Hami. And at this point two informants come to our aid, one the geographer Ptolemy [1] and the other a Chinese scholiast on the *Shih-chi* of Ssŭ Ma-ch'ien.[2] The former mentions the Issedones by name and locates them in his geography east of Lop-nor ; the latter tells us that this region was at an earlier date the country of the nomad horde known to the Chinese as the Wu-sun.

Ptolemy's knowledge of the lands east of the Pamirs is derived through Marinus of Tyre from Maës Titianus, a Greek silk-merchant who sent agents to China, apparently during the first half of the second century A.D. Ptolemy gives a very fair description of the main physical features on or near the Pamirs-China silk-routes, and his rivers and mountain ranges can be identified with a high degree of probability ; thus the river Oechardes is the Tarim, while of mountains the Auxacii are the T'ien-shan, the Asmiraei the Kurruk-tagh, the Casii the K'un-lun-shan and Altyn-tagh, and the Thagurus the Nan-shan. Between the Asmi-raean and Casian ranges, according to Ptolemy, are ' the

favour a curve which leads far to the south. F. W. Thomas identifies the Argippaean mountains with the Hindu Kush, S. S. Casson with the Kopet-dagh. But these interpretations bring the route within the confines of the Persian empire, which included Sogdiana and Chorasmia, and of this there is no hint in Herodotus.

[1] Ptolemy, IV, 16.

[2] *Shih-chi*, 110. See Hirth, *The Story of Chang Ch'ien* in the *Journal of the American Oriental Society*, vol. 37, pp. 89–152.

great nation Issedones.' That is, in the region of Lop-nor.

It need hardly be pointed out that Ptolemy's location of the Issedones in this part of the world, whatever be the precise interpretation of the site, provides a most decisive confirmation of the theory which independently, by examination of Herodotus, has put the Argippaei at the foot of the Altai, while on the other hand it is quite incompatible with the view which identifies the Argippaean mountains with the Urals. The only defence for the Urals hypothesis would be to stress the fact that Maës Titianus is nearly six centuries later than Herodotus and to urge either that Ptolemy's mention of the Issedones is a learned error due to an accidental similarity of name between two entirely unrelated peoples, or else that the Issedones had in the meantime migrated eastwards. The first hypothesis is possible, but has nothing to support it, and must be regarded as unlikely ; the second may be dismissed, inasmuch as all the known migrations through Central Asia in the period concerned are from east to west, and it is inconceivable that the migration of a large horde in the contrary direction could have entirely escaped all notice in Chinese records. We may take it then that the Issedones of Ptolemy are the same people as the Issedones of Aristeas and Herodotus, and that their position in Ptolemy's ethnography is not far from where they ought to be by the account in Herodotus.

A difficulty, however, arises. The Issedones are the only people of all those mentioned by Ptolemy in the lands between the Pamirs and China whom he specifies as ' a great nation.' And yet contemporary Chinese records which give such a detailed account of the ' western regions ' do not show us any people on the site of Ptolemy's Issedones with a name remotely resembling theirs. How is this to be explained ? Fortunately a clue is provided by a Chinese scholiast on the *Shih-chi*. He tells us that in the time of the Contending States in China, in the fifth or fourth century B.C., the horde of the Wu-sun, which had had its pastures near Kua-chou (modern An-hsi on the Su-lo-ho in extreme west Kansu), migrated to the north-west. Subsequently the Su-lo-ho country was occupied by the Yue-chi who were driven out by the Hiung-nu about 170 B.C. ; the Wu-sun during the first half of the second century seem to have had their territory round the eastern T'ien-shan in vassalage to the Hiung-nu, but about the middle of the century they moved west and took the country round Lake Issyk-kul, where they survive as a distinct people until the fifth century A.D. In the first two centuries A.D., the Yue-chi having gone west of the Pamirs, the Wu-sun were the most powerful horde in the neighbourhood of the Tarim, and would have well deserved to be singled out as a ' great nation.' They were not, however, actually on a silk route, and the trading agents of Maës probably would not have had any very clear idea of their whereabouts. At the same time it is quite likely, in view of many analogies in cases of barbarian migrations,[1] that the name of the Wu-sun had clung to a district or place [2] in their long since abandoned homeland east of Lop-nor through which the silk routes passed. If we remember that Ptolemy's information is derived from Maës and that Maës compiled it from the reports of his agents who had most of it from hearsay through interpreters, it is not hard to see how confusion might have arisen.

[1] There is a parallel in the same passage of Ptolemy in the name of Thagurus applied to the Nan-shan. It certainly represents Tocharus, but the Tocharians had gone west with the Yue-chi : cf. Hüan-tsang's ' old T'u-huo-lo country ' (see Minns, *Greeks and Scythians*, p. 111, note).

[2] Ptolemy gives two places called respectively Issedon Scythica and Issedon Serica, the Tarim basin being divided by him into Scythia extra Imaum and Serica, i.e. the part under Chinese control. Issedon Serica appears to be near Lop-nor, and perhaps it was this place which retaining the Wu-sun name from former times caused all the confusion. Issedon Scythica was apparently much further west near the foot of the T'ien-shan, and I hazard the suggestion that this was a real contemporary Wu-sun emporium tapping the Pamirs-China trade route north of the Tarim. The Wu-sun lived north of the T'ien-shan, but they must have held the Muzart and other passes communicating to the south.

Minns takes the view that Ptolemy's Issedones are an anachronism in the site given them ; on the other hand he identifies them, not with the Wu-sun, but with the Yue-chi, and even suggests that Ngüt-shi, an older form of the name Yue-chi, might be verbally equivalent. But this seems a little hard even with Chinese transliteration, whereas Wu-sun (= Ü-sun) really does look something like the Greek form. Further, in the time of Maës the Yue-chi, having gone west of the Pamirs, were quite out of the picture, while the Wu-sun, though north of the T'ien-shan, were still in the vicinity, making the error more likely. If we are to make an identification, therefore, it appears more satisfactory to take the Issedones to be the people called by the Chinese the Wu-sun.

Chinese sources give us no idea as to the northward extent of the Wu-sun territory in the fifth century B.C., but as they were a numerous and important people it seems quite likely that it included the Hami district and south-eastern Dzungaria where, following Herodotus, we were looking for the Issedones. We may take them, on a summing up of all the evidence, as extending in the time of Herodotus from the Altyn-tagh in the south to beyond the Bogdo-ola and Barkul mountains in the north. And now let us continue our travel to the east. Beyond the Issedones dwell the one-eyed Arimaspi and their griffins ; but let not that deter us ; we are already more than half-way across Asia.

It was from the Arimaspi that Aristeas called his poem of travel the *Arimaspea*, though he did not claim himself to have reached them, but only to have heard of them from the Issedones. In the few lines of the *Arimaspea* preserved by Tzetzes he says that the Arimaspi dwell beyond the Issedones to the north, that they are many and mighty in war, rich in horses, in sheep and in cattle, shaggy. of hair, the sturdiest of all men, and one-eyed. They are recognizable from this description as warlike, pastoral nomads ; as for their eyes, Aristeas had never seen them, so he was not proof against legend or misunderstanding.

There can be no doubt that the Arimaspi belong to Mongolia and represent the group of tribes which figure in Chinese history as Hien-yün or Hiung-nu.

That the Arimaspi were producers of gold is indicated by Herodotus, III, 116 : ' The greatest quantity of gold is evidently found in the north of Europe, but I am unable to say for certain how it is obtained, though it is alleged that the Arimaspi, a one-eyed people, steal it from the griffins.' The gold may have come from the Southern Altai, east of Dzungaria—the name Altai (Altain-ola) means ' golden mountains '—and been traded through the Issedones to the Argippaei, from whom the Scythian traders could have purchased it. An abnormally large gold supply is indeed required by archaeology for the Pontic Scythian state in the days of its power. Borovka [1] stresses ' the wealth of Scythian culture in gold.' ' Never before or since,' he asserts, ' apparently not even in the days of the Maikop civilization, was gold in such universal use in this region. And scarcely any other culture, not even " Mycenae rich in gold " can rival Scythia for its superfluity of gold. Siberia is the sole exception. . . . The use of gold among the Scythians had assumed extraordinary proportions, even when measured by modern standards.'

As we are not told by Herodotus of any valuable products of the land of the Argippaei—which seems rather to have been specially unproductive,[2] it is hard to imagine why traders should have gone so far to visit them unless it were to buy the gold of the Arimaspi. That there was a commercial centre in the Argippaean country is suggested by the assertion that they ' are accounted sacred ' and that ' no one injures them, nor do they possess any weapon of war ' ; the tendency among primitive peoples for markets to grow up round religious sanctuaries is well known. A religious link between the Scythians and the Argippaei is further indicated by the remarkable similarity between the name of the latter and that of the deity

[1] G. Borovka, *Scythian Art* (1928).    [2] Herodotus, IV, 23.

Argimpasa,[1] who according to Herodotus was the Scythian equivalent of Aphrodite. It is reasonable to assume that some holy place of the Argippaei was the point at which traders from the west and from the east, Scythians and Issedones, bartered their goods, and that by such barter the gold of the Arimaspi came west in considerable quantities to Pontic Scythia.

If, as Aristeas says, the Scythians had been first driven to migrate by the Issedones, they must themselves have been originally located in Dzungaria. The evidence of archaeology is fully compatible with this supposition. To quote again from Borovka's *Scythian Art* : ' My journey to Mongolia in 1924, together with the results of excavations there and a rapidly increasing body of indications from various regions, convinced me that this Scythian cultural province extended right to the frontiers of China and was to some extent unitary throughout its whole area. . . . None of the cultures with which the Scythians came in contact on their westward advance possessed anything comparable. In the interior of Europe, in Greece, in Asia Minor, in Mesopotamia and in Persia a totally different style of art was current. On the other hand a thoroughly analogous style ruled in the eastern countries bordering upon Scythia from the Caspian to beyond Lake Baikal. . . . The most intimate relationship is bespoken not only by the agreement in artistic style but also by the types of everyday utensils—the knives and daggers, the mirrors and huge cauldrons and a host of other articles show the same shapes here as there, and are typical of this cultural province in the East, while they are utterly foreign to the civilizations of Hither Asia and Europe.'

The account of the Scythian migration given by Aristeas appeared to Herodotus to be incompatible with the current

---

[1] Herodotus, IV, 59. 'Αρίππασα is given by codd. Laur., LXX, 3, Romanus Angel. August., and Laur. conv. suppr., 207. For Αργιππαῖοι. in IV, 23, there are variants 'Ογγεμπαῖοι (cod. Vaticanus, 123, Zenob. v. 25), 'Ογγιεμπαῖοι (codd. Sancroftianus and Vindobonensis) and Aremphaei (Mela). Stein reads Αργεμπαῖοι.

story of the Scythians themselves that they had been driven
west by the Massagetae. But the two versions can easily
be reconciled if we take into account the normal character
of primitive historical memory [1] and suppose that the conflict with the Massagetae represents a later stage of the
migration than that with the Issedones. The Massagetae
appear from Herodotus to have lived east of the Aral and
north of the Oxus ; hence if the Scythians had moved
from Dzungaria to the Pontic steppes they must in any
case have passed near them. Probably the Scythians,
squeezed out of their old territory and looking for a new
one, first attempted to seize that of the Massagetae ; perhaps there was a prolonged, indecisive struggle lasting a
generation or more, until at last the wanderers yielded to
the emphatic ' Pass along, please ! ' of the Massagetae,
crossed the Volga and turned out the Cimmerians from
their domain on the shores of the Sea of Azov. In the
Aristeas version the Scythians are certainly represented as
passive ; the Arimaspi drive the Issedones, and the Issedones in turn drive the Scythians. But the bare statement
in the Scythian tradition that the crossing of the Araxes
was due to pressure from the Massagetae is not incompatible with the view that the rôle of the Massagetae had
been in the first place defensive.

So far then Aristeas is credible. And now we come to
the Hyperboreans who dwelt beyond the Arimaspi and
' reached to the sea ' and did not take any part in the disturbance which led to the Scythian migration. Who can
they be ?

It was Tomaschek who first suggested that they might
be the Chinese. The majority of Herodotean commentators, careful and cautious men with a dislike of great distances and a horror of the intervening griffins, have refused
to entertain such an idea. But now that we have reached
Mongolia it will be hard indeed if we are not to arrive

[1] Compare the vagueness and brevity of the Magyars' memory of
their migrations. See C. A. Macartney, *The Magyars in the Ninth
Century* (1930).

at the sea of which Aristeas speaks. Let us not turn back now, but hold on our way, until the waters of the Gulf of Pe-chih-li extend before our eyes, and we can cry, ' Thalassa ! Thalassa ! '

It is generally agreed that the original Hyperboreans were a tribe somewhere in the Balkans which had at one time sent offerings to the shrine of Apollo at Delos by way of Dodona, Malis, Carystus and Tenos (Herodotus, IV, 33) ; the bearers were called by the Delians περφερέες, as Herodotus tells us, and Ahrens has shown this to be the equivalent of a northern dialect ὑπέρβοροι, meaning ' bringers over ' (of the offerings). But a popular etymology connected ὑπέρβοροι with βορέας, the north wind, and made them the people ' beyond the north wind,' a fancy which was natural enough, seeing that the offerings *had* come from somewhere to the north and from an otherwise unknown people. And so a Greek traveller, hearing of a people who *were* beyond the north wind, would identify them with the Hyperboreans of tradition.

But, it will be at once objected, how could the Chinese possibly have been supposed to be in the north ? Is not Peking in the latitude of Lemnos and actually far to the south of the starting-point of the Argippaean trade route at the mouth of the Don ? The answer is that away from familiar land-marks the ancient Greek traveller had virtually no criterion of direction over a long journey, that he was ignorant of the relation of climatic zones to continental mass, and that the Chinese do live ' beyond the north wind ' in the sense that they enjoy a comparatively mild climate on the other side of the terrible winter cold of Central Asia.

The disabilities under which the Greeks laboured in the matter of judging direction are seldom adequately realized. They are well brought out by M. Cary in his introduction to *The Ancient Explorers.*[1] ' For the taking of latitudes,' he says, ' the ancients used a simple pointer which cast its shadow on a disc or a hemispherical bowl. This instrument, if accurately suspended in a vertical plane, must have given

[1] M. Cary and E. H. Warmington, *The Ancient Explorers* (1929), p. 5.

readings as good as those of the early modern astrolabe, though of course it was less precise than the present-day sextant. In the hands of men of science like Eratosthenes and Hipparchus it yielded important contributions to geographic knowledge ; but it does not appear to have been extensively used by practical travellers. Hence the great majority of figures of latitude in Ptolemy's Geography could not be derived from direct measurement of the sun's inclination, but had to be inferred from the observed length of a midsummer night or from the data of maps and itineraries. The fixing of longitudes remained throughout antiquity a mere matter of dead reckoning. . . . The ancients possessed no real substitute for the compass, no device that was always available and nearly always accurate. The difficulties into which they accordingly fell may be plentifully illustrated from faulty orientations in ancient geographers. The cases in which these are 45 degrees out of their reckoning are so numerous as not to be worth collecting ; in some instances the error amounts to a full right angle. Thus Herodotus imagined the pass of Thermopylae as running from north to south, and Strabo described the Pyrenees as extending in the same direction. Under such conditions ancient travellers proceeding without some familiar landmark to guide them stood in danger of losing their way irretrievably.'

With their deficiencies of geographical equipment the Greeks naturally tended to rely on a climatic criterion of direction and to assume a far-northern situation for the regions of the most intense cold. The winter cold of Scythia certainly made a profound impression on the Greek mind. Herodotus says that ' the winter continues eight months and during the other four it is cold there,'[1] an exaggeration, for the winter is not more than half the year and the summer days are of great heat—although in the deserts the nights are chill even in summer. But it was the cold which impressed itself on the Greek, for an inhabitant of Greece has not much to learn about heat, but a great deal to learn

[1] Herodotus, IV, 28.

about cold. And if the winter of the Ukraine is intense, even more so is that of the great plains of Kazakstan in the same latitudes. The winter of Uralsk (in the latitude of London) is colder than that of Finland, and the Ural river there is frozen from November to the middle of April. The prevailing winter winds are from north, north-east or east ; they are of biting keenness and bring appalling blizzards which are the great scourge of the nomad herdsmen. In a two days' blizzard in 1827, recorded by Helmersen, the Kazaks of the Inner Horde lost 280,000 horses, 30,480 oxen and 1,012,000 sheep. In Mongolia the climate is rendered still more severe by the greater elevation.

On a journey to Dzungaria and back Aristeas would have had experience of the Central Asian blizzards, and there is some excuse for him if he imagined that he was ascending to high latitudes. Even in our age of geographical enlightenment it is not everyone who is aware, without reference to the map, that Liverpool is in the latitude of Labrador and New York in that of Madrid.

It has already been shown that Herodotus from his ignorance of the course of the Don made an initial error of fully 45 degrees in the direction of the Argippaean trade route. And there was no further independently known landmark by which to make a correction. The geography of this part of the world is for Herodotus, as it were, one-dimensional ; its plotting must be dependent on internal directives without aid from external relations. Had the Sauromatae-Hyperboreans series overlapped at any point with the Asiatic geography known from Persian sources, its eastern direction must have been recognized, but actually the two great avenues of sight across Asia remain unconnected,[1] and the Argippaei and their neighbours are assigned to the far north. Even so, even taking literally the notes of direction given, the series goes a long way to the east in longitude, for there are two eastward inclinations before reaching the Argippaei, and the Issedones dwell east of the

[1] Except in that the Massagetae are ἄντιον the Issedones. But the preposition is too vague to be really significant.

Argippaei. There is no question therefore of the Hyperboreans being due north of the Sea of Azov. But both Aristeas and Herodotus believed them to belong, if existing, to high latitudes, and their sea to be in the north ; in contrast to which the Black Sea is called ' the southern '.

But the Hyperboreans, though they are in the furthest north, are beyond the north wind, beyond the reign of the blizzards. In Dzungaria Aristeas heard of a heaven-favoured country on the other side of the snow peaks of the T'ien-shan and the wind-swept desolation of the Gobi, of a land of plenty and of a settled, agricultural people dwelling by a never-frozen sea.

There is another early version of the Hyperborean legend, which may be derived either from Aristeas or from some other source, and which is preserved in fragments of the geographers Hellanicus and Damastes,[1] contemporaries of Herodotus. They put the Hyperboreans on the shores of the northern ocean beyond the ' Rhipaean ' mountains, and add that they are vegetarians. These further items of information both fit in with the Chinese hypothesis. As agricultural, the Chinese are certainly vegetarians relative to the exclusively pastoral and hunting tribes of Central Asia ; as for the mountains, they should represent one or more of the great Central Asian ranges, the Altai, the Tarbagatai, the Dzungarian Ala-tau or the T'ien-shan.

The Rhipaean mountains were originally called simply Rhipae, i.e., ' the Blasts ' (of wind). The association of the word ῥιπή with the north wind is already found in Homer's ὑπὸ ῥιπῆς βορέαο.[2] Its use apparently for the proper name of a mountain first occurs in Alcman's magnificent phrase—

Ῥιπᾶν ὄρος ἀνθέον ὕλᾳ,
Νυκτὸς μελαίνας στέρνον.

—' the Mountain of Winds clad in forest, the bosom of black Night.'[3] Aristotle[4] has ' the mountains called Rhipae beyond the extremity of Scythia.' The later Greek geo-

[1] Jacoby, frs. 1 and 187.  
[2] Il., 15, 171 ; 19, 358.  
[3] Alcman, 42 (Bergk.).  
[4] Meteor., 1, 13, 19.

graphers, whose precision was so often in excess of their knowledge, located them in the middle of European Russia, and supposed the great rivers of the Black Sea basin to be fed from them. And modern scholars, discovering that there is no great mountain range in the middle of European Russia, have pronounced them to be a baseless invention.

But if the argument we have followed is correct the poetic fancy of Alcman had its root in a fact, a fact not unworthy of such lyric splendour of commemoration. Perhaps it was through the lines of the *Arimaspea*, wherein Aristeas gave all the experience of his inspired journey, that Alcman *saw* with the eye of the mind the peaks of Bielukha or Bog-do-ola, towering above the vast empty steppe, savage with dark forests [1] and gleaming snows, the cradle of great winds.

There is no reason to doubt but that Aristeas did actually make the journey to the Issedones. Since the Scythians traded with the Argippaei, he had only to join a Scythian caravan in order to go that far, and at the Argippaean mart he could attach himself to a party of Issedones returning to their country. The hardships and difficulties of the journey were not greater for Aristeas than they were for Zemarchus, Plano Carpini and others who are admitted to have achieved in mediaeval times what is claimed to have been done in the seventh or sixth century B.C. The web of legend, which by the time of Herodotus had enveloped the name of the Apollo-inspired traveller, need not prevent us from assigning to him the distinction of having been the first civilized European to pass the Dzungarian Gate and to learn of the existence of China.

The fact that Herodotus could obtain no contemporary report on the Hyperboreans points to a fading of the Issedones' knowledge of them in the course of time. The Issedones must originally have lived nearer to China, but by the westward movement described by Aristeas had been

---

[1] The mountains of Central Asia are often treeless, but some ranges bear forests. See D. Carruthers, *Through unknown Mongolia* (2 vols., 1913).

pushed farther away, and the Arimaspi intervened, holding probably not only central Mongolia but also the greater part of modern Kansu. It may seem incredible that if the Issedones were as far to the south-east as An-hsi they should not have been well informed about the Chinese. But it is only necessary to recall how completely in the time of Chang Ch'ien China was cut off by the Hiung-nu from all communication with, or knowledge of, ' the western regions ', in order to understand the drying up of the channel of information which had been still available for Aristeas. And in the fifth century China was no longer a united power, but under the nominal sway of the Chou dynasty was broken up into a swarm of petty feudal principalities ; for the Issedones the Chinese were remote and inconsiderable compared with the near and formidable Arimaspi, and in the absence of any great through commerce to China, such as silk was to make in the future, they were practically out of the picture.

And just as the Hyperboreans disappeared in the interval between Aristeas and Herodotus, so also, soon after Herodotus, all the nations from the Budini to the Arimaspi vanished from the view of the Greek world. They had been known to the Greeks only through the Scythian-Argippaean trade, and there can be little doubt that this trade was interrupted somewhere about the end of the fifth century B.C. Its duration coincided with the period of the power and prosperity of the Scythian empire, which afforded a surplus of goods—probably metalwork, horse-trappings and rugs—to exchange for the Arimaspian gold, and made it possible to send out large caravans. In the fourth and third centuries the Scythian state was undermined and finally destroyed by inroads of Sarmatians from the east and Celts and Bastarnae from the west. In Central Asia likewise there was probably a new turmoil and a breaking of such commercial links as had existed. And so it comes about that the later Greek geographers have hardly any knowledge of the lands which were traversed by the Scythian traders in the time of Herodotus. Herodotus knew the Caspian to be an enclosed sea ;

after him it was generally believed to be an inlet of the
Ocean from the north, and the error was not definitely
corrected until the second century A.D. The geography
of Strabo shows no trace of the Argippaean trade route or
of any memory of it ; the peoples of the series from the
Budini onwards have disappeared as though they had never
been.

The silk trade in classical times brought to Europe new
knowledge of China, both by the sea route from Egypt and
by the overland route across the Pamirs and through the
Tarim basin. But for more than a millennium after Aristeas
no European traveller, as far as we know, traversed Central
Asia by a way leading north of the Caspian—not until
in A.D. 569 a Byzantine embassy went thus to the camp-
capital of the Western Turks in Dzungaria.

# CHAPTER II

## Chang Ch'ien

IN the fifth and fourth centuries B.C. the Achaemenid Persian empire, which reached westward to the Mediterranean and the Aegean, extended to the north-east as far as the river Iaxartes, the modern Syr Darya. In the angle between the Hindu Kush mountains and the river Oxus (Amu Darya) making its way across the plain to the Aral Sea, was the province of Bactria ; between the Oxus and Iaxartes, to the north and north-east of Bactria, was Sogdiana. Both these lands were thus part of the Aral basin, the western watershed of the great Pamir divide ; on the other side of a line high up in the great mountain wilderness the streams flowed eastward to join the Tarim or to lose themselves in the sands of the Takla-makan desert, the Tarim itself being destined to disappear in the marshes of Lop-nor. This way, across a vast distance of desert and steppe with occasional oases watered from the mountain ranges to north and south, was China. But between China and Persia there was, as far as we know, no communication or intercourse. Each was to the other utterly unknown ; the mountains and the deserts interposed an as yet unsurmounted barrier.

We have found reason to believe that in the fifth century gold from Mongolia was traded to European Scythia, and that a Greek traveller had penetrated along that trade route to the east of the Dzungarian Gate and had heard something of China and the Pacific. But if knowledge of China reached the Greeks by way of Scythia—and was therefore, as we have seen, referred to the far north—there is no evidence whatever for such knowledge gained by way of Persia, which was for the Greeks virtually synonymous with Asia and ' the East.' Not only was there no rumour of lands further east than the Pamirs, but there was not even any report of the Pamirs themselves. Herodotus knew what tribute was paid to the Persian treasury by Bactria and Sogdiana, he knew of the contingents they supplied to the great army with which Xerxes invaded Greece, but he did not know of any great mountain ranges in that quarter. If he had information of the Altai, he had none of the Pamirs, the Hindu Kush or the Himalayas, on or within the confines of the Persian empire and in actual distance nearer to Greece. Speaking of the plain east of the Caspian he merely says that it is ' limitless in prospect ' (ἄπειρον ἐς ἄποψιν).[1]

At the end of the fifth century, Ctesias of Cnidus, a Greek physician at the Persian court, was able to tell his countrymen of the existence of mountains to the north of India and north-east of Iran. But Greek knowledge had not advanced further than this at the time when Alexander of Macedon undertook the conquest of Persia, and meanwhile the old Scythian-Argippaean trade had been discontinued, so that there was no longer a chance that its real relation to the eastern parts of Asia might be discovered and that the information given by Aristeas and Herodotus might be combined with new knowledge to give a general idea of the lands towards China. As it was, the geographical equipment available in the latter half of the fourth century B.C. is indicated by W. W. Tarn in a comment on Alexander's plans for the invasion of India : ' He [Alexander] never knew of the existence of northern or eastern Asia—of Siberia and Chinese Turkestan, China and further India ; to the end of his life " Asia " meant to him, as to everyone, the empire of Darius I. He never knew of the Ganges or eastern Hindustan, which were unknown to Greeks prior to Magasthenes, or of the Indian peninsula, though later Nearchus and Onesicritus collected dim reports of " islands " further south. There is no evidence that he even knew

[1] Herodotus, I, 204.

of the Rajputana desert, which Herodotus had known. " India " to Alexander, when he invaded it, meant the country of the Indus, which, following Aristotle, he thought was a broad-based peninsula jutting *eastward* into the sea from the land mass of Iran. Along the north side of it, like a backbone, ran a chain of mountains, Aristotle's " Parnassus " (i.e. Paropanisus) ; the rest was a plain traversed by the Indus and its tributaries. Ocean, which was near the Iaxartes, washed the northern base of these mountains, and flowed round the eastern end of the peninsula.' [1]

In 329 B.C. Alexander in his great march of conquest traversed Bactria and Sogdiana to the Iaxartes, and stood on the extreme limit of Persian dominion to the northeast. To his right the mountain-locked valley led up to the Terek Pass over the divide into the Tarim basin ; to his left extended the open steppe towards the desert of Kizil Kum ; in front of him, across the Iaxartes, rose the high pastures of the Kendyr Tau, now the domain of the Kara Kirghiz and then of the independent Sakas. Here was nothing but a promontory of the civilized world thrust out into an unprofitable wilderness ; this way there was nothing more for Alexander to conquer. It only remained to secure this march of the new empire against the outer barbarism of the nomads, and for the purpose Alexander planted a Graeco-Macedonian colony on the bank of the Iaxartes, on the site of the modern Khojent. This was called 'Alexandria the Furthest.' While its walls were being built Alexander crossed the river as a demonstration, and, with the aid of his catapults, inflicted a severe defeat on a force of Sakas which had gathered to oppose him. After this he left a garrison in Khojent, placed other garrisons in key positions elsewhere in Sogdiana and in Bactria, and proceeded south for his invasion of India.

After the death of Alexander in 324 Bactria and Sogdiana were held for nearly two centuries by Greek rulers—for

[1] W. W. Tarn, *Alexander : The Conquest of the Far East* (*Cambridge Ancient History*, vol. VI, chap. 13).

about seventy years by the Seleucids ruling from Antioch in Syria, and for a further ninety or thereabouts by local dynasts making their capital at the town of Bactra (Balkh).

The history of this remote corner of the Hellenistic world is still very little known, but it is clear that, far from being, as might be expected by its distance from Greece, one of the least hellenized of the regions conquered by Alexander, it received a stronger Greek element than any other east of Syria. It was for the Seleucid kingdom *the* frontier covering Iran and Mesopotamia. Alexander's Indian conquests, including the Kabul valley, had been ceded by Seleucus in 302 to the new Maurya empire of North India, but the latter showed no disposition to expand further into Iran, and entered into the most friendly relations with the Seleucids. There was, therefore, no danger from India to Greek power in Western Asia, nor was there any considerable menace from the unsubdued tribes of Arabia or the Caucasus. The greatest peril to be anticipated was from the Saka nomads beyond the Iaxartes. The Achaemenids had held this march in great strength, as is shown sufficiently by the formidable resistance which Sogdiana offered to Alexander after the greater part of the Persian empire, including the seats of the central government, was already in the hands of the conqueror. After the conquest was completed the Greeks merely ' took over ' from the Persians the old frontier system. Greek colonies were planted, consisting of military garrisons with a complement of civilian camp-followers, and the vine was cultivated by them in the oases of Bokhara and Samarkand. By reason of the need for a strong frontier guard against the Sakas Hellenism here flourished in a highly concentrated form, flourished so vigorously that even after it had been cut off from European Greece and the main centres of Hellenistic life it remained as an independent centre for the diffusion of Greek cultural influence.

Of the Bactrian coinage, which constitutes the greater part of the evidence now available for an estimate of the culture of Hellenistic Central Asia, Professor E. J. Rapson observes [1] : ' The coins struck in Bactria are purely Greek in style, in language and in weight. They are the most noble examples of Greek art as applied to portraiture. No rivals to the lifelike portraits of Euthydemus and Demetrius appeared in the world until after the lapse of sixteen centuries, when the Greek spirit was again kindled at the renaissance and manifested itself in the medals of the great Italian artists.' It was this fine artistic tradition of the Bactrian Greeks which afterwards gave initiation in Greek taste to the Saka and Kushan conquerors of Bactria and North-west India ; reinforced under the Kushan empire by influences of Syro-Hellenistic-Roman art and blended with the native art of India, it eventually gave rise to the Gandhāra school whose forms were carried by Buddhism to China and Japan.

The formation of a separate Greek state in Bactria about 255 B.C. was due mainly to the neglect by the Seleucids of this part of their empire. The primary concern of the policy of the Seleucid kings was to restrain the power of the Ptolemaic kingdom of Egypt and to avoid being driven away from the Mediterranean littoral. They had fixed their capital at Antioch in Syria in the extreme west of their dominions ; there was a viceroy at Seleucia on the Tigris to look after the affairs of the east, but even so the kingdom was geographically lop-sided. When therefore Diodotus, a satrap of Bactria, declared his independence about the middle of the third century, he had strong support from the Greek colonists, who had developed a local patriotism and chafed under the sway of a king in Syria too busy with constant wars and troubles in the west to pay attention to the needs of the distant Saka frontier.

The secession of Bactria did not avail to secure Greek ascendency in Iran, for it was immediately followed by another revolt against the Seleucids, that of the non-Greek Parthians, and the kingdom formed by the latter gradually grew until it had eaten up all that was left of the Seleucid

[1] E. J. Rapson, *The Successors of Alexander the Great* in *The Cambridge History of India* (vol. I, chap. 22).

dominions east of the Zagros and had cut off Bactria from the rest of the Greek world. But Bactria itself withstood the Parthians, and while holding them at bay on the west, entered on a career of expansion to the south and east. Strabo declares [1] that ' the Greeks who occasioned its [Bactria's] revolt became so powerful by means of its fertility and the advantages of the country that they became masters of Ariāna [the Herāt region] and India, according to Apollodorus of Artemita. . . . They extended their empire also as far as the Seres and the Phauni.'

The conquests of the Bactrian Greeks in India are attested by other evidence ; they included the Kābul valley, the Punjab, Sind and Kāthiāwār, and were rendered possible by the collapse of the great Indian Maurya empire. The mention of the Seres, however, introduces a problem. The Seres were a people named from the product by which they were known ; both the product and its name are Chinese —ssŭ, whence through Latin is derived the English word silk.[2] In most classical authors the Seres are from other indications quite definitely to be identified with the Chinese. The Phauni with whom the Seres are coupled in the above quoted passage of Strabo are the Hiung-nu of Chinese, the Huns of European history (Chuni, Phuni, Χοῦνοι, Φοῦνοι, Οὖννοι, Sanskrit Hūṇa), the great nomad power of Mongolia in the third and second centuries B.C.

The difficulty is that there is nothing in Chinese records of this period suggesting the close approach to China at this time of a nation which can be identified with the Bactrian Greeks. The solution appears to be that the extension of Bactrian ascendency as far as the Seres refers, not to the real Chinese, but to some people further to the west who traded in silk. There is nothing to show that

---

[1] Strabo, XI, 516 (Trans. M'Crindle, *Ancient India* (pp. 100–1).

[2] It is probable that the Greek σηρικόν was not an adjective formed from σήρ, but derived from a form of the Chinese word with a final k (cf. Mongol *sirkek*) ; from what seemed an adjectival form the Greeks then derived a suitable substantive. (See Yule, *Cathay and the Way thither*, vol. I, p. 20, note 2).

silk of *Bombyx mori*, the mulberry silk-moth, was at this time produced anywhere outside China. But the Seres were simply ' the silk-people,' and under conditions of geographical ignorance the name might be loosely applied to intermediaries in the commerce of the article as well as to the actual producers. There can be no doubt that in several other instances apart from the passage under consideration the name is so applied. We are forced to conclude therefore that what the Bactrians actually did was to cross the Pamirs and subdue the nearer oases of the Tarim basin, perhaps Kashgar and Khotan, thereby coming in contact with a silk-buying people also of the Tarim basin. This would be fully compatible with the mention of the Phauni as a limit, for the Hiung-nu suzerainty at this time extended far to the west, both north and south of the T'ien-shan ; a little later on, when Chang Ch'ien visited Ferghana in 128 B.C., it reached even to the K'ang-kü tribes in the neighbourhood of Tashkent.[1]

We cannot say then that the passage in Strabo is evidence for any contact with, or knowledge of, the Chinese, but it does show that the Bactrian Greeks had some acquaintance, however slight, with silk which had originally come from China.[2] Outside this passage, however, there is no other Greek or Latin reference to the Seres or to silk which belongs to a date earlier than the embassy of Chang Ch'ien to the Ta Yue-chi in 128.[3] And when Chang Ch'ien made his

---

[1] *Shih chi*, 123.

[2] Unless of course the mention of the Seres is an anachronism, a note of locality used by a historian writing when the silk trade was already in full swing in the first century B.C. But the date of the *Parthica* of Apollodorus from which Strabo quotes is not known.

[3] The alleged reference to the Seres in Ctesias is undoubtedly an interpolation ; the mention in Strabo supposed to be quoted from Onesicritus is certainly not so quoted, as is shown by the words τινὲς φασί which separate it from the Onesicritus passage (Strabo, XV, 1, 34 and 37). Nor is there any ground for the assertion that Aristotle refers to silk in the passage *De Animal. Hist.*, V, 24, though it is a very persistent one and in spite of past refutations has just reappeared in the article *Silk and Sericulture* in the latest (14th) edition of the *Encyclopaedia Britannica*. Aristotle refers to a silk-like insect product which

journey to the west, whatever silk trade had formerly existed in the Tarim basin had been discontinued in the turmoil following on the migration of the Yue-chi.

It was this same migration of the Yue-chi which both drove the Greeks out of Bactria and provided the motive for Chang Ch'ien's epoch-making mission. It was the most violent and the most important ethnic movement in Central Asia since the great Scythian migration some six centuries before. It resulted from a struggle between the Yue-chi and the Hiung-nu of Mongolia in which the former were worsted. The Yue-chi were living to the north of the Nan-shan in what is now West Kansu ; after a final crushing defeat by the Hiung-nu they sought refuge in flight, and migrating to the north-west in about 165 B.C. invaded the territories of the Wu-sun in the Ili basin and of the

was spun in the island of Cos, perhaps a ' wild silk ' in the widest sense of the term, but certainly not the silk of *Bombyx mori*, the true Chinese silk. Aristotle does not give the slightest hint that the material of the Coan textiles came from the east ; it is clearly a local product. Aristotle says : ' From a certain great grub, which has as it were horns, and differs from others, is produced by transformation first a caterpillar, then a *bombylius*, and then a *necydalus*. In six months the grub goes through all these changes of form. From this creature women disengage and reel off *bombycina* and then weave them ; the first to have woven this material is said to have been Pamphile, daughter of Plates, in Cos.' The use of the technical terms in the passage shows that Aristotle is dealing with a purely Greek industry, not with vague reports of a far distant foreign one.

As regards other alleged early mentions of silk the testimony of Nearchus must be considered as entirely invalidated by Arrian's editing, while the statements of Procopius (*Pers.*, I, 20 and *Vandals*, II, 6) that the stuffs anciently known as ' Medic ' had been the ' same as are now called Seric ' is a piece of antiquarianism that fails to convince. While we cannot prove that Chinese silk did not reach the Greek world before about 100 B.C., neither can we dissent from the conclusion of Coedès (*Textes d'auteurs grecs et latins relatifs à l'Extrême Orient*) : ' En bonne méthode on ne saurait se baser sur ces témoignages pour affirmer que les pays d'Extrême Orient ont été connus ou même soupçonnés des peuples méditerranéens avant le 1er siècle avant J.C.' The only exception which can be made to this generalization is in favour of the references due to the Scythian-Arimaspian trade discussed in Chapter I.

Saka tribes farther to the west. As we have only fragments of information, it is impossible to reconstruct in
detail the course of the migration, but it seems clear that
it passed to the north side of the T'ien-shan main range, a
route much to be preferred by a migrating people to the
deserts of the Tarim basin. The Yue-chi defeated the
Wu-sun, but did not occupy their country, probably because
they desired to put a greater distance between themselves
and their Hiung-nu enemies ; they seized instead the land
of the Sakas between the Iaxartes and Lake Issyk-kul, and
the dispossessed Sakas swarmed over Sogdiana. A little
later the Yue-chi, having suffered defeat at the hands of a
coalition of Hiung-nu and Wu-sun, again moved west, and
conquered both Sogdiana and Bactria soon after 140. The
Greeks withdrew over the Hindu Kush into the Kābul
valley where Greek rule survived for some time longer,
while the Sakas were scattered, the main body making their
way through the Herāt and Kandahār regions into Sind
where they founded ' Indo-Scythian ' states. The Yue-chi
themselves encamped to the north of the Oxus near
modern Bokhara and drew tribute from the native
Bactrians to the south of the river ; to the east in the
upper Iaxartes valley Ferghana became a separate and
independent kingdom.

Such was the situation when in 128 Chang Ch'ien
arrived in West Central Asia as ambassador of the Chinese
emperor Wu Ti. The occasion arose out of the almost
incessant warfare which went on between China, now
united under the Han dynasty, and the Hiung-nu. According to the *Shih-chi* [1] of Ssǔ Ma-chien the Emperor in
about 140 B.C. ' made inquiries among Hiung-nu prisoners
and they all reported that the Hiung-nu had overcome
the king of the Yue-chi and made a drinking cup out of
his skull ; the Yue-chi had decamped and were hiding
somewhere, all the time scheming how to take revenge on
the Hiung-nu, but had no ally to join them in strik

[1] Ch. 123, Trans. Hirth, *Story of Chang k'ien* in *Journal of the American
Oriental Society*, vol. 37, pp. 89–152.

a blow. The Chinese, hearing this report, desired to communicate with the Yue-chi, but as the way was through the territory of the Hiung-nu, the Emperor sought out men whom he could send.' It was Chang Ch'ien who was chosen for the mission ; he set out, was taken prisoner by the Hiung-nu, spent ten years in a not unpleasant captivity among them, escaped, and finally reached Ta-yüan (Ferghana), whose people ' having heard of the wealth and fertility of China [1] had tried in vain to communicate with it.' The Ta-yüan sent him on to the camp-court of the Yue-chi king near Bokhara, but there he found that the Yue-chi were too contented with their present good fortune to have any desire to resume warfare against the invincible Hiung-nu. So he returned to China, bringing with him a relic of the past Hellenism of Sogdiana, the seeds of the vine, and its name βότρυς, which became Chinese *p'u t'ao*. He brought with him also a great store of carefully and intelligently gathered geographical information in the light of which was planned the subsequent forward policy of China in Central Asia. According to the *Shih-chi* Chang Ch'ien had visited in person Ta-yüan (Ferghana), the Yue-chi (near Bokhara), the K'ang-kü (tribes near Samarkand and Tashkent) and Ta-hia (Bactria) ; he also reported from hearsay on the Wu-sun (round Lake Issykkul), the An-ts'ai (Aorsi north of the Aral and Caspian), An-si (Parthia), Li-kan (Seleucid Syria), T'iao-chih (Babylonia) and Yen-tu (India). ' The Son of Heaven, on hearing all this, reasoned as follows : Ta-yüan, Ta-hia and An-si are large countries, full of rare things, with a population living in fixed abodes and given to occupations somewhat like those of the Chinese, but with weak armies and setting great value on the rich produce of China ; in the north are the Yue-chi and the K'ang-kü, peoples of military strength—they might be made subservient to our interests by bribes.' From such thoughts new schemes ...d themselves in the mind of Wu Ti ; the Emperor

[1] Probably from the Yue-chi who must have brought west a report ...hina.

had a vision of a great web of diplomacy extending to the farthest west, and resolved to open up permanent relations with the lands beyond the Pamirs.

First of all an attempt was made to communicate with Bactria via India. This somewhat curious plan was due to the fact that Chang Ch'ien had seen in Ferghana certain bamboo and cloth goods of Chinese make, and on inquiring whence they came had been told that they were bought in Yen-tu (India). It appeared that Chinese wares reached India by indirect trading through the primitive tribes to the south-west of China. India itself had only now become known to China through being discovered by Chang Ch'ien from the north-west ; he by calculations of relative position estimated that it must lie between south-west China and Bactria, and that it might be expected to offer a safer road for embassies than the Tarim country or the Tibetan K'iang. There is a certain irony in the fact that access to India was only thought of as a means for reaching Bactria ; the Chinese had as yet no idea of the size and importance of India. However, the attempt to open up the Indian route failed, for the Chinese envoys could not penetrate to India, but were murdered or robbed of their diplomatic gifts by the intervening hill tribes.

So it was resolved to open up a north-western route, and war was resumed on a grand scale against the Hiung-nu. Operations were almost immediately successful, the Western Horde of the Hiung-nu was severely defeated and driven away to the north, and Chinese dominion was advanced as far as Lop-nor (121 B.C.). The way was now clear. During the next few years embassies were despatched to all the countries mentioned by Chang Ch'ien in his report, and the diplomatic ambitions of Wu Ti were to a great extent realized. According to the *Shih-chi* [1] : ' Such missions would be attended by several hundred men, or by a hundred men, according to their importance. At least five or six missions were sent out in the course of a year, and as a rule more than ten ; those sent to distant

[1] § 79 (Hirth, *op. cit.*).

countries would return home after eight or nine years, those
to nearer ones within a few years.' Chang Ch'ien had
reported that there was no sericulture in the western lands,
so that silk formed a large part of the ambassadorial gifts ;
those to the Wu-sun are specified as silk and gold.

It was now no longer a question merely of forming
military alliances for the perpetual struggle of China against
the Hiung-nu. This end was indeed still pursued, though
it was the co-operation of the Wu-sun rather than that of
the Yue-chi which was sought. But the new diplomacy
was for the most part directed towards other ends. It
was intended to glorify the Han court both at home and
abroad and at the same time to be an instrument of commerce in objects of luxury. From the *Shih-chi* we see that
no pains were spared to impress upon foreign nations the
greatness of China, whether by the sending out of embassies
or by the entertainment of return missions from the countries
visited. And the arrival at Ch'ang-an of the envoys of
kingdoms hitherto unknown, envoys clad in strange garb
and bearing for gifts things peculiar to their respective
countries, greatly added to the prestige of the house of Han
among its own subjects. Further, from the point of view
of the Emperor, the foreign products and curiosities received
as presents more than paid for the expenses of the diplomacy ;
in return for ordinary Chinese silks accepted as precious
things in Ferghana or Bactria or Parthia the Chinese court
received corresponding rarities from those lands. Thus the
exchange of embassies constituted a kind of trade, and
opened the way for further, non-official commerce by
creating habits and demands. The envoys themselves took
the opportunity to engage in private trading over and above
their proper duties, and sometimes even sold certain of the
presents which were destined for the ruler of the country
visited—delinquencies which if they were adverse to the
diplomatic designs of Wu Ti were certainly ' good for
trade.' Especially for *the* trade which now grew up and
was soon to extend its market westward to the Atlantic—
the commerce of silk.

Probably not all the embassies reached their destinations ; it was easy enough for envoys despatched to the extremities of the known world and dismayed by the distance or dangers of the road to collect a few curios from some fairly remote region and return with an imaginary account of countries they had not reached—nor would their story necessarily be rendered suspect by the fact that no return embassy came to Ch'ang-an. It is thus unlikely that any mission journeyed to Antioch, even if one was destined for Syria (Li-kan), as the *Shih-chi* avers [1] ; not only is there no trace of such an event from the Greek side—this might not be conclusive in view of the many gaps in the material for Hellenistic history— but we are also informed in the *Hou-han-shu* [2] that no Chinese envoy had been as far west as Babylonia before the time of Kan-ying who journeyed there in A.D. 97. With Parthia on the other hand China certainly entered into diplomatic relations ; we are told that ' when the first embassy was sent from China to An-si (Parthia), the king of An-si ordered 20,000 cavalry to meet it on the eastern frontier. . . . After the Chinese embassy had returned An-si sent forth an embassy to come and see the extent and great-ness of the Chinese empire. They offered to the Chinese court large birds' eggs [3] and jugglers from Li-kan.'

The climax of Wu Ti's forward policy in Central Asia was the conquest of Ferghana by the war of 104–100 B.C. The Emperor sent presents to the king of Ferghana and requested in return a number of the special breed of horses for which his realm was famous. But Ferghana was by this time ' overstocked with Chinese produce,' and there was reluctance to give away the precious horses. Deeming that Chinese power could not reach them the king and magnates of Ferghana rejected the demand ; the Chinese envoys used insulting language, and were in retaliation murdered at the frontier on their return journey. A Chinese army under a general named Li Kuang-li was sent to avenge them, but it was driven back after many of the troops had perished from starvation in the Tarim deserts.

[1] § 79 (Hirth, *op. cit.*).    [2] Ch. 88.    [3] Ostriches' eggs ?

Wu Ti, however, refused to admit defeat. 'The Emperor thought that his having sent an unsuccessful expedition against Ferghana, a small country, would cause Bactria and other neighbouring states to feel contempt for China, and that the pedigree horses of Ferghana would never be forth-coming.' A new army was therefore sent out—'60,000 men not counting those who followed as carriers of extra provisions; 100,000 oxen; more than 30,000 horses, myriads of donkeys, mules and camels, and a commissariat well stocked with supplies besides cross-bows and other arms. All parts of the empire had to bestir themselves in making contributions.' This force overcame the desert by dividing into columns which took different routes; on reaching Ferghana it won a decisive victory and obtained the submission of the country. Subsequently ' China sent more than ten embassies to countries west of Ferghana to collect curiosities and at the same time to impress upon such countries the importance of the victory over Ferghana.'

Thus by the end of the second century B.C., within twenty-eight years of the discovery by Chang Ch'ien of China's 'New World,' Chinese arms had penetrated trium-phantly west of the Pamir divide, and regular intercourse with Western Asia had been established. And now through Western Asia an indirect trade gradually developed, linking China with Europe. During the early years of the first century the use of silk, which at the Parthian court probably dated from the coming of the first Chinese embassy, spread from Parthia to the Mediterranean. The taste won its way to Europe at a time when the unification by Rome of the whole Mediterranean world had given unprecedented stimulus to industry and commerce and had created an enormously rich ruling class with an appetite for every kind of exotic luxury. By the Augustan Age silk is familiar merchandise in Italy, and its Chinese name finds its way into the poetry of Propertius, Horace and Virgil.

In Ferghana, in the valley of the upper Iaxartes, the army of Li Kuang-li advancing from the east encamped perhaps on the very ground which two hundred and twenty-seven years before had seen the tents of Alexander of Macedon. The great march of Alexander from the Hellespont to the Pamirs and the Punjab spread Greek settlements over Western Asia and brought Mesopotamia, Iran and India into one world of intercommunication with the lands of the Mediterranean. But it did nothing to open a road to China, which remained separate, secluded, utterly unknown, as it had been on another planet. Between Alexandria the Furthest and the Chinese pale in Kansu there intervened such a barrier of natural wilderness as did not anywhere confront the traveller between Spain and Bengal. A modern traveller has called the Takla-makan 'the most appalling desert on the face of the earth.' The bridging of this gap was accomplished not from the west but from the east, not by the Persians or by the Greeks but by the Chinese themselves. It was the Chinese who, first by an exploring diplomacy and then by force of arms, broke through to the land which alike for Achaemenid and Macedonian had been nothing but a cul-de-sac.

# CHAPTER III

## The Traffic of Silk

IN the Vicus Tuscus in Rome there was during the early
centuries of our era a market for Chinese silk. The
traffic of this silk was the most far-reaching large-scale
commerce of antiquity. Since the silk might be produced
in the littoral of the Yellow Sea and since Roman fashionable society existed for its demand in Spain, Gaul and
Britain, the trade drew the threads of its exquisite material
as a bond of economic unity across the whole of the Old
World from the Pacific to the Atlantic.

The silk trade was, however, but a part of Rome's commerce with non-Roman Asia. Trade between the Mediterranean, Iran and India had existed for centuries before
the imperialism of Wu Ti brought China into this circle
of economic intercourse, and though exact figures are
lacking, it is certain that throughout Roman imperial
times the trade with India was far larger than that with
China. The silk trade has its own peculiar problems for
the historian, but in many ways it is inseparable from the
Rome-India trade, which by its pre-existence and permanently greater importance determined the principal
channels of commercial intercourse and the structure of
the market in Western Asia. The study of silk, therefore,
involves a consideration of the origins and development of
the commerce between the Roman empire and India [1]—the
commerce through which, as Pliny says,[2] ' India is brought
near by lust for gain.'

[1] See the admirable work by E. H. Warmington ; *The Commerce
between the Roman Empire and India* (1928).
[2] Pliny, VI, 101.

The Achaemenid Persian empire had held under a single sway a territory extending from the Indus to the Mediterranean, and a Carian, Scylax of Caryanda, under orders from Darius I sailed from the Indus round Arabia and up the Red Sea to Arsinoe near the modern Suez. There was a certain amount of Mediterranean-India trade ; by it, for instance, peacocks were introduced into Greece from India in the fifth century B.C. But the total was evidently small, and it did not greatly increase during the Hellenistic period. The unification by Alexander of Greece and Persia, the provision made in the new empire for the Greek mercantile class and for the organization everywhere of urban life on the Greek model, and the release into circulation of the immense hoarded treasures of Susa and Persepolis gave promise of vast economic expansion. But the political disintegration of the Macedonian empire and the concentration of both the Seleucid and Ptolemaic policies on the maintenance of the balance of power in the Mediterranean were adverse factors. The Seleucids held the ports at the head of the Persian Gulf, and after the loss of the Indus provinces they marched with the Maurya empire by land at the Hindu Kush passes and in Seistan, so that their subjects could either sail to India by sea from Babylonia or go overland across Persia. But from the first they allowed the Persian Gulf traffic to fall into the hands of independent intermediaries, the Gerrhaean Arabs of Gerrha on the southern shore of the Gulf, while from 250 B.C. onwards the overland trade was intercepted by the rebel Bactrians and Parthians. The great rivals of the Seleucids, the Ptolemies of Egypt, held part of the western shore of the Red Sea, and it was thus possible for their subjects to reach India by a continuous voyage ; but the use of the monsoons for sailing to India was not yet known to the Greeks, the royal monopoly of foreign trade maintained by the Ptolemies restricted enterprise, and here again the trade with India fell into the hands of middlemen, in this case chiefly the Sabaeans of the Yemen. Meanwhile, in the Mediterranean the Hellenistic period

was marked by a series of great wars and outbursts of
piracy which disorganized long-distance commerce and
retarded the accumulation of wealth.

   The costs of ancient commerce fell under three heads :
(*a*) transport, (*b*) tariffs and tolls, and (*c*) losses from requisi-
tion, brigandage and piracy.  Of these the first, transport
costs, were susceptible of only slight variations ;  in the
other two categories on the other hand enormous reductions
or increases were always possible.  Let us suppose for the
sake of argument that a commodity produced in a place
A is demanded in a place E and that its traffic passes
through intermediate stages B, C and D ;  let us suppose
further that of these stages B is a wild region infested by
savage tribes ;  that C is a weak state unable to suppress
brigands within its borders and comprising a number of
petty feudatory states with rights of levying toll ;  while D,
a strong state, is normally at war with the state in control
of E.  This would be quite a typical situation in ancient
commerce.  And we are assuming provisionally that there
are no middleman profits, that the merchants of E buy
directly from those of A, either by going to them in their
own country or meeting them in one of the intermediate
stages of the route, and liable only to the customs dues
in C and D and possible highway robbery in B or C.  If,
of course, C or D or both prevent direct exchange and
give the transit trade to their own merchants, the profits
of the latter must also be added to the cost of the commodity before it can be sold to the consumer by the merchant
of E.  It can be imagined, then, that the sale price of the
commodity in E does not remotely resemble its cost price
in A.  But if we now suppose that D and E become united
under a single political authority, that A effectively con-
quers the savage tract B, and that C eliminates its brigands
and sub-states, the price may be expected to drop con-
siderably, even if there is a profiteering ring of merchants
in C trying to keep it up.  And if finally we suppose
that the merchants of E find a direct way by sea to
A with only a slight risk from pirates, we are con-

fronted with possibilities of price-cutting that are almost fantastic.

In other words, prices in such a commerce may be reduced by eliminating tolls and middleman profits, and by suppressing brigandage and piracy. The middleman or toll-levying power may be either abolished by armed conquest or checked by a vigorous diplomacy or outflanked by the discovery of new and more direct channels of trade. Brigandage and piracy may be suppressed by a state or states policing the trade-routes, or they may be rendered more or less innocuous by the sheer size and strength of the commercial expeditions themselves ; the latter kind of immunity can only be obtained by commerce when it is on a large scale, and implies a large demand and purchasing power in the country of import and considerable sums of capital available for investment in commercial enterprises. In all these ways commercial costs, and following them selling prices, may be reduced. Demand and purchasing power operate as factors in price-cutting by increasing turnover as well as by enlarging the trade and thereby giving it a greater capacity for self-protection against robbery. Increased prosperity in the locality of demand swells the volume of the trade even if there is no drop in prices ; and with a drop in prices the trade expands still further. A consideration of these general principles serves to explain in outline the vast economic expansion, involving the greater part of the Old World, which followed on the final establishment of the *Pax Romana* by the victory of Augustus at Actium in 31 B.C. The unification of the entire Mediterranean world and of the Egyptian Red Sea littoral under the peaceful rule of a single autocrat ; the elimination within the empire of all tolls and exactions with the exception of the comparatively insignificant provincial customs ; the suppression of brigandage and piracy in the empire and its seas ; the concentration of vast wealth in the hands of the Roman ruling class combined with an avid taste for all rare and exotic objects of luxury ; the existence of a money economy with banking and credit

facilities and an advanced technique of production in agriculture, mining and manufacture—all these factors went
to make a boom in the trade between the Mediterranean
and India, and to them all was added by the middle of
the first century A.D. the discovery of the direct passage
from the Red Sea to India by the use of the monsoons.

It was the all-sea way between Roman Egypt and Indian
ports, at first by coasting voyage round the south of Arabia
and later by the use of the monsoons, which was the supreme
price-regulating factor in Rome's oriental commerce during
the two and a half centuries after Actium.  The overland
and Persian Gulf routes from India to Syria were controlled
by Parthia and her vassal states ; the caravan route across
Arabia from Gerrha on the Persian Gulf to Petra near the
head of the Red Sea was controlled by the Nabataean
Arabs when it was not rendered impassable by tribal
anarchy.  But from the time when Roman subjects established regular direct relations with the Indian exporters
by the all-sea route, the Parthian and Arab middlemen intercepting the other routes had to adjust their prices if they
were to compete in the Roman market.

As already mentioned, the all-sea route itself had been
intercepted by middlemen in the time of the Ptolemies,
and it was destined to be again intercepted in the third
century A.D.  As the latter event involved the Chinese
silk trade, it may be as well to follow the history of the
all-sea route in somewhat closer detail in order to make
clear the conditions on which its maintenance depended.
In the Hellenistic period the Sabaeans, who at the end of
the second century B.C. became merged with the Himyarites
and are afterwards generally known by that name, held
the Yemen with their ports at Arabia Eudaemon (Aden)
and Ocelis a little farther to the west.  They themselves
traded with India, and they used their power to prevent
Indian ships from entering the Red Sea and Egyptian
ships from leaving it.  The barrier they set up was seldom
passed before 30 B.C.  But after the annexation of Egypt
as the private domain of Augustus, the whole power of

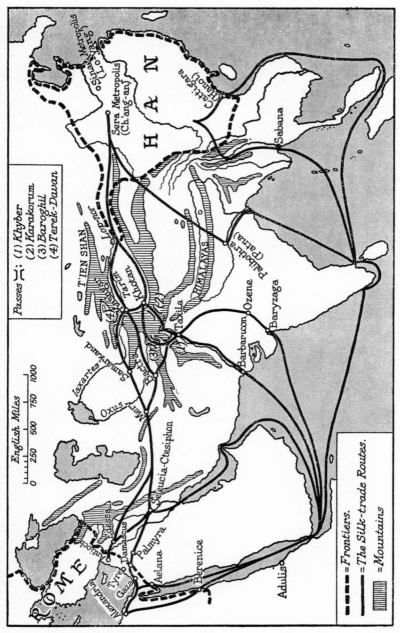

ROUTES OF THE SILK TRADE BETWEEN CHINA AND ROME IN THE FIRST AND SECOND CENTURIES A.D.

73

imperial Rome was available to back Egyptian commerce.
In 25 B.C. a military expedition under Aelius Gallus was
sent through south-west Arabia, and though it achieved
no spectacular success it appears to have served well as a
demonstration. At some later date, according to the
*Periplus of the Erythraean Sea* of the time of Nero, a Roman
expedition made a temporary occupation of Aden. We
have hardly any information about these events, but it
is clear that Rome became the paramount power in the
Red Sea. The Roman mercantile interest was further in
a position to apply economic pressure to the Himyarites,
for Rome was the chief market for the incense and perfumes
of South Arabia, and the custom could be allotted between
the various kingdoms according to their good behaviour.
The Himyarites therefore ceased to molest the direct
voyagers ; Roman ships were free to sail to India, and
some Indian ships came to Egypt. Strabo tells us that in
the reign of Augustus as many as 120 ships set out in a
single year from the Egyptian Red Sea ports Myos Hormos
and Berenice, bound for lands outside the Straits of Bab-el-
Mandeb, and that some even sailed as far as the Ganges.[1]
This was before the discovery of the use of the monsoons ;
coasting was still the only method. It was in the reign
of Tiberius that a Roman [2] merchant first made a voyage
from the Gulf of Aden to the mouth of the Indus by
striking out into the open sea and committing himself to
the south-west summer monsoon. The technique of the
use of the monsoons was gradually developed until at last
' about A.D. 50 a nameless merchant, bolder than the rest,
by ordering his helmsman to pull constantly on his rudder,
and his sailors to make a shift of the yard, found an open-
sea route from the Gulf of Aden in an arc of a circle (bent

[1] Strabo, II, 118 ; XV, 686 ; XVII, 798, 815.

[2] ' Roman ' in these pages is to be understood as ' Roman subject.'
The ' Romans ' engaged in the oriental trade appear to have been
almost exclusively Greeks or Semites (usually bilingual and half-
hellenized), natives of Syria and Egypt. But they were often backed
financially as well as politically by ' real ' Romans.

northwards) to the South Indian coast, which he touched near the greatest of all Indian marts, the town of Muziris (modern Cranganore).' [1]  Thus it was now possible to reach by direct open-sea sailing any one of the three main centres of commerce on the west coast of India, Barbaricon at the mouth of the Indus, Baryzaga on the Gulf of Cambay or Muziris in Malabar.  A journey could be made from Italy to India in sixteen weeks, including the land stage through Egypt ; India had indeed been ' brought near by lust for gain.'  And towards the end of the first century Roman merchants went further.  The west-coast ports continued to be the termini for the great majority of Roman ships, but a few passed round Cape Comorin, and from the Coromandel coast the monsoons were again used to cut the Bay of Bengal, and open-sea voyages were made, first to the ports at the mouths of the Irrawaddy and Salwen, and then to Sumatra and the Straits of Malacca.  Finally by sailing round the Malay Peninsula Roman merchants found an all-sea route to China (Tongking, which was then Chinese territory), though it was never brought into regular use.

Thus direct maritime commerce based on the Red Sea ports of Roman Egypt opened up the whole southern coastline of Asia and even penetrated into the Pacific. Not all, indeed, of the long-distance voyagers in the Indian Ocean were Roman subjects.  Indian ships sailed to Egypt on the one hand and to China on the other,[2] the Arabs ranged perhaps as far.  But whoever actually carried the trade, there was in the second century at any rate no absolute barrier to prevent a Roman subject from sailing from Egypt to Tongking or to any intermediate point, and to this extent a market of free competition prevailed. No middleman power was able to corner the traffic, and piracy could be defied wherever the scale of profit was sufficient for the fitting out of expeditions of one or more large ships carrying armed guards in addition to the crew.

[1] E. H. Warmington, *The Ancient Explorers*, p. 77.

[2] *Milindapañha*, 359, quoted in the Introduction (see p. 22).  Cf. Dion Chrysostom (*Or.*, ed. Arnim, 22 and 40) for Indians at Alexandria.

It was the maritime routes, therefore, which determined the movement of prices in the Roman oriental trade as long as direct voyaging was possible, breaking down or at least modifying the great middleman monopolies of the land routes. And the price-cutting attack of the sea traffic against the land led often to a diversion of trade routes to the sea for the purpose of outflanking land intermediaries.

Such were the general conditions governing Rome's oriental commerce, of which the silk trade formed an important, yet minor, part. Silk, as we have seen, was probably introduced into Western Asia by the Parthians when they had been made familiar with it by the presents of Chinese embassies ; after a while the Parthians bought it not only for their own consumption but also to sell further west. Silk thus first reached the Mediterranean by an overland route, via Seleucia (on the Tigris) and Antioch, and this continued to be the main channel of the trade. But with the great expansion of direct commerce in the Indian Ocean Roman shipping from the Red Sea tapped the silk trade, not merely by the all-sea route from Egypt to Tongking which was discovered late and was never decisive in its effects, but also at ports in Burma, in Bengal, in North-west India and in the Persian Gulf. By the competition of these various routes the trade was developed until at Rome in about 380, in the words of Ammianus Marcellinus, ' the use of silk which was once confined to the nobility has now spread to all classes without distinction, even to the lowest.'

Silk brought to Rome by the land route came in the first stage from the north-west of China along the northern rim of the Nan-shan mountain range through modern Kan-chou, Su-chou and An-hsi-chou. Thence to Kashgar by either of two routes, the one passing to the north, the other to the south of the terrible Takla-makan desert. From Kashgar there were again alternative roads. One crossed by the Terek Davan pass into Ferghana and then by Samarkand to Antiochia Margiana (Merv) ; the other went over the Pamirs by a route the exact course of which

is much disputed, but which probably parted from the
Samarkand route at Irkeshtam, turned to the left across
the Taun-murun Pass, descended through the Wakhshāb
valley, crossed the upper Oxus, passed through Badakshan
to Bactra (Balkh) and then on to Merv. These two ways
will henceforth be referred to as the Samarkand and Balkh
routes respectively. From Merv the road ran west-south-
west across northern Iran, through Hecatompylos (the old
Parthian capital near Damgan) and Ecbatana (Hamadan)
to Seleucia-Ctesiphon on the Tigris (just below modern
Baghdad—Seleucia the old viceregal city of the Seleucids
and Ctesiphon the court town of the Parthians planted
on the opposite, i.e. left, bank of the river). From Seleucia
the trade normally followed the old royal road of the
Achaemenids and Seleucids through northern Mesopotamia
to Syria, crossing the Euphrates at Zeugma, where there
was a Roman legionary camp, and arriving at Antioch ;
from there goods could be shipped to Italy by the port of
Apamea, but as the silk was usually destined for manufacture in the cities of southern Syria which specialized in
textile and dyeing industries, notably Berytus, Tyre, Sidon
and Gaza, the greater part of the trade had to go south
from Antioch after having come west-north-west to Antioch
from Seleucia. Hence arose the demand for short cuts
across the Syrian Desert and the use of the route to Damascus
via Circesium and Palmyra or the even straighter way
from Seleucia through Petra. But the greater directness
of these routes was more than cancelled by their liability
to Bedawin raids, and they could only attract large custom
if some one power held undisputed sway in the great desert
tract, a condition which was fulfilled by Palmyra in the
second and third centuries A.D., but not appreciably in the
first.

The whole route from Kansu to the borders of the Roman
empire may be divided into four ' control stages ' according
to the political authority or group of authorities which
was dominant in each section. The four stages are as
follows :

I. From Kansu to the Pamirs, the tract which is most conveniently called Kashgaria, the part of the present province of Sinkiang which lies south of the T'ien-shan divide, including the Tarim basin and the desert region east of Lop-nor.

II. From the Pamirs to the Merv oasis, that is, Bactria or Sogdiana, according to whether the Balkh or Samarkand route was followed.

III. From Merv to Seleucia inclusive.

IV. From a point a little way to the west of Seleucia to the Roman frontier on the Euphrates at Zeugma.

Of these, stages II and III admit of the simplest historical generalization for the opening centuries of our era. Bactria and Sogdiana were controlled from about 140 B.C. to about A.D. 450 by the Yue-chi, at first by the confederacy of their five tribes, then—throughout the first two and a half centuries A.D.—under the Kushan dynasty, and in the last phase under the Kidara. In the early fifth century Sogdiana and Bactria were conquered by the Ephthalites or White Huns, and from them passed in about 560 under the sway of the Turks. Thus we have in this area a succession of more or less unitary powers with a few brief intervals of confusion. In stage III the story for our purposes is soon told ; the road from Merv to Seleucia was under the direct control of the Parthian Arsacid kings from 129 B.C. to A.D. 224 and after that date, until the Arab conquest in the seventh century, of the Persian Sassanids.

Stages I and IV of the land route, however, were of constantly fluctuating allegiance. Since the successful conclusion of Wu Ti's campaign against Ferghana in 100 B.C. China has several times won and maintained for a while a supremacy over Kashgaria, and it is to-day part of the Chinese province of Sinkiang. But real Chinese control has been the exception rather than the rule ; it has always meant a strain on the resources of China and has been possible only for Chinese dynasties at the height of their power. In the early part of the first century A.D., when the Han dynasty declined, was broken by the usurpation of Wang Mang (A.D. 9–25), and restored after civil war, Chinese power in Kashgaria was at a very low ebb. A brilliant revival followed, especially with the campaigns of General Pan Ch'ao between A.D. 73 and 100, but a decline soon again set in, and there was no further great offensive of Chinese imperialism until the seventh century when the T'ang dynasty surpassed the record of the Han in the range of its conquests. In the periods of Chinese retreat, Kashgaria was either divided among the petty principalities of its oases, or else annexed by far-reaching nomad powers centred in Mongolia, Dzungaria or Tibet. It should be pointed out that physically Kashgaria alternates between patches of extremely fertile oasis and stretches of desert too sterile even for a nomad pastoralism ; hence it has never been itself the seat either of strong states of sedentary culture or of great nomad hordes.

Whenever Chinese dominion extended westward to the Pamirs it was possible for Chinese merchants to trade direct with Bactria and Sogdiana, but at other times the trade was conducted, or at any rate taxed, by intermediary states and tribes. These intermediaries were sometimes confused under the name of Seres with the real Chinese by Greek and Latin writers. Thus Pliny, speaking of an embassy sent to the Emperor Claudius by a king of Taprobane (Ceylon) says [1] : ' The Seres, too, who dwell beyond the mountains of Emodus [the Himalayas], and who are known to us by the commerce which is carried on with them, had been seen by these people [i.e. the envoys from Ceylon] ; the father of Rachias [the chief envoy], had visited their country, and they themselves on their travels had met with people of the Seres. They described these as surpassing the ordinary stature of mankind, as having red hair, blue eyes, hoarse voices, and no common language for communication. The rest of what they told was just as we have it from our own [i.e. Roman] traders. The goods carried thither are deposited on the further side of a certain river beside what the Seres have for sale, and the

[1] Pliny, *Nat. Hist.*, 6, 24.

latter, if content with the bargain, carry them off; acting, in fact, as if in contempt of the luxury to which they ministered, and just as if they saw in the mind's eye the object and destination and result of this traffic.' [1] This statement clearly does not refer to the real Chinese; it is to be taken rather as indicating tribesmen of the Pamirs, among whom a considerable blonde element survives at the present day.[2] The silent barter trade is likewise suitable to primitive mountaineers but not to any civilized people. We may believe therefore that the Pamir highlanders kept the silk trade in being even when there was no great imperial power in Kashgaria to link up with the Yue-chi and the Parthians. It had needed the imperialism of Wu Ti to establish the silk commerce, but once established it could survive severe stress from political disintegration, because the profit to be derived from it had become obvious to even the more barbaric peoples along the route. In Kashgaria itself the little states of Turfan, Kucha, Ak-su, Khotan, Yarkand and Kashgar all had a share in the trade, while the Wu-sun from the north and the Tibetans from the south were inclined to take bites out of it.

The complication and mutability of political affairs along stage I of the overland silk route were paralleled to a lesser degree by conditions in stage IV, the last section of the route. Between the country directly ruled by the Parthian kings and Roman Syria there intervened several petty kingdoms, the most important of which was Osrhoene with its capital at Edessa ; the majority of these were nominally vassals of Parthia, but actually northern Mesopotamia and still more the desert tract in the angle between Syria and the Euphrates were a no man's land wherein Roman policy sought to maintain buffer states against Parthia. Parthia was strong enough to resist absorption by Rome, but was never strong enough to centralize its ' empire,' and a core

[1] The point of this remark lies in Pliny's objection to oriental luxuries in general, and in particular to the semi-transparent silk gauzes worn in Roman fashionable society.
[2] Especially among the Galchas.

of directly ruled territory extending from Babylonia in the
west to Merv and Kandahar in the east was surrounded to
north, west and south by a belt of semi-independent feudatory states.   On the side of Parthia towards Syria the
centrifugal tendencies of Parthian vassals were encouraged
by Rome as a means of weakening Parthia after the Roman
appetite for annexation east of the Euphrates had been
restrained by the costly failures of Crassus and Antony
against the elusive Parthian power.   Thus the kingdom
of Osrhoene which had been founded by an Arab tribe
out of the wreck of the Seleucid empire towards the end
of the second century B.C. was maintained in virtual independence, and its court was a cockpit for the intrigues of
Roman and Parthian diplomacy.   In Mesopotamia to the
south-east of Osrhoene were several semi-independent Arab
tribes which cut into the Seleucia-Antioch trade route,
while in the desert to the south of the Euphrates was Palmyra owing nominal allegiance to Rome.   This was the
situation, except for the period of Trajan's Parthian war
(A.D. 114–117), until 165 when as a result of a three years'
war north-west Mesopotamia was ceded by Parthia to Rome.
The independence of Osrhoene was finally brought to an
end by Caracalla in 216.   Soon afterwards the concentration of government under the Persian Sassanid dynasty
which had supplanted the Arsacids at Ctesiphon brought
direct Persian into contact with direct Roman rule, and
the destruction of Palmyra by Aurelian in 273 after its
brief career as a great power concludes the era of buffer
states on the Euphrates.   But as long as the buffer states
lasted they were of great economic importance, and both
Osrhoene and Palmyra grew rich as commercial intermediaries between Rome and Parthia.

With so many powerful middlemen it is little wonder
that the silk trade between Rome and China by the overland route was almost always indirect.   We do not know
for certain that any Roman subject ever reached China
or any Chinese ever reached the borders of Rome by overland travel.   There are, however, two travel records, the

one from the Chinese side and the other from the Roman, which reveal the endeavour from both ends to establish direct intercourse, which served as standard geographical ' authorities ' in their respective literatures, and which provide us with much valuable information. One of these sources is the report of the Chinese envoy Kan Ying, who in A.D. 97 was sent out with instructions to proceed to Ta Ts'in (the Roman empire), but did not go farther than T'iao-chih (Babylonia) ; the information about Western Asia which he obtained from experience and by hearsay became the principal ingredient in Chinese accounts of the countries west of Parthia. The corresponding Roman source is the work of a Greek merchant Maës Titianus which has perished, but was used both by Marinus of Tyre and by Ptolemy—who tells us of Maës ' not that he made the journey himself, but he had sent agents to the Seres.' The date of these trading ventures is uncertain, but it was probably about A.D. 120–140, after Hadrian had concluded peace with Parthia and after Chinese power in Central Asia had declined from the point to which it had been carried by the wars of Pan Ch'ao ; the decline is indicated by Ptolemy's division of Kashgaria between Serica, i.e. Chinese dominion, and Scythia extra Imaum, i.e. independent states.

The journey of Kan Ying is related in the *Hou-han-shu* [1] as follows : ' The *tu-hu* [general] Pan Ch'ao sent Kan Ying as an ambassador to Ta Ts'in, and he arrived in T'iao-chih on the coast of the great sea. When he was about to take his passage across the great sea, the sailors of the western border of An-hsi [Parthia] told him that the sea was very vast, that it could be traversed within three months, but with unfavourable winds might take two years, . . . that there was something in the sea which made a man long for home, and that many men lost their lives on it. When he heard this, Ying did not go any farther.'

The sea route on which Kan Ying was unwilling to ven-

[1] Ch. 88.

ture was, as is clear from this and other Chinese references, the way from Babylonia down the Persian Gulf, round southern Arabia and up the Red Sea, either to an Egyptian port or, if bound for Syria, to Aelana at the head of the Gulf of Akaba. The *Hou-han-shu* gives, following the passage above quoted, details of the road to Babylonia as far as a city called Yü-lo, whence ships sailed south and then turned round to the north to reach Ta Ts'in. In another account [1] it is said that the voyage was to the west following the coast in a great detour and coming to an arm of the sea with land to east and west of it (either the Red Sea itself or the Gulf of Akaba). We know from Roman sources that there was a traffic between Babylonia and Egypt by this roundabout sea route, though we are not told that it was used for silk.

But why, if Kan Ying did not like the idea of a sea voyage, did it not occur to him to try going overland to Syria? The answer appears to be that he was told by the Parthians of the sea route but not of the land route. It was the aim of the Parthians to put off Kan Ying if possible without giving offence. They had been afraid to refuse passage to the embassy in view of the formidable reputation of the conquering general who had sent it, but at the same time they were exceedingly anxious to prevent an intercourse between Chinese and Romans, which would reveal to each the profiteering of the Parthian merchants and perhaps lead to measures to cut them out. The *Hou-han-shu* shows an insight into the situation when it says that ' the kings of Ta Ts'in always desired to send embassies to China, but the Parthians wished to carry on trade with Ta Ts'in in Chinese silks and therefore cut them off from communication.' So when Kan Ying came west, the Parthians saw to it that he learnt nothing about the land route, but guided him to the starting-point of the sea route and there terrified him with tales of the perils of the sea. They had judged well the man with whom they were dealing, for it is clear that Kan Ying was from the landward

[1] *Wei-shu*, 102.

side of China and knew nothing of the sea. In the account of his embassy in the *Chin-shu* [1] we are told as part of his report that ' the great sea crossed on the way to Ta Ts'in is salt and bitter and unfit for drinking '—a statement which would be absurd from one familiar with the sea, but is quite intelligible in relation to the great lakes of Central Asia, which may be either fresh or salt. [2] So Kan Ying was headed off from his objective, and it was only later on that the Chinese learnt of the continued overland route between Seleucia and Syria. The *Wei-lio* [3] which describes the latter remarks that ' formerly only the sea routes were heard of ; the overland route was not known to exist.'

The journeys made by the agents of the silk merchant Maës Titianus [4] were across Parthia and must have been by special privilege granted by the Parthian court ; we are told that Maës was a hereditary merchant, so he probably began with a fortune large enough to gain his ends either by direct bribery of Parthian magnates or by obtaining the good offices of Roman imperial diplomacy. The agents straightened out the first part of the overland route by going from Zeugma to Ecbatana through the country of the Garamaeans (south-east of Mosul) ; beyond Merv they followed the route by Bactra over the Pamirs into Kashgaria. But they do not appear from Ptolemy to have reached China itself, and certainly there is no trace in the Han records of the arrival of Roman subjects by the overland route. On the other hand, they brought back information which, although arranged by Ptolemy with an exactness that is quite illusory, was nevertheless the most important contribution made to the Greek geography of Eastern Asia. From Ptolemy's description, derived from Maës through Marinus of Tyre, we can recognize the chief mountain ranges, the rivers Tarim and Hoang-ho, and the city of Ch'ang-an in Shen-si, the former Han

[1] Ch. 97.    [2] Balkash and Baikal are both fresh.
[3] Quoted in the *San-kuo-chih*, ch. 30.
[4] Ptolemy I, 11, 4–8 ; 12, 2–10 ; VI, 31, 1 ; 16, 1–8.

capital.[1] But no hint was obtained of sea to the east of China, and the information Ptolemy received from voyagers to Tongking—who sailed up the Gulf of Tongking but did not go east of Hainan—was not sufficient to contradict his belief that the Indian Ocean was enclosed to the east and south by land. Thus Ptolemy continues China to the east with unknown land, in this respect showing a decline in knowledge from Pomponius Mela and Pliny[2] who, both drawing from a common source, put the Seres on the shores of the Ocean in the extreme east of Asia.

Apart from the overland route the Chinese silk trade was, as already stated, tapped by Roman shipping from the Red Sea. The nearest point at which overland commerce from the east could be sidetracked so as to cut out a middleman was of course in the Persian Gulf, and the use of the seaway round Arabia for silk is suggested by the story of Kan Ying. It would indeed be going too far to argue, as Hirth[3] does, that the diversion from Seleucia and round by sea to Aelana was the normal route of the traffic. This route to the Roman empire was the only one of which for reasons of policy the Chinese were allowed to know, but that does not prove that it carried the bulk of the silk trade or even any at all. The roundabout sea way might be convenient for trade between Babylonia and Egypt, but the silk imports were for the most part destined for manufacturing processes in Syria, and the natural course of goods bound for Syria and having come as far as Seleucia would be to finish the journey by land. We have seen, however, that quasi-independent states with inhabitants of great commercial enterprise intervened between Seleucia and Roman Syria, the middle powers of stage IV of the China-Rome overland route. Hence the importance of the sea way round

[1] Sera Metropolis. Lo-yang in Honan was the capital in the time of Maës ; it is called Sinae Metropolis by Ptolemy, who knew it by the Tongking route ; the change of capital led to the idea that the Seres and Sinae were different nations.

[2] Mela, *De situ orbis*, I, 2 and III, 7 ; Pliny, *Nat. Hist.*, VI, 20.

[3] F. Hirth, *China and the Roman Orient*, pp. 169–72.

Arabia ; it could always be used to defeat by a direct trading with Parthia profiteering and extortion by Osrhoene and Palmyra and the desert tribes. It is true that lower Babylonia also was occupied by a separate kingdom vassal to Parthia, namely Mesene or Characene, but there is reason to believe that, at any rate before the time of Trajan's Parthian wars, the control of the Arsacid suzerain over Mesene was much more effective than it was over the states towards the Roman frontier. So the Persian Gulf route in spite of its deviousness enabled Roman merchants to tap trade coming through Parthia, and the land middle-men between Rome and Parthia could only recapture it by lowering prices.

Farther east the Roman merchants established a connec-tion by sea which could cut out not only stage IV but also stage III of the overland silk trade, not only the Euphrates buffer states, but also Parthia itself. The evidence for this is supplied by that invaluable anonymous work *The Periplus of the Erythraean Sea*, probably dating from the reign of Nero, which gives the following note on the silk trade and on China : ' Behind this country [Chryse, i.e. Lower Burma and the Malay Peninsula] the sea comes to an end some-where in Thin [1] ; and in the interior of that country, some-what to the north, there is a very great city called Thinae, from which raw silk and silk thread and silk stuffs are brought overland through Bactria to Baryzaga, as they are on the other hand by the Ganges River to Limyrice [Coro-mandel coast]. It is not easy, however, to get to this Thin, and few and far between are those who come from it.'

The route to Baryzaga through Bactria, of which this passage speaks, was a result of the founding of the Kushan empire in India. The Yue-chi tribes, who held Bactria

[1] This is the earliest occurrence in European literature of this name (*Thin, Sin, Chin, China*) ; it is at least a century later than the use of the name *Seres*, and comes by the sea route, whereas *Seres* was a name of the land route. Thin probably represents a Further Indian name for China derived from the great dynasty of Ts'in or Ch'in which preceded the Han. For a summary of the controversy about the word see Yule, *Cathay and the Way thither*, ed. Cordier, vol. I, pp. 1–14.

and Sogdiana, stage II of the overland silk route, were early in the first century A.D. united under the sway of the Kushan dynasty, and soon built up a great empire over North-west India, the ports of which were now thronged with merchants from Roman Egypt. With the extension of Kushan ascendency from Samarkand to the Indian Ocean it became profitable both for Kushan and for Roman merchants to enter into direct commercial relations and divert trade from Parthia. Thus silk brought from Kashgar over the Pamirs to Bactria might, instead of being sent on through Parthian Merv, be taken over one of the passes of the Hindu Kush and through the Khyber to the great city of Taxila near the modern Rawalpindi ; thence down to the Indus to Barbaricon or by way east of the Thar to Baryzaga on the Gulf of Cambay. The *Periplus* mentions silk as exported from Barbaricon as well as from Baryzaga.

The silk trade down the Ganges on the other hand was not a diversion from the overland route to Syria, but linked up with a route from China to India across Tibet. According to Ptolemy [1] : ' They say that there is not only a road from these lands [of the Seres and Sinae] to Bactriana by the Stone Tower [in the Pamirs], but also one to India which goes through Palimbothra [Pataliputra, now Patna].' This probably followed the line of the present route from Kansu to Lhasa, and thence across the Himalayas through Sikkim ; from Patna silk could be taken down the Ganges to ports on the Bay of Bengal visited by Roman merchants. There was yet another connection with Roman shipping by a route from China to the coasts of Burma where there were two considerable emporia, Tacola near Rangoon and Sabana near Moulmein, outlets for the Irrawaddy and Salwen valleys respectively. The *Wei-shu* [2] indicates the routes used, remarking that ' there is a connection by sea [of Ta Ts'in] with the principalities of Yi-chou [Yunnan] and Yung-ch'ang [near Bhamo].'

[1] I, 17.
[2] Ch. 102. Cf. *Hou-han-shu*, 86, and *San-kuo-chih*, 30, quoted by Hirth, *China and the Roman Orient*.

Finally the net of Roman commerce in the Indian Ocean reached out to Tong-king with the port of Cattigara (probably Hanoi), Ptolemy's ' harbour of the Sinae ' [1] at the head of the ' Great Gulf.' The Chinese had annexed the Tongking coast to their empire while Kwang-tung to the east was still held by unsubdued tribes, and Tong-king was in Han times China's main channel of communication to the south. The pioneer of Roman commerce in the seas beyond Malaya was a certain Alexander, who had previously led the way in experiments in open-sea sailing with the monsoons in the Bay of Bengal. Sometime before the middle of the second century A.D. he made a voyage to Cattigara, touching at Zabae (apparently near Saigon), and wrote an account of his travels, which, like the report of Maës Titianus on the land route to China, was used by Marinus of Tyre and Ptolemy for their geographies.

The confusion in these writers about the waters round the Malay Peninsula suggests that Alexander did not sail through the Straits of Malacca, but crossed the Isthmus of Kra and took passage in a native ship on the other side for his exploring visit to Cattigara. However, the all-sea route must soon have been discovered by Alexander's successors. Indian ships already used it ; the *Milindapañha* speaks of the voyage to China, and the age of Hindu colonial expansion to Java and Cambodia had begun. But the Malayan seas were infested, as they have always been, with pirates, and only a few Roman merchants were found to brave their perils at so great distance from Egypt. Apart from Alexander's voyage, the only notices of them are from the Chinese side. In the year A.D. 166, according to the *Hou-han-shu*, ' the king of Ta Ts'in, An-tun [Antoninus, Marcus Aurelius] sent an embassy which coming from the border of Jih-nan [Annam] offered ivory, rhinoceros-horn and tortoise-shell. From that time dates [direct] intercourse [with Ta Ts'in]. But the fact that the list of tribute includes no jewels throws doubt on the tradition.' This embassy is also mentioned by the *Liang-shu* [2] which adds,

[1] Ptolemy, VII, 2.  [2] Ch. 54.

apparently alluding to the same period, that 'merchants
of Ta Ts'in often visit Fu-nan [Siam], Jih-nan [Annam]
and Chiao-chih [Tong-king], but that few from those countries have been to Ta Ts'in.' The *Liang-shu* also records
that a Roman merchant named Lun (Leo ?), arriving in
Tongking in 226, was sent on to the court of Sun-ch'üan,
emperor of the Wu dynasty, at Nanking, and was questioned by the latter about his country.   On his return to
Ta Ts'in the Wu emperor sent an official named Liu Hsien
to accompany him with a present of dwarfs for the Roman
court.   But the envoy died on the way, and the imperial
compliments of Nanking were not conveyed to Rome.   In
284, however, a second Roman 'embassy' arrived in China
and presented 30,000 rolls of thin aghal-wood.

It is clear from these accounts that the Roman 'embassies' were merely private commercial missions assuming
an official status to further their ends ;  their presents were
products not of the Roman empire but of the Indies.   It
was no doubt customary for Roman merchants trading far
to the east to sell their Roman cargoes in India and then
carry Indian goods to Malaya and beyond.   There is no
trace in contemporary Roman history of any embassy sent
to, or received from, the Chinese.   The only attempt at
official communication seems to have been that made by
Sun-ch'üan.   The Roman visit in 166 has been convincingly
interpreted as an enterprise of Roman silk merchants to
meet the crisis caused by the Parthian wars of Marcus
Aurelius, which resulted in the destruction of Seleucia and
complete interruption for a while of the overland route
from China.   It is almost certain that the Han court was
aware that the 'embassy' was fraudulent, since it only
brought products of Further India as presents, but the
Chinese were flattered by the pretence of 'tribute,' and
no doubt the envoys were permitted to load a good cargo
of silk at Cattigara.

The attainment of Chinese ports by Roman merchants
towards the end of the second century seemed to promise
a new era of economic expansion ;  with the Mediterranean

a Roman lake and Roman direct commerce extending from the Red Sea to the Pacific it might have been expected that the third and fourth centuries would show a prosperity in the Roman world surpassing that of the first and second. In the event it was of course quite otherwise. Rome's story in the third century is one not of advance but of decline. Prolonged political and economic troubles diminished her purchasing power and a debased coinage upset her foreign trade, while at the same time she was unable to prevent the interception of the Red Sea route by Nubians, Abyssinians and Arabs. A few Roman merchants slipped or bribed their way through the cordon thus drawn, and among these were the visitors to China in 226 and 284. But even the voyage to India soon became exceptional. From the early years of the third century to the middle of the sixth, when the Chinese silkworm was introduced into the Roman empire, the silk traffic was in the hands of middlemen, and during most of the time the supply for Rome was an almost absolute monopoly of Persia. This period, however, belongs to another chapter. In the preceding pages we have viewed the trade only as an expanding activity, ever increasing its sales and opening up new routes which compete with one another. It has grown swiftly from small beginnings until at the zenith of its prosperity in the age of the Antonines silken fabrics are well nigh as familiar in Londinium as in Lo-yang.

The silk trade not only brought profits to the merchants who engaged in it ; it also provided the raw material for important manufacturing industries in Syria and Egypt, especially in Syria, where the finest Roman textile industry centred round the supply of the most famous of ancient dyes, the Tyrian purple. There is no evidence that there was ever in the Roman world a taste for Chinese patterned silks. Silk appears to have reached the Roman frontier in various forms, but always to have undergone subsequently some finishing process. The most usual of such processes was of a rather curious kind. We learn from ancient sources, both classical and Chinese, that the main demand of Roman fashion was for semi-transparent silk gauzes and that, in order to make these, close-textured Chinese silks were split and re-woven. Ma Tuan-lin says [1] that the people of Ta Ts'in bought Chinese *chien-su* (close-textured, plain silk-stuffs) and unravelled them to make *ling* (light-textured fabrics), and this is confirmed by Pliny [2] who declares that the Seres send to Rome ' the fleecy product of their forests ' and thus ' furnish our women with the double task of first unravelling and then reweaving the threads, . . . and all that a Roman lady may exhibit her charms in transparent gauze.' The form which silk manu-facture thus took in the Roman empire must be attributed to the endeavour to imitate in silk the earlier *bombycina* or ' Coan garments,' silk-like textures of extreme delicacy which had long been a local product of the island of Cos and had attained a wide popularity for light summer clothing, not only among women but also among men. The habit of wearing garments of this kind, which in Pliny's phrase ' render women naked ' (*ut denudet feminas vestis*) and were humorously said to be made of glass, seems to have spread through Roman fashionable society from the *demi-monde*, in spite of the protests of such moralists as Pliny and Seneca [3] ; but in the first century A.D. silk had generally superseded the Coan material [4] for their produc-tion. A great part of the silk import was treated in this way. Other silk stuffs were merely dyed to suit Roman taste, while silk thread was used for embroidery or mustered with wool and linen for the mixed fabrics of which large quantities were turned out by Syrian workshops.

For Rome the trade in silk and trade with China were virtually identical, and it was strictly appropriate that the nation should be named after the beautiful merchandise

---

[1] *Wên-hsien-t'ung-k'ao*, ch. 330.  [2] *Nat. Hist.*, VI, 20.

[3] Seneca, *De beneficiis*, VII, 9 : Video sericas vestes, si vestes vocandae sunt, in quibus nihil est quo defendi aut corpus, aut denique pudor possit.

[4] Just what this was is disputed, but it was an insect product like silk itself. See note on page 60.

which it sent forth. But though we may reckon that silk constituted at least 90 per cent. of China's export to Rome, there were also two or three other items on the Chinese side of the commerce. Pliny represents the Seres as sending to Rome, besides their silks, very valuable skins and the most highly prized kind of iron.[1] The trade in skins is attested by the statement of the *Periplus* that Seric skins were exported from Barbaricon, which, as we have seen, was also a mart for silk. The skins were perhaps of Central Asian snow-leopards and martens and Siberian sables. As regards the iron, however, doubt has been cast on Pliny's statement [2] on the ground that the *Periplus* does not indicate the export of iron from the same marts as silk, while there was a trade in Indian iron and steel, some of which may have come through the Chera Tamils and been wrongly attributed to the Seres on account of a confusion between the names Seres and Cheres. The objection certainly has some force, yet if we are to accept the *Periplus* as evidence Pliny was quite right in attributing a trade in furs to the Chinese, and the balance of probability is in favour of his having been right about the iron also ; as there was a large and highly skilled iron industry in North China in Han times, and Yule suggests that Pliny's iron was ' that fine cast-iron, otherwise unknown to the ancients, which is still one of the distinguishing manufactures of China.'

More important probably in the volume and value of its trade than either furs or iron, though the Romans did not know that it came from China, was the cinnamon bark which held a high place among Roman luxuries. To quote Warmington [3] : ' The very best bark must have come to the Romans from the Chinese as it does to-day ; in Persian records cinnamon is always called " Chinese bark," and from the third century onwards it was brought to the Persian Gulf by the Chinese themselves. The inferior bark must have come from Malabar. Three hundred

---

[1] *Nat. Hist.*, XXXIV, 41.
[2] Warmington, *Commerce between the Roman Empire and India*, p. 257.
[3] Warmington, *op. cit.*, p. 190.

denarii were paid for the best, ten for the very woody, five for the worst, and the oil mixed with other aromatics fetched from thirty-five to three hundred denarii, while special preparations from the flowers and shoots reached fifteen hundred denarii! All were used in medicines, unguents, wines and in incenses for funerals.'

Cinnamon, both Chinese and Indian, was carried by Indian ships, and in Hellenistic times was sold by them to the Arab and Ethiopian middlemen of the Red Sea, from whom the Greeks obtained it. So deeply rooted was the idea that cinnamon was an Ethiopian or Arabian product, that even when the Romans opened up direct commercial relations with India they did not discover that cinnamon was an Indian, much less a Chinese, product. They did buy in India cinnamon-leaf which they called malabathrum —some of it came from China through Tibet and Sikkim, according to the *Periplus*—but they did not know that it had anything to do with cinnamon proper, and the lucrative trade in the latter remained with the secret of its origin as a monopoly of middlemen. The traffic of cinnamon provides the most remarkable example in ancient times of a commercial secret successfully kept in spite of conditions most conducive to its being divulged.

Chinese also, although it was never known in antiquity, was the drug rhubarb [1] which the Romans obtained from somewhere to the north-east of the Black Sea. It was called *rha* from the name of the Volga (as given by Ptolemy), and with a redundant adjective *rha ponticum*, i.e. Black Sea *rha*, by those who did not know that *rha* was also a proper name, and Dioscurides describes it as a root brought from beyond the Bosphorus. The interesting point in connection with rhubarb is that it appears not to have been brought in early times along any of the silk routes, but to have been on the other hand the only commodity brought from China to Rome by way north of the Caspian. It is true that some historians suppose that there was always a silk route down the Oxus and around to the north or across

[1] See Warmington, *op. cit.*, pp. 207–8.

the Caspian to the Black Sea, and assign to the trade they thus imagine a part in determining Roman policy in Armenia, Iberia and on the Cimmerian Bosphorus.[1] But there is really no evidence for a regular silk trade along such a route in the first two centuries A.D. Some Indian traffic is alleged to have passed this way in the time of Alexander the Great, and we hear of it again at the time of Pompey's career in the east, but not later. In the absence of any great dominant power in Central Asia the route was hopelessly exposed to tribal raiding, and with such risks could not possibly compete for regular trade with the main overland or sea routes from India and China after the latter had been properly opened up.

Strabo,[2] speaking of his own time, says explicitly of the Caspian that ' there are no vessels upon the sea nor is it turned to any use,' and his belief that the Caspian was an inlet of the Ocean from the north is hardly compatible with the existence of an important trade passing to the north of it from Central Asia to the Sea of Azov. If, therefore, rhubarb, an insignificant item of Rome's oriental commerce, was brought by such a route, we must seek an explanation in exceptional circumstances. The Aorsi (An-ts'ai), who bordered on the north of the Caspian and were later on merged with the Alani, were one of the peoples to whom Chang Ch'ien is alleged in the *Shih-chi* to have despatched embassies. Perhaps rhubarb was among the diplomatic presents sent to the Aorsi and in the sequel its medicinal use ' took on ' with them ; later a Roman merchant discovered it among them, and it was marked

[1] See Warmington, pp. 26–8. The allusion in Strabo, XI, 6, 1, to the trade carried on by the Aorsi is not in any case contemporary but refers to the time of Pharnaces ; apart from this, the statement that they ' transported on camels merchandise of India and Babylonia, receiving it from the Armenians and Medes ' can only mean that they took it from the south along the *west* side of the Caspian and sold it in the north and north-west to Finnish and Sarmatian tribes and Bosporan Greeks. There is nothing in this passage about a trade from the Oxus.

[2] XI, 7.

down in the Roman market as their peculiar product. The Aorsi would have been in no hurry to clear up the misunderstanding, and probably charged prices which more than paid them for the trouble of obtaining the drug for Rome ; the demand was small, and Roman merchants, not knowing that it came originally from China, would not have tried to obtain it along the silk routes. But by the middle of the sixth century it is known, no longer as *rha ponticum*, but as *rha barbarum*, which suggests that it had by then found a way to Barbaricon, the great mart at the mouth of the Indus.[1] The Indian route probably at once cut out the Volga by the lower price it could afford ; in any case the northern trade in the drug must have been upset by the Hunnish and ensuing migrations across the steppes.

With furs, iron, cinnamon and rhubarb as a supplement to silk we come to the end of the list of Chinese contributions to the economy of Rome, and it only remains to ask what Rome gave for exchange in her Chinese trade. Fortunately we have Chinese lists of Ta Ts'in products which give us a fairly good idea. There was indeed no commodity from the other side which could be set against silk for scale and insistence of demand ; it was the Roman demand for silk rather than a Chinese demand for any Roman product which made the commerce, and it is therefore correctly referred to from any point of view as the silk trade. The Roman exports which reached China were, however, not unimportant. They fall into three categories —glass, textiles and miscellaneous.

According to a Chinese source the people of Ta Ts'in were not equalled by any other nation in the manufacture of glass. The Roman glass industry was centred at Alexandria, Tyre and Sidon and had attained to a high degree of technical skill ; it had a market throughout non-Roman Asia. Crude glass was exported, also glass vessels and

---

[1] In modern times Chinese rhubarb has been called ' Chinese,' ' Indian,' ' Russian ' or ' Turkey ' according to its route of export from China.

mirrors, but above all imitation jewellery and ornaments in coloured glass. In Han times glass ranked in China with jade and crystal among the precious materials, and the profits to be made from trade in it must have been very considerable. Gradually its rarity value disappeared, but there continued to be a large demand ; China did not produce glass for herself until the early fifth century, when the technique of glass-making was introduced by Yue-chi artisans.

Textiles of wool, of linen and even of silk passed to China from the workshops of Syria and Egypt. Fragments of a Syrian woollen textile of the first century B.C. have been found in Mongolia. According to Ma Tuan-lin ' the countries on the west of the sea ' (Hai-hsi-kuo), identified with Ta Ts'in,[1] produced rugs of all kinds, and their colours were superior to those of the industry in ' the countries on the east of the sea,' i.e. Babylonia and Persia, the sea being the stretch round Arabia from the Persian Gulf to the Red Sea, the maritime route known to Kan Ying. The note is interesting not only as an indication of trade but also as an expression of Chinese opinion on the merits of Levant Roman textile art in the first centuries of our era. Our Chinese sources also mention gold-thread embroideries, ' gold-coloured cloth,' a fine cloth made of ' water-sheep-down ' which was probably byssus, mustered goods and ling of various colours. The ling, as we have seen, was Chinese silk re-woven into gauzes, and some of it appears to have been exported to China ; it was so unlike the Chinese silks that for a long time its origin was not recognized and it was believed by the Chinese that the Romans themselves produced some sort of silk. Such a belief finds expression in the Hou-han-shu and is repeated by scholars in later works even after the real method of producing ling had become known.

[1] Politically Ta Ts'in (= Hai-hsi-kuo) was the Roman empire ; geographically it was Egypt and Syria. Most of the descriptions apply only to Syria, and An-tu (Antioch) was supposed to be the capital of Ta Ts'in. The Wei-lio shows a knowledge of Egypt, of the Nile, of Alexandria (Ch'ih-san) and of the Mediterranean (' another great sea ').

In the category of miscellaneous exports must be included corals and pearls from the Red Sea, amber from the Baltic, several kinds of precious stones cut or uncut, asbestos cloth, storax and a few other drugs and perfumes. Several of these commodities were not Roman products at all, but re-exports, and there were others sold by Roman merchants which never even came within Roman frontiers, but were both bought and sold again in the course of trading voyages. Thus Roman ships from Egypt exchanged wares in southern Arabia for the local incense and brought it to Barbaricon, where they could barter it for silk ; similarly they bought Indian cargoes with the proceeds of sales in India and traded with them farther east, and so again from Further India. The ' tribute ' articles brought to the Han court in 166, ivory, rhinoceros horn and tortoise-shell, imply a commerce of this kind.

In the absence of statistics we have no means of comparing the total values of import and export between China and Rome. But for Rome's oriental foreign trade as a whole we know that there was a serious adverse balance which was made up by bullion or specie payments. Pliny,[1] writing in the 'seventies of the first century A.D., declares that India took away from the Roman empire annually not less than 55 million sesterces (on the ordinary computation about £600,000), and, in another passage, that India, the Seres and Arabia together drained away at least 100 million (over £1,000,000)—' so dearly do we pay for our luxuries and our women.' Dion Chrysostom [2] likewise laments that Rome paid tribute to foreigners by giving away good money in return for articles of frivolous luxury. The great hoards of Roman coins found in India bear out the idea of a great eastward flow of specie from the Roman empire, and an old Tamil poem speaks of Yavana (Roman Greek) ships coming to Malabar with gold and going away laden with pepper.

There can be no doubt that the demand of the Roman

---

[1] *Nat. Hist.*, VI, 101 and XII, 84.
[2] *Or.*, LXXIX, 5–6 (Arnim).

upper class for oriental luxuries, notably spices, perfumes, gems and silk, was far in excess of any corresponding demand for Roman produce in non-Roman Asia, and that the great oriental demand, in accordance with the traditional treasure-hoarding habits of Asiatic monarchies, was just for the precious metals themselves, the gold and silver that were the basis of the whole monetized economic system of the Roman world. In this commerce the more primitive economy sucked the life-blood of the more advanced. The habit of hoarding, particularly characteristic of India, meant in any case the withdrawal of specie from circulation over long periods, and there was the further risk of total loss in times of trouble when treasure hoards were usually buried in some secret place ; thus the balance of trade against Rome was not rectified, as it would be in free trade between states of similar economy. There has been in modern times an adverse balance in European trade with the East, but its harmful effects have been cancelled out by other economic factors, of which not the least has been the comparative abundance in the supply of the money-metals. But the drain of Roman currency took place at a time when the known sources of supply of these metals within the Roman empire were becoming exhausted and unable to keep pace with the ordinary wear and tear of coin due to a rapid circulation.

It is clear that the figures given by Pliny refer not to the volume of Rome's oriental trade but to the excess of imports over exports, and in relation to the prevailing conditions of economic life they indicate a very serious drain of precious metals from the empire. The outflow of silver at any rate appears to have been checked under Vespasian, and in the second century there are signs that an increase of barter reduced the adverse balance, but the harm had already been done under the Julio-Claudian emperors, though the consequences were not immediately apparent. It cannot be denied that the drain of bullion and specie by the oriental trade was one of the major factors in the economic decline of the Roman world. It may be conjectured that the net money loss to Rome from the oriental trade between the battle of Actium and the death of Commodus was something like £100,000,000.

Pliny divides his 100 million sesterces per annum between India, the Seres and Arabia, giving 55 million to India and the other 45 million to the Seres and Arabia together in proportions of which we are not told ; we might put the share of the Seres at anywhere between 10 and 30 millions. But here there is a difficulty ; there have been scarcely any finds of Roman coins in China, nothing to compare even remotely with the great hoards which have turned up in India. It appears unlikely, therefore, that Roman money reached China at all except to a quite negligible amount. The discrepancy between this evidence and Pliny's statement may be explained in two ways. One is to assume with Warmington,[1] as in the case of the Seric iron, that there was a confusion between the Seres and the Cheras (Tamils of Malabar) owing to the similarity of name ; on this hypothesis the Malabar trade would be reckoned separately from that of India, and the Chinese would not be mentioned at all. But even if there was a confusion between the Cheras and the Seres, it is hard to see why the total for India should not include the figure for the Malabar trade, which would be that of the Cheras ; the Seres, whoever they are meant to be, are certainly thought of by Pliny in this passage as external to India. And as Pliny makes so much of silk as a type of the luxury which he deplores, we should expect him to make some mention of the real Seres, the silk producers, in his summary of Rome's luxury bill. If we admit, however, that he does refer to them, there is another explanation possible for the apparently erroneous statement which includes them among the nations which divided the spoil of Rome's adverse balance.

If we ask how Pliny or his informant arrived at the figures quoted, it is at once clear that the statement cannot be accepted just as it stands. There were no international

[1] Warmington, *op. cit.*, p. 276.

trade returns which could be consulted, and it would have been impossible to ascertain just how much was bought and sold in any one foreign country. The only available evidence would have been that provided by the Imperial customs service, which would know roughly the amount of money taken out of the empire by merchants in a year and the relative values of the trades in various commodities. An estimate could thus be formed of the net adverse balance, and Arabia, China and India were considered as sharing in it in proportion to the total value of the imports from each. But such a method would be quite inadequate to the complexity of the market with its indirect commerce. Silk was produced by China, but the Romans bought it almost entirely from Parthians, Kushans and other middle-men. We may well believe that the Romans failed to balance with exports their great purchases of silk, but that does not prove that Roman specie payments ever reached China in any large amount ; they were more probably absorbed by middlemen, who had goods of their own as well as Roman products to sell to the Chinese. In saying that the Seres took away Roman currency Pliny merely means to point out the silk traffic as one of the principal factors in making the adverse balance ; it was of very little concern to him who actually received the money that Rome lost.

It is of course true that the evidence from coin finds or the lack of them only applies to specie, and it can be argued that payments in the silk trade may have been by uncoined metal. Bullion was no doubt often used for commercial transactions, but the most striking feature of the commerce of the first two centuries of our era is the immense popularity of Roman currency in India, and there is no reason to believe that it would have been less popular in China if it had once penetrated there. It is hard to see why bullion payments should have been more common in the silk than in the pepper or pearl trades, and we are therefore forced to conclude that the Roman export of precious metals did not reach China to any large amount either as bullion or as specie. The progress of archaeology in China may still greatly modify the evidence as to coin finds, but apart from such evidence it is likely on general grounds that the money-metals tended to stay with the middlemen in indirect commerce, and provisionally we are entitled to assert that this is what happened in the silk trade.

# CHAPTER IV

## The Smuggled Moth

THE third century of our era is the time in European history which divides the classical from the mediaeval. The development of the European classical culture from its Homeric origins through the age of the Hellenic city-states and that of the Hellenistic monarchies culminates in the Greco-Roman civilization of the two centuries after Actium. That was the greatest organization of material culture the world had yet seen ; politically also the Roman *municipia* preserved much of the old, typical, city-state life, and intellectually the tradition of Greek science was maintained up to the time of Ptolemy and Galen. Then from the closing years of the second century A.D. there is decline, swift and catastrophic. The imperial power of Rome is consumed by incessant civil strife and is unable to prevent the ravages of barbarian invasion ; the coinage is repeatedly debased ; everywhere there is a decline of productivity and purchasing power, abandoned fields and mines, decrease of trade, reversion from a monetized to a natural economy ; the service of municipal government, from being a privilege, becomes a burden ; taxes multiply as wealth diminishes ; the tale of ancient science that began with Thales of Miletus draws to a close, and Diophantus is the last and loneliest of its great names. The decline is indeed arrested, and followed by revival with Diocletian and Constantine. But the revival cannot afford any comparison of power and prosperity with the age before Marcus Aurelius, and its basis of spiritual culture is entirely different. The revived empire is Christian, its monarchy is established in alliance with the organized Church, and all the subtlety of the

Greek intellect is now devoted to theology. Territorially the Roman empire has lost little since the time of Trajan and its political forms are but little altered, yet in essentials we have already passed from the civilization which we call classical to that which we call mediaeval, and it is with true insight that the editors of the *Cambridge Medieval History* have made it begin with Constantine. There is a greater change in cultural atmosphere between Trajan and Theodosius I than there is on the one hand between Pericles and Trajan or on the other between Theodosius I and Charlemagne.

In the history of world commerce the third century is as decisive as in the domestic history of Europe. Rome's oriental trade which had grown to such vast dimensions reflected the decline of the empire ; the great event was the interception of the Red Sea commerce by Abyssinians and Arabs. It was an event the decision of which was not reversed for more than a millennium. The revival of Roman power under Diocletian and his successors did not avail to reopen the all-important sea corridor ; Egypt and the Isthmus of Suez were held until the Arab conquest in 641, but there was virtually no unimpeded, direct communication between a European nation and the ' Indies ' from the time of Caracalla to the voyage of Vasco da Gama to Calicut in 1498.

In the silk trade there was, as we have seen, during the first two centuries A.D. a competition of routes and even, towards the end, direct access to China for Roman merchants. Silk could be fetched from the Persian Gulf to avoid Palmyra, Osrhoene and the desert Arabs, from Barbaricon or Baryzaga to avoid Parthia ; or it might come through Bengal or Burma—though these routes had their own middlemen ; or it might be obtained by a voyage all the way from Egypt to Tongking. But all these sea routes had to pass the Straits of Bab-el-Mandeb, and a power holding the Straits could intercept them one and all. After the Abyssinians had obtained control of the entrance to the Red Sea Roman subjects could only buy

Indian and Chinese products either from them or from the Persians, or if they did sail in the Indian Ocean, it was only by arrangement with Abyssinia. Even so, there was still a check on prices as long as there was competition between Abyssinia and Persia. In the course of time, however, arrangements between the merchants of the two nations made the silk trade a Persian monopoly, a situation intolerable for buyers to whom the material had become almost a necessity of life. An acute crisis was reached when in 540 Justinian attempted to fix a maximum price to be paid for imported silk, and the Persian traders refused to sell at all. But, faced with the dreadful prospect of a silkless city, the Byzantine genius rose to the occasion, and a formidable economic problem was solved by the smuggling of silk-moth eggs from Kashgaria and the introduction of sericulture into Europe.

To return to the 'melancholy third century' as Chapot calls it. The diminution of Roman power and prestige coincided with the growth of the Abyssinian kingdom of Axum, the kings of which according to Abyssinian tradition were descended from the son of Solomon and the Queen of Sheba. The city of Axum itself was far inland near the modern Adowa, but the kingdom had a port, Adulis, near the lower end of the Red Sea, and Adulis became the centre of a great maritime commerce. The Axumites became the paramount power in the narrow waters of Bab-el-Mandeb and the Gulf of Aden, and claimed a suzerainty over the Himyarites of Yemen ; they shared with the latter the sea trade to India, and Roman subjects could now only participate with their permission, a permission for which a price must be paid. The kings of Axum in the third century usurped control of a traffic which, though reduced in volume, was still extremely lucrative, and they consolidated their power from the proceeds ; when, in the fourth century, the Roman empire revived, they were too strong and well established to be overawed, and Rome was too much occupied with threats to her frontiers to contemplate a military expedition so far afield as Abyssinia.

The interception of the Red Sea routes by the Axumites, added to the economic troubles affecting trade throughout the Roman empire in the third century, caused acute distress in Alexandria, then the greatest commercial city of the Mediterranean. Disastrous also for Alexandria was the competition of Palmyra, whose successful organization of a protected caravan service across the Syrian desert more and more diverted Roman-Indian traffic from the Red Sea and Egypt to the Persian Gulf and Syria. Now that the Red Sea as well as the Persian Gulf was dominated by a middleman power, the routes from the former had lost their peculiar advantage, and the growing military strength of Palmyra safeguarded the marches of Syria at a time when Roman arms were too weak to prevent the roads from the Nile to Myos Hormos and Berenice from being raided by the Blemmyes, wild nomads of the Nubian deserts. But the relations between Alexandria and Palmyra were not merely those of jealous competition. Alexandria was the leading producer of the manufactured goods with which Rome paid for her oriental trade, and as the Roman coinage became more and more debased, the market had to be maintained by barter. Palmyra was not a city of industry, but only of transit. Thus a section of the Alexandrian mercantile interest was involved in close commercial relations with the power which in the second half of the third century attempted to supersede Rome as ruler of the Levant.

Palmyra had the status of a free city under Roman suzerainty ; her tolls were regulated by Rome and she was required to assist in the defence of the Roman frontier against Parthian and subsequently (from 224) Persian aggression. Her position was therefore that of a feudatory, and as Rome became more and more dependent on her military strength, she aspired to change places with her suzerain. The favours bestowed on the Palmyrenes by the Emperor Gallienus in recognition of their services against Persia caused jealousy and discontent in the Roman regular army in Syria, which mutinied and proclaimed the two sons of a general named Macrianus as joint-emperors (261). Palmyra remained loyal to Gallienus and in his name crushed the revolt, incidentally occupying Roman Syria and Mesopotamia and invading Egypt. Egypt now set up an emperor of its own in the person of the imperial prefect Aemilianus, but Theodotus, a general adhering to Gallienus, recovered Alexandria after bitter street-fighting, which left a large part of the city in ruins (263). The ruthless repression only aggravated the misery of Egypt, a fresh revolt broke out under the leadership of a certain Timagenes, and the Palmyrenes sent an army into Egypt which conquered the whole country with the exception of Alexandria itself, which was retained by a Roman garrison (269). Palmyra was now openly at war with Rome without even the pretence of taking sides in Roman civil strife, and while one Palmyrene army invaded Egypt, another was sent through Anatolia to the Bosphorus.

In 271 Egypt was reconquered by a lieutenant of the Emperor Aurelian, and in the following year Aurelian himself, after his great victories over the Teutonic invaders of the Empire, marched against the Palmyrenes, defeated them in a great battle before the walls of Emesa in Syria, and boldly crossing the desert, besieged and captured Palmyra. The city was spared, but its prosperity had passed with its military strength ; the Roman garrison established by Aurelian could not carry on the work of safeguarding the desert routes which had been performed by the Palmyrene ascendency. The trade was gone, and the economic crisis in Egypt became yet more acute. A ring of Alexandrian merchants were now convinced that the only hope lay in the restoration of Palmyrene power, and under the leadership of Firmus, a trader in papyrus and glue, they intrigued with a faction at Palmyra which was in favour of renewing the struggle against Rome. In the year after its capture Palmyra revolted, and Alexandria rose simultaneously. But the allies were no match for the grim Aurelian ; Palmyra was captured a second time and utterly destroyed, and the insurrection at Alexandria was crushed with relentless severity.

As a commercial centre Alexandria never really recovered from these misfortunes. With the Red Sea traffic intercepted by the Axumites and Himyarites and the shorter land routes to Babylonia given over to the anarchy of desert tribes, the centre of gravity in commerce shifted northwards from Egypt. The Persian Sassanids had made their dominion over the lands of their inheritance more concentrated than that of the Parthian Arsacids had ever been ; they marched directly with the Romans in Mesopotamia, and conditions for trade there were now more favourable than they had been since the Seleucids ruled from the Mediterranean to the Persian Gulf. The independence of Osrhoene had been terminated by Caracalla, and the desert stronghold of Hatra, which had defied Roman and Parthian alike, had been reduced by Shapur I. The trade which Palmyra lost did not return to the Red Sea, but was diverted northward to the Mesopotamian routes through Hierapolis and Samosata.

The tendency of commerce to flow towards Mesopotamia was made more pronounced by the founding of Constantinople as the new capital of the Roman empire in 330. As long as the city of Rome was the chief centre of demand for oriental luxuries, carriage by sea in the Mediterranean was necessary, and Syria was no better situated than Egypt for the forwarding of goods, but with the migration of wealth and fashion to the shores of the Bosphorus merchandise could be sent straight to its goal by land from the crossings of the Euphrates ; this was greatly to the disadvantage of Egypt, for oriental goods received at the Red Sea ports had first to be conveyed by land and river to Alexandria and then by ship round Anatolia and through the Dardanelles. Further, a new overland route was developed to effect the maximum economy of distance ; from Herat and Merv it led to Constantinople through Armenia well to the north of the old Mesopotamian routes. Thus in the fourth and fifth centuries Syria and

Armenia came to hold the primacy, which had formerly belonged to Egypt, in the transmission of the oriental commerce. Egypt continued to deal with the imports of Ethiopian and Arabian produce and to receive some traffic from the Indian Ocean, but the bulk of Indian and Chinese imports, and above all of the silk trade, now passed through Persian territory to Syria and Armenia, coming either by all-land routes or up the Persian Gulf.

On the other side of the Persian and Axumite-Himyarite barriers which now shut in the Roman world the conditions of commerce underwent little change. In China the period from A.D. 200 to 600 was for the most part one of political disintegration and confusion, but the production of silk was not much affected ; the trade was too well established to be easily given up, and whatever royal power held north-western China had an interest in taxing it, while it was the very life-blood of the oasis-cities of Kashgaria, which grew rich on it and exerted all their strength to maintain it. The trade itself seems to have been mainly conducted by Sogdian caravans from Samarkand, as a result of which the Sogdian dialect of Iranian became a *lingua franca* from the Pamirs to Kansu. Meanwhile the maritime commerce from the coasts of South China to the Indian Ocean was not only continued but enlarged, the great factor in its development being the colonization by emigrants from India of coastal districts of Further India and Indonesia.

The eastward expansion of Indian population, culture and commercial enterprise from India proper, which probably began with the Christian Era, belongs mainly to the period we are now considering (*c.* A.D. 200–600) ; the greatest achievements of Indian energy abroad are roughly contemporary with India's ' Golden Age ' at home, the days of the Gupta dynasty (320–480). The Sanskrit inscription of Vo-can in Champa (French Cochin-China) is attributed to the third century at the latest, and the conquest of Fu-nan (Cambodia) by colonists from India some time before 265 is attested by the Chinese

Ts'in-shu. There were undoubtedly Hindu kingdoms in the Malay Peninsula, Sumatra, Java and Borneo by A.D. 400. The people of these states, which had been founded by sea-faring, were the chief intermediaries of trade by sea between China and India ; merchandise destined for lands farther west than India was taken to Ceylon, which was frequented by Persian, Arab and Ethiopian shipping. The sea route from Ceylon to China was taken at the end of the fourth century by the Chinese Buddhist pilgrim Fa Hsien on his way back from India, which he had reached overland via Khotan ; a little over a century later intercourse by sea had become a powerful cultural factor, as is shown by the South Indian influences in the art of the Liang dynasty which had its capital at Nanking (502–556).

From the Roman side important evidence as to the traffic of the Indian Ocean in the first half of the sixth century is provided by Cosmas Indicopleustes in his *Universal Christian Topography*, that fantastic medley of theology and geography which fills out an argument of crazy ingenuity with a mass of generally accurate and, for the historian, superlatively valuable, information. Cosmas, it seems, had himself voyaged in the Red Sea and round Arabia, and had gathered accounts of India and Ceylon from the rare Roman merchants who still went there ; his knowledge of regions more remote was presumably derived through the same channel from the geographical gossip of Ceylon. He knows China under the name of Tzinitza, also written Tzinista (cf. *Thin* of the *Periplus*, *Sinae* of Ptolemy, Sanskrit *Chinasthāna*, Persian *Chinistan*, *Tzinisthan* of the Syriac inscription at Si-an, all deriving probably from Ts'in).

Speaking of the supposed existence of the Earthly Paradise, which nearly a thousand years later was to haunt the imagination of Columbus, Cosmas says : ' If Paradise were really in this world, surely there would be among those who are so zealous in learning and finding out everything many who would not allow themselves to be deterred from reaching it ? When we see that there are men who cannot be put off from going to the ends of the earth to fetch silk just for greed of money, how can we believe that they would be put off from making the journey to see Paradise ? The country of silk, I may mention, is in the furthest part of the Indies, lying to the left as you enter the Indian Sea, but a vast distance further than the Persian Gulf or the island which the Indians call Selediba and the Greeks Taprobane [i.e. Ceylon]. Tzinitza is the name of the country, and the Ocean surrounds it to the left just as the same Ocean surrounds Barbary to the right.[1] . . . It lies very much to the left, so that loads of silk passing on through several different nations in succession over the land reach Persia in a comparatively short time, but the distance by sea is very much greater. For the voyager to Tzinista has to turn up from Taprobane and the regions beyond [i.e. Malaya], as far as the Persian Gulf extends into Persia,[2] and further there is no small distance to be covered in sailing over the whole of the India Sea from the Persian Gulf to Taprobane and thence to the regions beyond. Thus it is obvious that any one who comes by the overland route from Tzinista to Persia makes a very short cut ; which accounts for the fact that such quantities of silk are always to be found in Persia. Further than Tzinista there is neither navigation nor inhabited land.'

Of Ceylon Cosmas says : ' From all India and Persia and Ethiopia many ships come to this island, and it also sends out many of its own, being in a central position. From the further regions, that is, Tzinista and other exporting countries, Taprobane imports silk, aloes-wood, cloves, sandal-wood and so on, according to the production of each place.'

It is clear from the account given by Cosmas that the bulk of Roman silk imports early in the sixth century came

[1] Barbary is here Somaliland. Left and right are to be understood from the point of view of one sailing out from the Red Sea into the Indian Ocean. Cosmas means that the Ocean extends both round the east of Asia and the south of Africa.

[2] The Persian Gulf includes here part of the Arabian Sea as well as the Gulf proper. The meaning is that China is as far north from the line Aden—Ceylon—Singapore as is the head of the Persian Gulf.

overland, but that there was a regular supply through Ceylon. From their interception of the overland routes the Persians were in a position to control prices if only they could corner the supply in Ceylon ; if on the other hand the Axumites buying from Ceylon were to compete with them in the Roman market, it would be impossible for them to establish a monopoly. That they actually succeeded in making their corner must be attributed to a bargain between Persian and Axumite mercantile rings, for both middleman nations had a common interest in squeezing their Roman customers, and it was natural that they should come to an agreement for sharing the commerce which either might take. The silk trade carried on mainly by land tended to be a monopoly of the Persians ; the trades in the spices of South India tended no less to be a monopoly of the Axumites. But the Persians could interfere with the Axumite monopoly of spices just as effectively as the Axumites could interfere with the Persian monopoly of silk. Economic interest dictated a give-and-take policy by which each side refrained from competition against the geographically natural monopolies of the other and both derived benefit at the expense of the Roman buyer.

It was probably by some such bargain rather than by superior mercantile organization that the Persians cornered the silk supply, rendering Rome liable to intolerable profiteering and to complete interruption of the traffic in time of political conflict with Persia. So galling did the Persian monopoly become that Justinian made the silk trade a subject of diplomatic negotiation with Ela Atzbeha, the contemporary king of Axum, and the latter agreed to obtain silk from Ceylon for the Romans. But the scheme was a failure, and we may suspect that it was frustrated by the vested interests of the Axumite merchants themselves. The Sassanids could have had no sort of political ascendency in Ceylon, which lay far outside the limits of their power, and there is no reason why the Axumites should not have been able to buy silk in Ceylon if they had really made up their minds to do so. But to engage in a cut-throat competition which would invite retaliation on their own lucrative corner was not at all to their liking, and it was not through them that Justinian finally attained his end.

It is impossible to determine the date at which Chinese ships began to sail in the Indian Ocean, but it is unlikely that they came in any considerable numbers before the seventh century. The only direct evidence for earlier voyages is Ma'sūdi,[1] who says, quoting a tradition of the city of Hira (in Babylonia), that at a time some generations before the Mohammedan conquest ships of India and China had been wont to ascend the Euphrates to that point. Chinese ships certainly came to the Persian Gulf in the early days of Islam,[2] and there is no reason why a few should not have made the voyage earlier, but probably in the four centuries between the Han and the T'ang the Hindu colonies of Malaya and Indonesia intervened as effectively in commerce between the Indian Ocean and the Pacific as did the Abyssinians and Arabs between the Indian Ocean and the Red Sea. The assertion made by War-mington [3] that Indians and Chinese frequented a fair held at Batnae in Mesopotamia does not seem to have any foundation, as the passage adduced in Ammianus Mar-cellinus [4] merely states that Indian and Chinese goods were sold there (*ad commercanda quae Indi mittunt et Seres, aliaque plurima vehi terra marique consueta*).

In the Roman empire, after the reorganization of the state and restoration of currency stability by Diocletian and Constantine, the total purchasing power available was greatly reduced from what it had been in the first two centuries A.D., but the standards of living of the upper class had not at all declined from their former extravagance, and the demand for silk relative to that for other luxuries tended to increase. To the older Roman tradition of luxury the Byzantines added a new and more distinctively

[1] Ma'sūdi, *Prairies d'Or* (tr. de Meynard and de Courteille), I, p. 216 *seqq.*

[2] *Op. cit.*, I, p. 308.          [3] *Op. cit.*, p. 138.

[4] XIV, 3, 3, 11.

oriental taste for sumptuous raiment.  If we are to attach
any credence to the descriptions of contemporary social
life in the sermons of John Chrysostom, the change from
paganism to Christianity had affected not at all the frivolity
and prodigality of aristocratic society, and the austere
ecclesiastic, whose virtue was to his age ' as a lamp burning
in front of sore eyes,' declaims especially against the lavish
use of silk and brocade.  Already before the economic
crisis of the third century the Syrian boy priest Elagabalus,
who for four years held the Roman principate, had surpassed all previous imperial records in textile luxury ;  he
clothed himself exclusively in silk and never wore the same
garment twice.

A little later, when the economic situation was at its
worst and silk is said to have been worth its weight in
gold, we are told that the Emperor Aurelian would neither
wear silk himself nor allow his wife to do so.  But with
the return of better times in the fourth century the tendencies
of taste apparent under the Severi renewed themselves in
full flood, and at once took hold of Constantine's new
capital and of a court which set itself to imitate as suitable
for the new type of monarchy the dress and manners of
the Persian Sassanids.  The Byzanto-Roman age had need
of silk both to express its intense, innovating passion for
colour, and to serve the hieratic and ceremonious magnificence which characterized its social forms.  And in
course of time the use of silk spread farther and farther
down the social scale.  Ammianus,[1] writing in the latter
part of the fourth century, says that ' the use of silk, once
confined to the nobility, has now spread to all classes
without distinction, even to the lowest,' and in a description
of the pomp at the baptism of the infant Emperor Theodosius
II in 401 we are told that ' all the city [i.e. Constantinople]
was crowned with garlands and decked out in garments
made of silk and gold jewels and all kinds of ornaments,
so that no one could describe the adornment of the city.'
Such language is without doubt loose and exaggerated ;

[1] XXIII, 6.

silk-wearing must really have been always confined to a small fraction of the population even in the metropolis ; nevertheless the testimony is valid for a spread of the custom to people of comparatively humble station.   Further, the extent of the market for silk in the Roman empire of the sixth century is indicated by the fragment of Menander Protector wherein the Sogdians urge their Turkish conquerors to open up relations with the Romans ' seeing that they consumed silk more largely than any other country.'

During the fifth and sixth centuries the demand for silk in Europe probably remained almost constant, but the conditions of the market altered greatly, and silk became involved in politics in a manner hitherto unprecedented.   The new situation arose from the loss of the western provinces of the Roman empire to German kingdoms.   In Italy, Gaul, Spain and Africa the demand for oriental luxuries continued, only the consuming class consisted now for the most part of Germans, and the states they formed were either partially or entirely independent of Constantinople.   But the Byzanto-Roman power extending from the Caucasus to Egypt controlled all the routes by which Chinese silk or Indian spices and gems normally reached the Mediterranean countries.   Hitherto the Roman empire as a unit had been the terminus of these trades, for the barbarians beyond the Rhine and Danube had as a rule neither the wealth nor the inclination to purchase such luxuries from Rome, but now that German tribes had entered into possession of rich and populous Roman provinces and had acquired expensive tastes, especially in objects of more obvious luxury, the Byzantines found themselves in the position of middlemen for the lands west of the Adriatic and the Gulf of Sidra and enjoying the same advantages at the expense of Goths and Franks that the Persians and Axumites held at theirs.   The advantages, however, thus accruing to the diminished Roman empire were not suffered by the government of Constantinople to be used merely for the profit of mercantile rings, even though the imperial revenue might have a share in such profit. The luxuries which the Byzantines could alone supply to Europe were employed as one of the most potent instruments of the astute diplomacy by which, from the end of the Western 'empire' in Italy in 476 to the capture of Constantinople in 1204, they strove to 'manage' the barbarians of the north and west.

The barbarian soldiers of fortune, Germans, Alans and Huns, who in the fourth century filled the ranks of the Roman armies and rose to the highest posts of command, readily assimilated Roman tastes in material goods and the externals of civilized life, and communicated these tastes to their uncouth country cousins of the 'federate' tribes dwelling either within or just beyond the Roman frontier. The result of such education is manifest in the items of the ransom demanded by Alaric from the city of Rome when he laid siege to it in 408—5,000 pounds of gold, 30,000 of silver, 4,000 tunics of silk, 3,000 scarlet-dyed skins and 3,000 pounds of pepper. This and other similar revelations of Teutonic desires led the bureaucracy of Constantinople to conclude that for the new epoch in international affairs it possessed in monopoly means of bribery quite as effective as expenditure of money-metals, and immeasurably cheaper for the state. In the delicate negotiations of 448 between the Byzantine court and Attila we find a clear recognition of the diplomatic value of oriental produce. In his narrative of the embassy sent to Attila the historian Priscus shows us the method in practice.[1] On the way to Attila's headquarters beyond the Danube the Roman embassy entertains to dinner two Hunnish magnates and their retinue, who had previously come to Constantinople and were now returning with the Romans. 'In the course of the feast, as the barbarians lauded Attila and we lauded the Emperor, Bigilas remarked that it was not fair to compare a man and a god, meaning Attila by the man and Theodosius by the god. The Huns grew excited and hot at this remark. But we turned the conversation in another direction, and soothed their wounded

[1] *Exc. de leg.* Tr. Bury in *History of the Later Roman Empire*, vol. I, p. 279.

feelings ; and after dinner, when we separated, Maximin presented Edecon and Orestes with silk garments and Indian gems.' Later on, after crossing the Danube the Roman envoys were entertained at a village by a widow of Attila's brother Bleda, and in return presented her with ' things which are esteemed by the barbarians as not produced in their country—three silver *phialae*, red skins, Indian pepper, palm fruit and other delicacies.'

Byzantine persuasion in the early Middle Ages made full use of ' things which are esteemed by the barbarians as not produced in their country,' and that not only for presents and bribes, but also to enhance that magnificence of Constantinople and its court which more than any force of arms maintained the prestige of the imperial power. Where an Augustus or a Trajan had confronted the barbarian world with straightforward pride as master of the Roman legions, the Emperor of New Rome had no longer command of such military strength and therefore studied other ways of impressing the primitive mind ; with the aid of the bureaucracy and the Church he surrounded himself with an atmosphere of mystery and marvel, with a bewildering complication of formality and ritual, and with deft suggestions of a potency subtle and occult but none the less effective in its operation. For the reception of rustic tribesmen, formidable fighters but children in the sphere of civilized statecraft, the etiquette of the Byzantine court was a mighty engine of hypnotic propaganda, its key secret the wearing of carefully chosen costumes in a superb stage setting. A modern writer,[1] using as material the revelations of the *arcana imperii* left us by the Emperor Constantine Porphyrogenitus, sketches a picture which enables us to some extent to enter into the experience of a barbarian chief who has made the journey to Constantinople. ' He has been royally entertained, under the vigilant care of imperial officials he has seen the wonders of the capital, and to-day he is to have audience with the Emperor. Through a dazzling maze of marble corridors, through

[1] Norman H. Baynes, *The Byzantine Empire*, p. 72.

chambers rich with mosaic and cloth of gold, through long
lines of palace guards in white uniforms, amidst patricians,
bishops, generals and senators, to the music of organs and
church choirs he passes, supported by eunuchs, until at
last oppressed with interminable splendour he falls prostrate
in the presence of the silent, motionless, hieratic figure of
the Lord of New Rome, the heir of Constantine, seated on
the throne of the Cæsars ; before he can rise, Emperor and
throne have been caught aloft, and with vestments changed
since last he gazed the sovereign looks down upon him,
surely as God regarding mortal men.'

The needs of the new diplomacy led the Roman state
to concern itself far more with the regulation of commerce
than it had done in former times.  The use of objects of
luxury as instruments of diplomacy required that they
should not be obtainable except by favour of the Byzantine
government ;  for the effective stage-managing of the
imperial court it was necessary that its peculiar splendours
should not be reproduced elsewhere.  Hence the state
must control the commerce of those commodities which
were destined to serve political rather than mercantile ends.

In the fifth century, partly in order to control the supply
for such reasons of state as have been indicated, and partly
also to ensure the advantages of collective bargaining
against the Persian middleman ring,the imperial government
took over from private merchants the function of importing
silk.  The general conditions of trade on the Roman-
Persian frontier were not unfavourable for such a measure,
as both powers had, chiefly as a precaution against espionage,
agreed on a policy of restricting commerce across the frontier
to certain towns specified by treaty, the merchants of each
country being forbidden to penetrate farther, or by intermediate routes, into the territory of the other.  By 408 [1]
an agreement was in force by which Roman Callinicum
and Persian Nisibis in Mesopotamia and Persian Artaxata
in Armenia were named as the legitimate marts for Roman-
Persian commercial relations.  This arrangement endured

[1] *Codex Justinianus*, IV, 63, 4.

for the next two centuries, except that Dubios (Dovin) was substituted later on for Artaxata as the Armenian mart. Since the partition of Armenia between the two great powers in about 390, Rome and Persia had been in direct contact from the Caucasus to the Syrian Desert, and the three towns chosen represented the three main lines of trade between east and west. Callinicum on the Euphrates served the old Seleucia (Ctesiphon)-Antioch road. But now that all roads led to Constantinople a great part of the traffic, especially in silk, passed farther to the north, going by land across Anatolia, either from Ecbatana (Hamadan) through Nisibis and Samosata or from Rhages (Rai) through Artaxata (or Dubios) and Satala.[1]

At Callinicum, Nisibis or Artaxata the agents of the treasury (commerciarii) purchased the raw silk from the Persian traders. Most of it was then sold to Roman private manufacturers ; the rest was sent to state workshops which supplied the court with ceremonial robes. In times of scarcity the state naturally served itself first, and it could also better afford to accumulate large reserve stocks than could the private enterprises, which were usually on a small scale ; hence the interruptions to which the raw silk trade was liable tended to increase the scope of state inter-vention and drive out the private manufacturer. A severe crisis arose in 540 on the outbreak of a war with Persia. Justinian ordered the commerciarii not to pay more than 15 gold solidi for a pound of silk, but the Persian merchants refused to sell at the price, and in the ensuing deadlock many of the private firms went bankrupt. In 542, there-fore, silk manufacture was declared a state monopoly, and so it remained even after the crisis had passed.

Stringent regulations were enacted to prevent the export from the empire by mere merchants of the more valuable silk products. The law on the subject is known to us mainly from the Eparchikon Biblion, a work dating from the tenth century, but there is good reason to believe that many

[1] After the partition of Armenia it is probable that there was also a direct route from Merv to Artaxata across the southern Caspian.

of the rules contained in that collection had been in force from a much earlier period. Their general aim was certainly to maintain a rarity value for the output of the more highly skilled branches of the industry ; hence a rigorous inspection of all goods exported from the capital whether by native or by visiting foreign merchants. Liutprand, bishop of Cremona, suffered under the silk export regulations when he visited Constantinople in 968 as ambassador for Otto I ; he bought some purple silk stuffs for Otto, but had them confiscated by the customs officials. In his time the enforcement of the law had become a farce, for silk manufacture of the highest quality was by then widely spread in Islamic countries, and Constantinople was no longer the only source of supply for Europe ; but at any rate before the eighth century the Byzantines held a real monopoly.

The event whereby the Roman empire and thus ultimately Europe as a whole were rendered independent of China for the supply of raw silk took place just over ten years after the establishment of the state silk manufacture monopoly in 542. According to Procopius [1] 'certain monks from [the land of] the Indians,' hearing of Justinian's perplexities over the silk trade and his desire to be delivered from exploitation by the Persian middlemen, came to court and undertook—for a consideration—to smuggle silk-moth eggs into the empire and hatch them so as to enable New Rome to produce silk for herself. They said they had lived a long while in 'a country where there were many nations of the Indians and which was called Serinda,' and had learnt there the whole art of sericulture. When the Emperor had promised a sufficient reward, they returned 'to India' and thence smuggled the eggs from which they proceeded to hatch the silkworms and put them out on mulberry leaves.

A slightly different account of the same event is given by Theophanes. [2] According to him the smuggler was 'a certain Persian,' and the eggs were brought from 'the country

---

[1] *De bello Gothico*, IV, 17.
[2] In Müller's *Fragmenta Hist. Graec.*, IV, 270.

of the Seres' concealed in a hollow cane—presumably a bamboo. In this version there is no mention of monks or of India. But the discrepancy between the two authors can be to some extent resolved if we suppose the monks to have been Persian Nestorians and Serinda to have been some part of Further India close to China and practising sericulture, perhaps Cambodia or Champa. Christianity had spread from Persia to India ; Cosmas bears witness to the existence early in the sixth century of Christian communities at Kalliana near Bombay (with a bishop appointed from Persia), in Malabar and in Ceylon, ' though I do not know,' he adds, ' whether there are any Christians further on in that direction.' [1] As Ceylon had such close commercial relations by sea with the lands of Malaya and beyond, it is quite likely that some Christian missionaries had penetrated to the latter ; that the monks in the version of Procopius were not natives of Serinda is implied by the statement that they had lived there for a long time. If Serinda were Cambodia or Champa the inhabitants could be correctly described as Indians, inasmuch as both countries had been colonized by emigrants from India, while they might also be styled Seres, inasmuch as they produced silk. It has been suggested indeed that Serinda may have been Khotan or some part of Kashgaria, whither at some time not definitely known sericulture spread from China. But this view does not accord so well as the other with customary nomenclature ; it is true that in the sixth century, during the age of Buddhist ascendency in Central Asia, the culture of Khotan and other places in the Tarim basin was predominantly Indian in type, yet there is nothing to prove that that region was reckoned in current speech to be any part of India, whereas everything eastward to Annam is included in Ptolemy's 'India extra Gangem.'

But whoever he was and whether he came from Khotan or from Chryse, someone guilefully brought to Europe in a hollow stick, just as Prometheus stole fire from Heaven, the power of making silk. As for *Bombyx mori*, introduced

[1] *Topographia Christiana*, III, pp. 118–21 (M'Crindle).

after its long journey into a new world of mulberry leaves, it did not pine for the home of its ancestors, but obeyed the order to increase and multiply, and laboured dutifully in its humble way to create wealth for mankind, to embody the visions of artists, to serve the glory of the Church and the vanity of princes. Byzantine sericulture was first developed in Syria, where textile manufactures had so long been concentrated, and by the end of the sixth century appears to have been meeting the demand for the raw material. Then Syria and its industries fell into the hands of the Saracens, and the Byzantines made a new centre of silk production in the central part of Greece ; it brought there a prosperity unknown since the second century B.C. Meanwhile from Syria silk cultivation and manufacture were carried by the Arabs to Sicily and Spain. But as the silk industry of Syria had passed by conquest in the seventh century from the Romans to the Arabs, so that of Sicily passed by conquest in the eleventh from the Arabs to the Normans. The Normans added to the textile inheritance of Sicily by carrying off Greek silk operatives from Thebes and Corinth as spoil of their wars in the Balkans. From Sicily the arts of silk spread northward through Italy in the time of the Crusades, and contributed in no small measure to that great economic development of the Italian cities which was the condition of the Renaissance.

But with this later course of the history of silk in Europe we have left our theme, which is the trade in silk as a link between Europe and China. With the introduction of the silk-moth into the Roman empire the commerce in raw silk naturally began to dwindle and at length ceased altogether. Its demise, however, was not immediate, for it was many years, probably at least three decades, before the new Byzantine sericulture had really come of age, and was able to meet the needs of the manufacturers as regards both quantity and quality of produce. And in the interval between the smuggling of the eggs (between 552 and 554) and the achievement of complete independence in silk production a situation arose along the overland silk route which, had it occurred a century earlier, might have saved the Romans from much of their embarrassment in obtaining supplies from China.

In the middle of the sixth century was formed in Central Asia an empire larger than any that had yet been set up by a nomad nation. A tribe, the Asena (A-shih-na), of Hiung-nu descent, were living in 545 in West Kansu under the suzerainty of the Juan Juan, another tribe then dominant in western Mongolia. They came to be known by the name of Turks, possibly after amalgamation with other tribal elements ; according to a Chinese account the name Turk is derived from *türkü* (t'u-chüeh) meaning a helmet and applied to a helmet-shaped mountain in the Turks' country, appropriate as they specialized in the working of iron. The Turks revolted against the Juan Juan in 546 and destroyed them ; then entered on a career of conquest towards the west. They came into collision with the Ephthalites or White Huns who, as we have seen, had dominated Bactria and Sogdia for over a century ; in their struggle with the Ephthalites the Turks took advantage of the enmity between the former and Persia, and entered into an alliance with the Sassanid Khosru Naoshirvan. The Ephthalites were overcome by the allies between 563 and 567 and the Oxus became the boundary between the Persians and the Turks, Sogdia thus passing under Turkish rule.

The Persians found, however, that in getting rid of the Ephthalites they had obtained as neighbours to the northeast a still more aggressive and dangerous nomad power, and they sought to hold in check their former allies. There was a suspension of the silk traffic by the Persians ; it was carried on through the Sogdians across the Oxus and the Persians seem to have feared that it would be used for espionage and intrigue by the Turks.[1] Maniakh, a vassal

[1] The narrative of Menander on the two Turkish embassies to Persia does not make clear the motive of the Persians in stopping the silk trade. It may be that Persia was overstocked at this time and that there was a conspiracy to force up prices. The Persians could of course get silk at this time from Ceylon as well as from Sogdia.

prince of Sogdia, now suggested to Dizabul, the Khan of
the Turks, ' that it would be more for the interest of the
Turks to cultivate the friendship of the Romans, and to
transfer the sale of silk to them, seeing also that they consumed it more largely than any other people.  And Maniakh
added that he was quite ready to accompany a party of
Turkish envoys in order to promote the establishment
of friendly relations between the Turks and Romans.' [1]
Dizabul approved the proposal and sent Maniakh with a
Turkish embassy to Constantinople, where they arrived in
the year 568 ; the Turks had extended their dominion far
to the west on the north of the Aral and Caspian and as
far as the Sea of Azov, so that the embassy was able to
avoid Persia and come without hindrance to one of the
Byzantine outposts on the Black Sea.   In Maniakh's mission
we have a remarkable instance of partnership between
an urban commercial interest and a conquering nomad
horde—between the Sogdians, dwellers in the oases of
Bokhara and Samarkand and middlemen of the silk trade,
and the warrior Turks, barbarians, but already advanced
beyond the stage of mere plunder, able by their far-ranging
power to open new trade routes and hoping for a rich
revenue in tolls and duties.

The Turkish embassy was favourably received by the
reigning Emperor Justin II and a return embassy headed by
Zemarchus the Cilician was sent with Maniakh as escort
to the camp-court of the Turkish Khan at a place among
mountains which cannot be fully identified but was certainly
east of the Syr Darya (Iaxartes) and probably in a valley
of the Dzungarian Ala-tau near Kulja.  ' The party of
Zemarchus on their arrival were immediately summoned
to an interview with Dizabulus.  They found him in his
tent, seated on a golden chair with two wheels, which could
be drawn by a horse when required. . . .  The tent was
furnished with silken hangings in various colours cleverly
wrought.'  In another tent there was a throne resting on
four golden peacocks, and outside, ' a great array of waggons

[1] Menander Protector in C. Müller, *Fragm. hist. graec.*, vol. IV.

in which there was a vast quantity of silver plates and dishes, besides many figures of animals in silver, in no way inferior to our own.' The camp was indeed full of objects of luxury gathered together by the Khan in his northern stronghold, plunder and tribute from the oasis cities of the silk route from China to Persia or the production of slave artisans among the Turks. The entertainment of the Turkish court consisted of prolonged drinking bouts at which the Roman envoys attended, ' talking and listening,' says Menander, ' to such purpose as people do in their cups.' The description given by Menander of this Dzungarian nomad capital has much in common with Priscus' account of the court of Attila in Hungary, and agrees still more closely with the thirteenth-century descriptions of the Mongol courts. The hordes whose power was centred towards the east, however, had an advantage over their cousins in Europe in that they had access to abundant supplies of silk, and the splendour imparted to Turkish royalty by the lavish use of the material seems to have made a great impression on the Roman envoys, as it did also sixty years later on the Chinese Buddhist traveller Hiuen Tsang. In his time the power of the Turks was already waning, but the luxury of their court had developed ; the Khan, says Hiuen Tsang,[1] ' occupied a great tent adorned with gold flowers of dazzling richness. The officers of the court sat in two long rows on mats before the Khan, brilliantly attired in embroidered silk, the Khan's guards standing behind them.'

The friendly relations thus begun between the Romans and the Turks did not long endure, and the new silk route imagined by Maniakh never became a fact, for the reason that Constantinople had now begun to produce its own silk, so that the journey of Zemarchus did not open up a new era of travel and commerce across Central Asia. It marks indeed the close rather than the beginning of an epoch. Nevertheless, it has great significance ; after an interval of more than a thousand years it repeats on a

[1] *Histoire de la Vie de Hiuen Tsang*, pp. 55–6.

slightly different route the journey of Aristeas of Procon-
nessus. So far as we know, no Greek or Roman since the
time of Aristeas had travelled to the east north of the
Caspian or visited the lands north of the T'ien-shan. But
in the thirteenth and fourteenth centuries under the Tatar
supremacy the route from Tana at the mouth of the Don
(the ancient Tanais) *via* Astrakhan to Almalik, Karakorum
and Peking was to be one of the main lines of approach
from Europe to the Far East.

Owing to the loss of parts of Menander's account we have
no information as to the route followed by Zemarchus on
the way to the Khan's camp, and the narrative of the return
journey is not quite clear, but it appears that the embassy
returned from Talas on the Syr Darya—as far as which
place Zemarchus accompanied the Khan and his army
who were going to invade Persia—round the south of the
Aral and the north of the Caspian. According to Menander
Zemarchus with his party crossed the river Oech, and after
a long journey came to ' that wide lagoon,' i.e. the Aral ;
he then sent on an express messenger who ' with a dozen
Turks set out for Byzantium by a route which was without
water and altogether desert, but was the shortest way.' [1]
Zemarchus then ' travelled for twelve days along the
sandy shores of the lagoon ' and ' came to the streams of
the Ich and then to the Daich [Yaik, Ural] and then to the
Attila [Etil, Volga].' From the Volga the embassy made

[1] There can be no doubt at all that the route went north of the
Caspian ; it must have done so to avoid Persia, and the Ural and
Volga rivers are both recognizable from their names. But the supposition that the route was also north of the Aral is incompatible with the
shortest route being across the desert from any point where the party
coming from Talas (Turkestan, the town) might reach the Aral. The
shortest route round the north of the Aral would be the one skirting
the shore. But from the south side there would be a short cut across
the Ust Urt desert, while Zemarchus himself followed the Aral shore
to the north and then struck westward to the Emba (the Ich ?) over
a less arid tract. This would be roughly the route of the Itil-Urgenj
caravans of the Khazars and later Astrakhan-Khiva trade. Menander
clearly had no conception of the real geography of this part of the
world, and merely wrote from notes of the itinerary.

its way to Trebizond, using a pass of the Caucasus in the
country of the Alans, who were allies of the Romans, and
narrowly escaping an ambush of 4,000 Persians sent to
intercept them to the north of the Caucasus.

The episode of Roman-Turkish diplomatic intercourse
did not open up any communication between Constantinople
and China, but it introduced into Byzantine Greek literature
a strangely accurate account of China derived from Turkish
sources. The Turks by the extent of their empire were in
contact with the Chinese on the east as they were with the
Romans on the west. Through them came a description
of China under a name current in Central Asia. Theo-
phylactus Simocatta, an Egyptian Greek, writing soon after
628, tells of the land of Taugas somewhere near that of
the Turks, and never suspects that this nation was identical
with the Seres and Sinae of other authors. However, there
can be no doubt that it represents China. The name
Taugas appears to be identical with Tamghaj, used for
China by Arab and Persian writers, and the city of Khubdan
also mentioned by Simocatta is none other than Ch'ang-an
(Turkish *Khumdan*). The people of Taugas are described
as one of the greatest nations in the world in power and
population, having a hereditary royal succession, idolaters
but with just laws, producing silk and carrying on a great
commerce. Simocatta further speaks of a great river
dividing Taugas into two parts (the Yangtse) and of a recent
war between two states on opposite sides of the river ending
in the extinction of one of them (the struggle between the
Sui and Ch'ên dynasties, concluded by the victory of the
Sui and the unification of China under their sway in 588).

This is the most intimate glimpse we have of China in
European literature before Marco Polo. Yet Simocatta is
already a writer of the Dark Age ; he is merely a recorder
of gossip, albeit a conscientious one, and does not locate
his Taugas in any scheme of geographical relations except
to say that its chief city was 1500 miles from India and that
its people were said to be Indians white in colour from living
in the north. The spirit of scientific geography had by

now vanished from the Roman world. And for over six centuries after Simocatta we search in vain in extant Greek or Latin works for any mention showing a living knowledge of China. Whether as Seres, Sinae or Taugas China ceases to be visible within the horizon of European letters. The domestic production of silk by the Byzantines and the poverty of the rest of Europe under the stress of barbarian migrations had killed the silk traffic from China, and with its passing was snapped the great link of trade that had joined the lands of the Mediterranean and the Far East. At the same time the Arab conquest of Syria and Egypt finally cut off Europe from the Indian Ocean.

Nevertheless, from Chinese records we have evidence that there was not a complete break in communication even in the seventh and eighth centuries. Indeed it is probable that a mission from Fu-lin which was received in China in 643 was a genuine embassy of the Roman state, and if so it is the first case of true diplomatic intercourse between Europe and China.

From the middle of the sixth century the name Fu-lin appears in Chinese and soon supersedes the older name Ta Ts'in used to designate the Roman empire. The texts of the T'ang dynasty declare explicitly that Fu-lin is the same country that was formerly called Ta Ts'in. The *lin* in Fu-lin appears to come from an earlier *lam* representing the name Rome itself.[1]

In 588 after nearly four centuries of disunion and warring dynasties China was united under the house of Sui, and in 618 the Sui were supplanted by T'ang who ruled until 907, the most famous of all Chinese dynasties and the one under which national power reached its zenith. With the new era of integration there came a renewal of expansion towards the west and a revived interest in remote countries. According to the records the Sui Emperor Yang Ti (605–617) desired to open communication with Fu-lin but did not succeed in doing so. In the next two decades, however,

[1] See Cordier's note on p. 44 of his edition of *Cathay and the Way thither*.

under the first two T'ang emperors Chinese political domination was carried west of the Pamirs and almost to the Caspian. The vast empire of the Turks had now collapsed ; from 582 they had been divided between two separate khanates, known as the Northern, centred on the Orkhon, and the Western, which held sway from Turfan to Merv. Soon the Western horde was also split by internal strife, skilfully fostered by the Chinese, who as a result were able to annex the greater part of the Turkish dominions. Ferghana and Bactria were brought under Chinese control, and the kings of Samarkand received investiture from China. To the south-west the Sassanian kingdom was crumbling away ; after the long and ruinous war with Rome in the first quarter of the seventh century the Persians fell under the sway of the advancing Moslem Arabs by the battles of Kadisiya (637) and Nehavend (641). The Arabs, however, were not at once able to carry their conquests to the Caspian and the Oxus, and regions in the north and north-east of Persia became independent under local dynasties, notably Tabaristan (Mazandaran) on the southern shore of the Caspian. Armenia, which had been under Persian domination, turned to Constantinople with the break-up of the Sassanian kingdom and from 633 to 693 accepted Roman rule, the Roman empire being thus brought for a while, for the first and last time in its history, to the south-west corner of the Caspian.

The Emperor T'ai Tsung (627–650) received embassies from most of the states of Central Asia not under his rule, and in 643 one arrived from King Po-to-li of Fu-lin bringing a rich present. The *Ch'iu-t'ang-shu* mentions further embassies from Fu-lin in 667, 711 and 719, and in 742 a mission composed of ' priests of great virtue.' The same work also preserves a genuine piece of European history in stating that the Ta Shih (Arabs) under their commander-in-chief Mo-i besieged the capital city of Fu-lin ; this refers to the siege of Constantinople by the Caliph Moawiya in 671–678.

There is no trace in extant Byzantine historical sources of any of these embassies alleged from the Chinese side, and

this may seem to show that the so-called embassies were
really parties of merchants posing as diplomatic envoys in
order to improve their chances of doing business in China
and accepted as such by the Chinese court, which for the
sake of its prestige always welcomed 'tribute-bearing'
missions from remote countries. We have seen good
reason to believe that the Ta Ts'in embassies of the second
and third centuries were really private expeditions, and at
first sight it seems as though the series we are now considering
should be put in the same category. We cannot, however,
be quite so sure. There are considerations which point to
the authenticity of at any rate the first of these embassies.
With the Roman dominion extending over Persarmenia
from 633, with Chinese supremacy carried at about the
same time apparently as far as Merv, and with the storm
of Arab conquest sweeping up against Byzantium from the
south, what could be more likely than that the Roman
government should have endeavoured to cultivate friendly
relations with any great power which might conceivably
give assistance against the Arab foe ? The Byzantines had
grown accustomed to look to Central Asia for diversions
hostile to Persia ; the White Huns had often relieved the
pressure on Rome by attacking the Sassanians in the rear,
the Turkish alliance had been used against Persia, and
Heraclius had called down the Khazars on Persia from the
north. What more natural than that the Byzantines
should seek in the same direction for a counterpoise against
the nation which had supplanted the Sassanians in Persia?

The records of Byzantine history in the seventh and eighth
centuries are not so complete as to make the argument
from silence convincing. Nor is it necessary to assume,
that if the envoys really had an official mission they must
have been sent by the Emperor himself ; they may have
been dispatched by the Roman governor of Armenia with
the support of the semi-independent local princes ; the
Armenian nobility had a special regard for China since two
of its most powerful families, the Orpelians and the Mami-
gonians, claimed descent from Chinese royal exiles.

The embassies of 711 and 719, if they were genuine, could not have been sent from Armenia, which had by then fallen under Arab rule, but they may have been forwarded to China by the favour of the Khazars. This horde which had possessed itself of a territory from the Sea of Azov to the river Ural, had established its capital at Itil, a town built in the delta of the Volga ; this place became the centre of a flourishing commerce. Through their outpost Tmatarakha on the Straits of Kertch the Khazars kept up close relations, both commercial and political, with Constantinople ; the Emperor Justinian II was especially intimate with this people, for he took refuge with them during his exile and married a Khazar princess. The Khazars were also in touch with China ; they were themselves one of the nations who sent envoys to the T'ang court.

A Roman embassy which reached China in 711 must have been sent by Justinian II, who was murdered in that year. The time was one full of menace for Rome, and now if ever Rome and China had a common interest. From 705 to 715 reigned the Caliph Walid I, under whom the forward movement of Islam reached its climax. The Arabs advanced victoriously on all fronts. In the centre the Caliph's generals invaded Anatolia and prepared to lay siege to Constantinople, in the west Tarik conquered Spain, and in the north-east Kutaiba overran Sogdia and Khwarezm (Khiva) and crossing the Pamirs drove the Chinese from Kashgar ; he was directed by Hajjāj the Viceroy of Irak to conquer China even as Walid himself was proposing to subdue Rome. In 717 the Arabs made their supreme effort against Constantinople. It was certainly an occasion for sending a message to the Chinese urging them on against the common foe. The Chinese account suggests that the embassy reaching China in 719 was sent out by Leo the Syrian before his elevation to the throne in March 717. For although the name given in the Chinese text to the sender of the embassy is unrecognizable, the statement that he was not a king but a chief minister of Fu-lin surely

identifies him.  Before he was proclaimed Emperor Leo
was Patrician and general of the Anatolic theme, the leading
man of the empire under the insignificant Theodosius III ;
on him fell the task of beating back the Arabs in the decisive
struggle about to commence.  He had previously been
sent himself on a diplomatic mission to the Caucasus, so
that he was probably well informed about the countries
round the Caspian, and it is not at all hard to believe that
he sent an envoy to China as a move to meet the approaching
crisis.  That the party should have taken two years to
reach the court of China is not surprising in view of the
situation in Central Asia, where the Arabs now held the
main routes between the Caspian and the Pamirs.

It has been held that all the above Fu-lin embassies were
in fact Nestorian religious missions and that *Po-to-li* represents the title of Patriarch.  The envoys of 742 are indeed
described as priests ; but the senders of the 643 and 719
embassies are definitely stated to have been, the one a king
and the other a chief official.  The famous Si-an inscription
shows that Nestorian Christianity had been brought to
China in 635, and T'ai Tsung had issued an edict authorizing
its propagation in 638, but there is nothing whatever to
connect this with the embassy of 643, nor with any of the
subsequent embassies except that of 742.  Indeed it appears
to have been that one which established the connection
between Fu-lin (or Ta Ts'in) and the Christian religion,
for in 745, three years after the arrival of the ' priests of
great virtue ' in 742, the Emperor Hiuen Tsung explained
in an edict that the religion known as ' the Persian ' had
really come from Ta Ts'in.

The Nestorian missions themselves fall outside the scope
of this book.  Christianity is by origin an Asiatic religion,
and only belongs to European history in so far as it has
been adopted by European peoples.  The Nestorian form
of Christianity was confined to Asia, its language was
Syriac, and its centre of diffusion lay always outside the
Roman empire, under Persian or Arab domination.  The
Greek inheritance in the Syriac culture is not sufficient to

justify us in regarding it as an offshoot of that Hellenic
tradition which is Europe, and therefore we may pass it
over in a study of the relations between Europe and China.

After 742 two other Fu-lin embassies are mentioned in
Chinese annals, one in 1081 and another ten years later.
But it is almost certain that these are not Byzantine but
Seljuk. The sender in 1081 is called Mi-li-i-ling-kai-sa,
and this seems to represent Malik-i-Rûm Kaisar, that is,
the Seljuk ruler of Baghdad who possessed the territories in
Anatolia taken from the Eastern Roman empire by the
battle of Manzikert in 1071. Fu-lin had meant both the
Roman empire and the territories over which it extended ;
when these territories were occupied by another power
there was naturally a confusion in the use of the name.
Syria, which had been Roman and the only part of the
Roman empire really known to the Chinese, apparently
continued to be included in Fu-lin after the Arab conquest ;
thus a description of Fu-lin subsequent to that time includes
definitely Moslem traits. Similarly the Seljuks' conquest
of Anatolia made them identical with Fu-lin, and they
themselves called their Anatolian kingdom Rûm (Rome).
Having just migrated from Central Asia the Seljuk Turks
had a memory of China, and the idea of sending an envoy
thither to announce their new greatness would no doubt
appeal to the vanity of these *parvenus* in lands once
Roman.

# CHAPTER V

## Pax Tatarica

IN the year 1222 a Mongol army, sent by the great conqueror Chingiz Khan, entered Europe and defeated a confederacy of Russian princes on the banks of the Dnieper. Simultaneously another of Chingiz Khan's armies was advancing through North China. Sixty years later the Mongol empire at its zenith included both China in the east and Russia in the west, and a single suzerain power prevailed from the Black Sea to the Pacific. Later still, about the middle of the fourteenth century, we are informed in a merchant's handbook that 'the road you travel from Tana [at the mouth of the Don] to Cathay [China] is perfectly safe, whether by day or by night, according to what the merchants say who have used it.' This comment in a work written for the practical direction of traders sums up in one sentence the historical significance of the barbaric Mongol empire, the Pax Tatarica.[1]

The Mongol conquests restored mutual knowledge and communication between Europe and China after all contact had been lost for at least four centuries. Nor was there merely a restoration. The thirteenth and fourteenth centuries gave to Europe a knowledge of China such as

[1] For the Chingizid period Mongol and Tatar are interchangeable names, both designating the tribes represented by the modern Mongols. Mongol has now a linguistic significance; the peoples speaking Mongol languages are the Khalkas, Kalmuks, Buryats and some others. Tatar now denotes tribes of Turkish speech who once formed part of the Tatar (Mongol) empire, and replenished the Mongol armies in the west. The incorrect spelling 'Tartar' originated in the popular thirteenth-century pun which consigned the Tatars *ad sua Tartara*, that is, to hell.

had never been transmitted during even the most flourishing days of the ancient silk traffic. This was due not to a greater volume of trade than in antiquity, for the total of commerce was actually very much less, but to the development of relations of another type, relations of religious and diplomatic purpose. In antiquity a few Greeks and other Roman subjects had reached China, but only for trade ; the narrowness of their interests appears to have disqualified them from being bearers of a full general knowledge of China to the Roman world. The Byzantine embassies to China in the seventh century, which we have found reason to credit, mark a new kind of reaching out towards China, a new interest in remoter Asia for its religious-political possibilities as a source of aid against Islam. The grand strategy of Christendom, to crush the Saracen between hammer and anvil, is first conceived by the Byzantines, then lost sight of for half a millennium, and then revived on a more ambitious scale and with greater facilities for its execution by the Latins in the thirteenth century. A great idea of religious *Weltpolitik* gives character to the travel to China under the *Pax Tatarica*, and imbues it with a will to observe and know which is lacking in the purely commercial travel of antiquity.

The idea of obtaining a Chinese or Tatar alliance against the Moslem did not require necessarily that those peoples should be converted to Christianity. But apart from Crusade strategy the Catholic Church was anxious to preach the Gospel in the newly opened pagan world, and the missionary activity begun in the time of the Mongol empire was to persist long after the struggle with Islam had ceased to be of any moment. Before the thirteenth century Christianity had been represented in China by Nestorian missionaries from Mesopotamia ; now the Latin Catholicism of Europe entered the field and took the lead. Its missions in China were obliterated after 1368, when the Mongols who had favoured them were expelled from the country, but they were renewed after the Portuguese had opened the all-sea route from Europe to China, and from the sixteenth century up to the present day Christian religious propaganda has been one of the main factors in European-Chinese relations.

For China the period immediately preceding the Mongol conquest had been one of extreme seclusion ; it was the period of the Sung dynasty when China was most intensively Chinese. The T'ang dynasty after maintaining a Chinese ascendency in Central Asia during the seventh and eighth centuries had its dominion restricted to China itself, and was at length brought to an end in 907. Half a century of disunion and turmoil known as the Five Dynasties followed ; then, in 960, China came under the sway of the house of Sung which survived as a reigning dynasty until 1280, but during the greater part of its three centuries' epoch governed only South China. The Sung did not revive the Central Asian imperialism of Han and T'ang ; on the contrary they were unable to keep back the nomad hordes of Mongolia and Manchuria from North China, which was dominated first by the K'i-tan (Liao dynasty) and then by the Nü-chên (Kin dynasty) horde. Thus China was divided between North and South for over two centuries before being reunited under the Mongols. The nomad lords of the North were culturally assimilated by the Chinese, as had been all the other northern invaders of China, but the centre of gravity in the Chinese world was transferred to the South where the native Sung continued to rule. To escape the advance of the barbarians from the north the Sung moved their capital from Kaifêng in Honan first to Nanking and then to Hangchow. It was during the period of division that the names of Cathay (*K'i-tan, K'i-tai*) and Manzi (from *man-tzŭ*, a northern nickname meaning ' southern ruffians ') came into use to denote North and South China respectively ; persisting under the Mongols, they were adopted by Europeans, Cathay being extended to cover China as a whole, but also sometimes used in the narrower sense.

In West Asia was Islam intervening between China and Europe. In the eighth century the lands of the Oxus and

Iaxartes had been definitely annexed to the Caliphate, but from 874 to 999 the Moslem Persian Samanids ruled as an independent power with their capital at Bokhara. They were succeeded as lords of West Central Asia and Iran by Moslem Turkish dynasties, first the Ghaznevids and then the Seljuks. The latter in 1055 replaced the Persian Buwaihids as guardians of the now powerless Abbasid Caliph at Baghdad, and pushing on to the west defeated the Byzanto-Romans at the battle of Manzikert in 1071 and overran Anatolia, a blow from which the East Roman empire never fully recovered. The Seljuks also conquered Syria and Palestine and their oppression of Christians there provoked the First Crusade from Europe. The Seljuk Sultan Malik Shah (1072–91) ruled from the Mediterranean to the Pamirs, but after his death the Seljuk empire split up. At the time of the formation of the Mongol con-federacy by Chingiz Khan the chief power in West Asia was that of the Shahs of Khwarezm (Khiva) who ruled over Transoxiana and Persia, from the Sea of Aral to the Arabian Sea.

In Europe Latin Christendom had reached the nadir of its fortunes in the chaos of the ninth and tenth centuries. Soon after 1000 began the great forward movement that in spite of checks and reverses was never to be turned back again to the standards of the Dark Age. First the expulsion of the Arabs from Sicily by the Normans, then the first three Crusades with the Latins in Palestine, then the Fourth Crusade and the Latin empire at Constantinople. The Latins overturned the decaying East Roman empire just eighteen years before the Mongols first appeared in South Russia. It was therefore a vigorous, growing and expand-ing nationality that was Latin Europe when the most far-ranging dominion that the world had ever seen was estab-lished by Chingiz Khan and his successors. Its political extension was less remarkable than the economic energy it was developing. The city-state had been re-born in Italy, and Venice, once the vassal of the Byzantine empire, was now its exploiter, having diverted the Fourth Crusade for her own profit. Rival to Venice was Genoa, destined to steal a march on her with the Greek Restoration at Constantinople in 1261. In these and other Italian free cities there was in the thirteenth century an intensive economic vigour without contemporary parallel in the world. Islam was still formidable ; in the eleventh and twelfth centuries its arms had gained Anatolia and a great part of India, and the strength of Egypt had been sufficient to defeat the original aim of the Crusades. But in Christendom there was now a more significant vitality ; though internal disunion frustrated its military triumph, there was an evolution of economic power more ultimately decisive than the warfare in Palestine.

The Mongols in their advance encountered three separate worlds of civilization—the Chinese, the Islamic and the Christian-European. But these worlds were not at an equal distance from the Mongol homeland. China lay immediately to the south, the lands of Islam farther away, and Europe most remote of the three. The facts of distance had more than anything else to do with the delimitation of the Mongol realm. The Mongols indeed overran Russia and Persia before they had completed the conquest of China, and the extraordinary mobility of the Mongol armies seemed almost to make distance of no account, yet China was in the end completely subdued, whereas Western Europe was never seriously menaced. Even with enlistments from other nomad tribes the numbers of the Mongols remained comparatively small. Their main front throughout the period of their great conquests was always in China, a fact which has not generally been grasped by the historians who have treated only of their invasions of Europe. This was not merely because China was nearest to the Mongol homeland ; in population and taxable wealth it certainly exceeded any other equal area in the world. Nor was China easily conquered ; the Kin of the North were not finished until 1234, and the Sung of the South prolonged resistance until 1279. For an equal striking power against China, West Asia and Europe the Mongol imperial headquarters should have been moved to somewhere near the Aral Sea ; actually they were retained in Mongolia until 1264, and then transferred to Cambaluc (Peking) in China. In so far as separate centres of Tatar power were established farther west they only weakened the offensive strength of the empire as a whole.

The Mongol operations in the west were subsidiary to those on the Chinese front, and the conquests were often given up after being thoroughly plundered. Chingiz Khan, after making himself master of all the tribes of Mongolia, had begun the war against the Kin in North China in 1211. It was only in 1219 that he attacked the empire of Khwarezm, and decisively defeated its ruler Mohammed Shah, overrunning Transoxiana and Persia. From Persia in 1221 an army under the generals Chepe and Sabutai moved north-westwards round the eastern end of the Caucasus, overcoming successively the Georgians, the Kipchak or Kuman Turks of the Volga-Don steppes, and the Russians who mustered to resist the invaders on the Dnieper. But these conquests were not held ; not only did Chepe and Sabutai evacuate Europe, returning into Central Asia round the north of the Caspian, but Jalal-ud-Din, the Khwarezmian heir, was suffered to regain Persia. Then under Ogotai, the successor of Chingiz Khan, fresh expeditions were sent into West Asia and Europe simultaneously with assaults on Sung China and on Korea, the reduction of the Kin having been completed by 1234. Persia was now again overrun, Jalal-ud-Din swept away, and Georgia and Armenia subdued as far as the Black Sea.

Meanwhile on the front to the north of the Caspian and Caucasus Batu, a grandson of Chingiz Khan, was launched with about 150,000 men [1] against Europe. He conquered the Bulgarians of the Kama and most of Russia, capturing Ryazan, Kiev and other cities ; then dividing his forces into two columns, attacked Poland and Hungary in 1241. The northern army under Kaidu and Baidar

[1] The estimate is that of Capt. Liddell Hart in *Great Captains Unveiled*, chapter on Chingiz Khan and Sabutai.

defeated the Poles at Szydlow, took Cracow and Breslau,
and then crushed a German army under Duke Henry of
Silesia with the military orders of the Templars and Hos-
pitallers at Liegnitz.   Meanwhile the southern army under
Batu himself annihilated the Hungarians in the battle of
the Sajo, took Pesth and Gran, and carried its arms as
far as the Adriatic.   But the unbeaten Mongols made no
attempt to hold Poland and Hungary.   The Kumans and
Russians on the other hand were brought under permanent
control from a great Mongol camp fixed on the lower Volga.
Appeals from Russia led Pope Alexander IV to proclaim
a crusade against the Mongols ; the Mongols defeated this
at its inception by a great raid through Poland and a
second capture of Cracow in 1259, but again there was no
attempt to occupy Central Europe.   The Mongols combined
with an intense confidence in their battle prowess a sense
of the limits of their capacity for annexation.[1]

The conquest of Iran was not completed until 1256, when
the formidable religious-political power of the Ismā'īlīyah
sect, commonly known as ' the Assassins,' was destroyed by
the capture of their great fortress of Maimundiz together
with their leader.   Then in 1258 the Mongols advanced on
Baghdad, took and destroyed it, and put to death the
Abbasid Caliph Musta'sim.   From Baghdad they moved
west into Syria and took Aleppo and Damascus, riding to
the shores of the Mediterranean.   But in Syria in 1260
they met their first great defeat.

The destruction of Baghdad had meant that Cairo was
left the centre of the world of Islam and the Sultanate of
Egypt its champion.   Since the time of Saladin Egypt had
been a great military power, her armed strength based on
the army of Turkish and Circassian slaves known as Mamelukes.   Egypt had had to meet the full shock of the European Crusades and had been victorious.   Saladin recap-
tured Jerusalem from the Crusaders in 1187, and defeated

---

[1] The oft-repeated statement that the Mongols withdrew from Europe
to take part in the election of a new Grand Khan is incorrect.   The
Mongol retirement began before the death of Ogotai.

the Third Crusade (1189–92) ; the Fifth Crusade (1218–21)
met with disaster in an attack on Egypt itself, and so did
the Seventh Crusade, led by St. Louis, King of France,
in 1249. It was the Mameluke army, victor over an enterprise supported by all the chief monarchs of Latin Christendom, which now in 1260 challenged the Mongols in Syria.
It was led by the Mameluke Sultan Qutuz and his great
general Bibars ; the Mongols were under the command of
Kitbogha, who was a Christian and meditated the capture
of Jerusalem. At 'Ain Jalut Kitbogha was defeated and
slain by the Mamelukes, who followed up their victory by
retaking Damascus from the Mongols. From this time on
there was a struggle on equal terms between the Mongols
and Egypt for the possession of Syria.

In 1261 Bibars, who had made himself Sultan of Egypt
by murdering his predecessor Qutuz, legitimized his power
by bringing to Cairo an uncle of the last Abbasid Caliph
of Baghdad, who had been killed by the Mongols in 1258.
The Abbasid heir was proclaimed Caliph by Bibars, and
in return formally invested Bibars as Sultan. Thus Mameluke Egypt inherited the religious dignity of the Baghdad
Caliphate as well as the *de facto* leadership of Islam.

The Mongol empire after 1260 was divided into a suzerain
khanate and four vassal khanates, all held by descendants
of Chingiz Khan. Such partition had begun with the death
of Chingiz himself, who assigned territories in his will to
his various sons and grandsons. At first the sub-khanates
had been definitely subordinate to the suzerain line, but
as time went on they began more and more to assume the
character of independent states, and there were dissensions
between the various Chingizid families, though it was long
before the dynasty ceased to present a united front to the
world. The Chingizid suzerainty, the holder of which was
known to Europeans as the Great Khan, had as its special
domain Mongolia itself and China. It was willed by
Chingiz to his second surviving son Ogotai, and from Ogotai
descended to his son Kuyuk and his grandsons Kaidu and
Chapai ; the line of Ogotai having shown incapacity, the

Mongol *kuriltai* (diet) [1] transferred the over-khanate in 1251 to the house of Tule, the youngest of the sons of Chingiz. To the Tule line belong Mangu (1251–9), Kublai (1260–94) and the remaining emperors of the Mongol (Yüan) dynasty of China.

In Central Asia reigned the house of Chagatai, second son of Chingiz, holding Dzungaria, Kashgaria and Bokhara ; to the north-west were the domains of the Orda and Batu lines, descended from Juji, the eldest son of Chingiz who had died before his father. Orda's dynasty ruled to the north of the Aral Sea, and was known as the White Horde or Eastern Kipchak ; Batu's had Russia and the Volga lands as its province, and was known as the Golden Horde or Western Kipchak. In Persia and Mesopotamia from 1260 the house of Hulagu, brother of Mangu, of the Tule line, reigned with the title of *ilkhan*, whence their state is commonly referred to as the Ilkhanate. [2]

Latin Europe was in contact with the Tatar empire on two fronts, on a northern in Europe itself, and on a southern in Syria, where a Latin foothold had been gained by the Crusades. In Europe the contact was both by land across

---

[1] The Mongol khanate was formally elective in the diet of the Mongol tribesmen.

[2] Genealogical Tree of the Chingizids
(Suzerain khans in capitals)

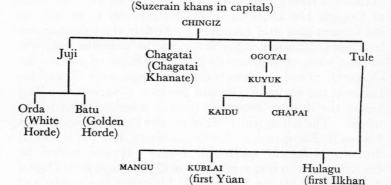

a march from the delta of the Danube to the upper Volga,
and by sea through the port-towns of the Crimea and
Black Sea coast.

On land the Golden Horde was separated from the inner
lands of Latin civilization by a barrier hard to traverse
either for commerce or for war. Between Italy, France
and West Germany on the one hand and the Don-Volga
steppes on the other intervened the vast territories of Hungary and Poland, lands but recently won for Latin Christendom, thinly inhabited before the arrival of the Mongols,
and now made emptier by their ravages. These powers
of the eastern frontier of the Latin world were not strong
enough to take the offensive against the Mongols, nor were
they wealthy enough to excite a great cupidity among them ;
at the same time their soil-clinging peoples with refuges in
forests and fens were hard for the steppe horsemen to bring
into subjection, and prevented the Golden Horde from
advancing its borders to the richer and more densely popu-
lated countries of Western Europe. The wild, half-savage
marchlands east of Cracow and Pesth made it an immense
distance by land from the Rhine to the Volga, and although
trade routes ran to the Golden Horde capitals Sarai (near
Stalingrad) and Bolgar (near Kazan) from Hungary, Poland
and the Baltic littoral, these were for a long time of less
importance for intercourse between Latins and Tatars than
the ports of the Black Sea frequented by Italian shipping.

In the interval between the time of Justinian and the
coming of the Mongols there had been a great increase
in the trade to the north from the Black Sea, due mainly
to the enterprise of the Scandinavian pirate-merchants from
the Baltic and their creation of the kingdom of Russia. A
large traffic now came to the Black Sea down the Dnieper
and the Don, and also down the Volga and across to the
Don by a portage at the close approach of the two rivers
near Stalingrad. Russian merchandise, consisting mainly
of furs, was carried over the Mediterranean from several
Black Sea ports of which the greatest in the thirteenth century was Soldaia or Sudak in the Crimea ; these towns

retained local autonomy under the Mongols on condition
of paying tribute, and they sent from the ships at their
quays to Sarai and Bolgar the luxuries required by the new
Tatar court. The power of the nomad conquerors ended
at the sea-shore ; they showed no disposition to venture
on to salt water, and where they could not plunder they
were ready enough to trade. Thus Soldaia, Matracha,
Kaffa and Tana [1] came to bear the same relation to the
Golden Horde as Olbia, Panticapaeum, Phanagoria and
Tanais had borne to the Scythians in ancient times. But
then it had been Greek enterprise that tapped the commerce of the Black Sea coasts ; now it was chiefly Italian.
From the Fourth Crusade in 1204 to the Greek Restoration
in 1261 the Black Sea was practically a Venetian lake ;
after 1261 the Genoese had the advantage, but the Venetians
remained a good second in the trade.

In Syria, as in the Crimea, the Latins were intruders
from the sea confronting the advance of the Tatars from
inland. But the Latin interest in Syria was not merely
commercial, as it was in the Crimea ; it was involved in
the great struggle of the Crusades, and affected not only
a few Italian trading cities, but also Catholic Christendom
as a whole. The Crusaders were strongly established in
Cyprus ; in Palestine after Jerusalem had been lost for the
second time they continued to hold Acre. Farther north
on the Gulf of Alexandretta was the kingdom of Little
Armenia with the port of Lajazzo (Laias), a great centre
of trade. Little Armenia was not merely Christian, but
Latin by adoption ; its church was united with Rome, its
crown had been accepted as a fief of the Western Empire,
and its fixed policy was one of alliance with the Latin
powers against Byzantines and Moslems. To these maritime Latin elements struggling to maintain themselves in
the Levant the attack of the Tatars on the rear of West
Asian Islam appeared as a divine intervention on behalf

[1] Tana on the left bank of the Don some 18 miles from its mouth
seems to have been only founded towards the end of the thirteenth
century. Its site was not quite the same as that of the ancient Tanais.

of the Christian cause. The warfare with Khwarezm and the Baghdad Caliphate, and later the prolonged and indecisive conflict with Egypt for the possession of Damascus and Aleppo, kept the Tatars in enmity to Islamic powers and disposed to adopt a neutral or even friendly attitude to the small Christian states in Asia. Little Armenia acknowledged Tatar suzerainty, as also did the Greek kingdom of Trebizond on the south-eastern shore of the Black Sea, and Lajazzo and Trebizond became the two chief ports for access to Tatar Persia from the Mediterranean.

It would in any case have been natural and in accordance with precedent for the Catholic Church to attempt the conversion of the new swarm of barbarians that had appeared in Europe ; only three centuries before the Magyars and the Vikings had been as terrible a scourge as the Tatars now threatened to become, yet they had been tamed by the missionaries of Rome. But over and above the established policy of assimilating barbarians through religious appeal there was in Latin Europe a special enthusiasm for the conversion of the Tatars, because their crushing blows against Islam seemed to mark them out as destined by God to be the destroyers of Egypt, the arch-enemy of Christendom.

The first approach made by the Church to the Great Khan of the Mongols was in 1245, four years after Batu's great invasion of Hungary and Poland, when the Pope sent from the Council at Lyons two embassies, one headed by the Franciscan John de Plano Carpini to journey through Poland and Russia, and the other under another Franciscan named Lorenzo to go by way of the Mediterranean and Armenia. The latter mission seems to have been turned back in Armenia, and no more is heard of it, but Carpini reached his destination in Mongolia, returned in 1247 with the Great Khan's reply to the Papal letter, and has left an invaluable record of his experiences and the information he gathered. After passing through Cracow and Kiev he came to the camp of the Mongol general Kurancha on the right bank of the Dnieper near Ekaterinoslav.

Kurancha with an army of 60,000 men guarded the western frontier of the Golden Horde and exacted tribute from the neighbouring Russian princes ; he sent on the embassy to the camp of his master Batu on the lower Volga a little way from the Caspian, and Batu forwarded it to the camp of the Great Khan which was at that time pitched not far from Karakorum in northern Mongolia. The Mongol rulers had not yet begun to live in built houses ; they held their courts in great tents, and frequently moved camp from one site to another ; yet in these camps in the wind-swept wilderness of the steppe the magnates arrayed themselves with a magnificence suitable to warriors who had plundered without restraint from Korea to Silesia. They wore the costliest furs, vaire and fox, ermine and sable, with velvets and silk brocades ; they displayed an abundance of gold and gems, not only on themselves and in their tents but also in the trappings of their horses.

Carpini arrived at the imperial camp in time to see the ceremonies at the election of Kuyuk, the Great Khan Designate, by the diet of the Mongol chiefs, which was held in a huge pavilion of white velvet. A great number of envoys, Chinese, Korean, Turkish, Persian and Russian, were present with tribute to lay before the Great Khan on his enthronement ; there were also many captives from all the lands overrun by the Mongol armies, including not a few Europeans, who were now employed at the court as secretaries, engineers, goldsmiths, jewellers and in other capacities. When at last Carpini was able to deliver his letters to Kuyuk, he was given a reply written in three versions, Mongolian, Persian and Latin, and this he took back to the Pope. As a diplomatic move the journey was hardly a success, for the Great Khan's answer was arrogant in the extreme, and gave little prospect of the spiritual submission of the Tatars to the Apostolic See.

The next Latin mission to the Great Khan, however, was sent at Tatar instigation. In 1248 King Louis IX of France came to Cyprus to prepare for the launching of the Seventh Crusade, and Ilchikadai, the general commanding the Mongol army in Persia, sent an envoy to him with the report that the Great Khan and his household were inclined to become Christians and a suggestion of a Tatar-Crusade alliance against Egypt. In response to these overtures Louis sent Andrew of Longumeau to Ilchikadai and on to the Great Khan to obtain a treaty. Andrew travelled through Armenia, Mazanderan and Khiva, skirting the southern and eastern shores of the Caspian ; the Great Khan's camp was found in Dzungaria, but Kuyuk had just died, and an insulting answer was returned by the Queen Ogul Gaimish who was acting as Regent. Nevertheless, a rumour of the conversion to Christianity of a son of Batu, Khan of the Golden Horde, induced St. Louis to make another attempt after the failure of his invasion of Egypt ; in 1252 he despatched William de Rubruck or Rubruquis, a Flemish Franciscan, with letters to the new Great Khan. Rubruquis went from Acre by Constantinople to Soldaia in the Crimea, and thence to the camp of Batu's supposedly Christian son in the steppe between the Don and the Volga ; this chief, however, turned out not to be a Christian at all, although one of his most influential lieutenants was one, and robbed Rubruquis of most of the books and vestments he had brought with him. After this disappointment the ambassador and his companions visited the camp of Batu himself, which was on the move down the Volga, and then made the long journey eastward across the steppes to Mongolia. Mangu, who was now Great Khan, received Rubruquis at his court and graciously offered peace to his master, the King of France, until the Mongols should have completed the conquest of the Saracens.

So far none of the Latin travellers who have left any record of themselves had reached China. But both Carpini and Rubruquis while in Mongolia obtained information on Cathay ; they knew that it was a great and populous country bordering on the Eastern Ocean, and Rubruquis perceived that it was identical with the Serica of antiquity. And they met with Chinese in Mongolia, for large numbers of Chinese artisans carried off captive by the Mongols were settled at Karakorum or attached to the Great Khan's court. Rubruquis notes that their skill as craftsmen was not surpassed anywhere in the world, that they produced silk of the finest quality and made wine from rice, that they wrote with a brush as if painting and combined all the letters of one word in a single figure—a closer observation on the Chinese written language than is to be found even in Marco Polo.

China itself, however, only became accessible to Europeans after Kublai Khan in 1264 had taken up his residence at his new capital of Khan Balig or Cambaluc (Peking, now Peiping) with a summer retreat at Shandu or Xanadu in the uplands to the north, thus shifting the centre of gravity of the Mongol realm from the Mongolian wilderness to within the confines of conquered Cathay. The first visitors to Kublai from Latin Europe were not emissaries from any ecclesiastical or political authority, but two Venetian merchants who had originally set out with a purely commercial aim. They were two brothers, Nicolo and Maffeo Polo, and in about 1260 they had journeyed from Soldaia in the Crimea to the court of the Golden Horde on the Volga, and had sold a stock of jewels to the reigning Khan, Batu's successor, for double their proper value. A war breaking out between the Golden Horde and Hulagu, founder of the Ilkhanate of Persia, made it difficult for them to return by the way they had come, so they went on further round the Caspian and across the Oxus to Bokhara, where they remained three years, and then received an invitation to come to the court of Kublai. Kublai gave them a warm welcome, questioned them at length about Europe, and appointed them as his ambassadors to carry letters to the Pope on their return to Italy ; in these letters he asked for a hundred missionaries of scholarly attainments to be sent to his court to instruct his Tatars and to dispute with the representatives of other religions.

The two Polos returned from their adventure by way of Persia and arrived at Acre in 1269. There was some delay before any answer to Kublai's letters could be obtained from Rome, the business of electing a new Pope being unusually prolonged, but at last the Apostolic See was occupied by Gregory X, and the Polos themselves were given Letters Apostolic and sent to Kublai together with two Dominicans, who were to stand for the hundred missionaries Kublai had requested. The two Dominicans turned back at Lajazzo, pleading as excuse the danger of Mameluke raids along the road in Little Armenia ; the two Polos, however, accompanied on this their second expedition to the Far East by Nicolo's young son Marco, braved these perils and in 1275 presented themselves before Kublai in his summer palace of Xanadu.

The Papacy has often been severely censured for not having responded more adequately to Kublai's invitation for missionary enterprise. It must be remembered, however, that bitter experience had taught the Church to distrust an affected zeal for the Christian religion in Tatar rulers, and to suspect ulterior motives in such overtures as Kublai's. And there can be little doubt that in fact the invitation was prompted less by the desire for instruction in Christianity—although the Khans certainly took pleasure in collecting the greatest possible variety of religious teachers at their courts and pitting them against one another in disputation—than by a wish to secure men of ability for secular employment, for the kind of service on which he actually employed the Polos when they arrived. China was too recently subdued for Kublai to be ready to employ large numbers of Chinese in the higher offices of the administration, while the Tatars were by nature unfitted for the complex tasks of civil government in China ; it was therefore his policy to make use of a staff of civilized foreigners in carrying on his rule, and among the foreigners to maintain a balance of distinct elements so as to make his own power more absolute. Persian Moslems and Uigur Nestorians were already enrolled by Kublai in his service, and he was anxious to add to it some picked men of the far-off Latin world, captives from which, the spoil of the great raids of 1241 and 1259, had established a high reputation

for ability in Mongolia.  In so far as this aim was understood in Rome, the Papacy may well have been reluctant
to send out brave and able men—for only brave men would
attempt the journey, and none without ability would be
suitable for upholding the Faith against its rivals—to be
lost to Europe and to be put to secular uses by the Emperor
of China.

However, the Polos returned to Kublai.  They went first
to Ormuz, evidently with the intention of taking a passage
to China by sea, but at Ormuz they changed their minds
and completed their journey via Balkh and Kashgar.  On
arriving at Kublai's court all three were at once taken into
the imperial service, in which they remained for seventeen
years, receiving high honour and promotion.  It was in
the accomplishment of missions which took him through
China from end to end that the young Marco gathered the
material for that narrative judged by a distinguished modern
critic [1] to be ' beyond question the best mediaeval picture
of Chinese civilization from a European source.'  When
the Polos at last returned to Europe they were still in the
Great Khan's service as far as Tabriz, for they escorted
on the sea voyage from China to Persia a Mongol princess
sent to be the bride of the Ilkhan Arghun.

The sojourn of the Polos in China opens a new era in
European knowledge of the Far East.  The Polos were, as
far as we know, the first Europeans to reside for any length
of time in China and to travel extensively within the country.
Rubruquis knew that in the Cathayans subdued beneath
the Mongol sway the Seres of classical antiquity had been
rediscovered ;  the Polos were for seventeen years in the
government service of this Cathay, and Marco was able
to give to Europe a detailed knowledge of it such as the
ancients had never had of the Seres.  Marco's book also
first made known in Europe the name of Japan (under the
form *Zipungu*) and the existence of numerous islands in the
ocean to the south-east of Asia where the ancients had
known only Java.

[1] C. R. Beazley, *The Dawn of Modern Geography*, vol. III, p. 94.

Besides the Polos themselves one other European appears in Marco's pages as contemporary with them in China. A German is mentioned as having been in the service of the the Polos and having assisted in the making of big mangonels for use in the siege of Siangyang. This passage presents serious difficulties in chronology, since the Polos cannot have arrived in China on their second visit before 1275, whereas Siangyang was captured in 1273 ; the best explanation appears to be, in spite of Marco's inclusion of himself in the reference to the incident, that the assistance at a siege was given by the elder Polos while Marco was away on a separate mission, and that the town besieged was wrongly identified by Marco with Siangyang. But there is no need to question the reality ot the German mangonel-maker, and a passage in Rubruquis gives a hint as to how this German reached China. The earlier traveller tells how a colony of German captives carried off by Batu in the war of 1241 had been settled in Dzungaria near the modern Kulja to work the gold mines ; Rubruquis was anxious to visit them but was not allowed to do so. This lonely fragment of the German people in the heart of Asia was no doubt a transplanted mining village from Silesia, and perhaps from here some specially skilled mechanic had been sent to China for service as an engineer with the Mongol army, for the Mongols were accustomed to leave the mechanical side of warfare to alien mercenaries or slaves.

Marco Polo's German belonged to a class of involuntary travellers whose most notable literary representative is Schiltberger ; but Schiltberger is exceptional in that he left a record of his experiences. As a rule the slave died without the commemoration of autobiography, and there is little of personal narrative that tells us of these lives uprooted and swept into exile by the storms of war. But there were many of them, and a few became richer in captivity and slavery than they could ever have been as free men in their own homes, for strange favours of fortune sometimes awaited the survivors of massacre and hardship, though not before misery and despair had killed whatever intellectual curiosity might have been evoked by surroundings more fantastic in contrast to their old homes than the scenes of fairy tales told to them as children.   There were men and women, brought up by the Danube or the Oder or still farther west, to whom captivity showed the peaks of the Altai and the rampart of Gog and Magog and the cities of Cathay, yet left with no thought but to make a living from day to day.   Only through such travellers as Carpini and Rubruquis do we get a glimpse of them and their enforced wanderings ;  Carpini says expressly that he relied on the reports of Christian captives among the Mongols for whatever had not come within his own experience, and it may be inferred that it was from one of them that he took his account of Cathay.   So that it was some unknown slave who had been the real pioneer in the European rediscovery of China !

Almost all European nationalities are included among the captives mentioned by Carpini and Rubruquis at the Great Khan's camp in Mongolia—the Russian goldsmith Kosmas who made Kuyuk's throne and the seal with which he stamped his letter in answer to the Pope ;  the Russian Temer, who had been an attendant of Prince Yaroslav of Suzdal and who assisted in the translation of Kuyuk's letter into Latin ;  William Buchier of Paris, a goldsmith, and his wife, a ' daughter of Lorraine, but born in Hungary,' both taken prisoners at Belgrade ;  a nephew of a Norman bishop from Belleville near Rouen, also a captive from Belgrade ;  a woman Paquette of Metz, made prisoner in Hungary and married to a Russian tent-maker ; Basil, son of an Englishman, but born in Hungary [1] ;  the Hungarian who acted as interpreter at Rubruquis' first reception by Mangu ;  a German girl who was thrown into trances

---

[1] These captives taken in Hungary, but of non-Hungarian origin, are important evidence for the extent of immigration into Hungary under the early Arpads.  The development which turned Hungary from a wilderness into a civilized state attracted settlers from all over Western Europe.

by the Mongol diviners ; the Greek charlatan and flatterer
Theodoulos who offered to act as a spy for the Mongols in
Europe.  What memoirs might not any one of these have
written !

On their return to Europe from China by the sea route
to Ormuz the Polos must have passed another European
bound for China and destined to give the Catholic Church
half a century of life there before the revolt which drove
the Mongols outside the Great Wall.  This was the Franciscan John of Monte Corvino, carrying a Papal letter to
Kublai and full of zeal to preach the gospel in the Orient,
a missionary pure and simple rather than an ecclesiastical
diplomat like the earlier friar travellers.  Between 1271,
when Gregory X had sent out the two faint-hearted Dominicans to accompany the Polos, and the commission given
to Monte Corvino by Nicholas IV in 1289, the Papacy had
made only one attempt to carry Catholic Christianity into
the Far East ;  this was in 1278, when a rumour reached
Rome, probably originating in the favour shown to the
Polos by Kublai on their return to China, that the Great
Khan had been converted to the Faith, and the Pope sent
out an embassy of five Franciscan friars with a letter *Caris-
simo filio Quolibey Magno Chamo, Imperatori et Moderatori
Omnium Tartarorum*.  The fortunes of this embassy are
unknown, but it does not appear ever to have reached
China.

Corvino, after preaching for fourteen years among the
Saracens of the Levant, came to Rome in 1289 and obtained
letters of credence to the Ilkhan of Persia and to Kublai.
He went first to Tabriz, thence to Ormuz and by sea to
India, and on to China by the Straits of Malacca, making
the voyage in the reverse direction to that of the Polos.
He reached Cambaluc in 1292 or 1293, and was allowed
to take up his residence there and preach ;  he was accompanied by a wealthy merchant, Peter of Lucolongo, who
had joined him at Tabriz and looked after the work financially.  Before he had been in Cambaluc six years Corvino
had built a church with a campanile and three bells.  In

1303 he was joined by another friar, Arnold of Cologne, and in 1305 he persuaded a Mongol envoy returning to Tabriz from Peking to carry a letter for him to the Vicar of the Franciscans in the Crimea. News of his success reached Rome, and in 1307 the Pope created him Archbishop of Cambaluc, and appointed seven bishops to assist him, of whom three reached China, three perished on the way, and one turned back. Three more suffragans were sent out in 1312. With these reinforcements the mission in Cambaluc was developed, and a new one was started at the great port of Zayton in South China. When Corvino died in 1328 there was a Latin Christian community in China numbering several thousands, and enjoying the favour of the Tatar dynasty, which made it a policy to patronize alien religions, whether Moslem, Tibetan Buddhist, Nestorian or Catholic, at the expense of the Confucian orthodoxy of China. The Catholic missionaries received a liberal allowance for food and clothing from the imperial treasury, were permitted to build a church just outside the wall of the palace in Cambaluc, and were received at court. At Zayton the preaching of the Gospel to the infidels seems to have led the friars to an earthly paradise instead of to martyrdom ; Andrew of Perugia built himself out of the imperial bounty a friary with ' apartments fit for any prelate ' in a garden outside the city, and a bath-house and a merchants' factory were maintained by the mission in the port itself.

The Latin community in China, however, did not have a chance to grow into an important power before the revolt of China in 1368 swept out the Mongols together with the various foreign elements they had patronized. The missionary effort languished rather than increased after the death of Corvino ; the distractions of the Church in Europe, the immense distance and dangers of the journey, and the difficulties of communication between Latin Europe and Peking made it hard to expand or even to keep up the strength of the missions, and Corvino found no worthy successor. China grew more remote again from Europe,

as the Ilkhanate and the Golden Horde became more and
more independent of their nominal suzerain at Cambaluc
and engrossed a greater share of Latin attention both in
diplomacy and religious propaganda.

Nevertheless, there was one more notable exchange of
diplomatic correspondence between the Papacy and the
Yüan court before the débâcle of the Tatars in China.    In
1338 an embassy from the last of the Yüan emperors of
China arrived in Avignon, asking for the Papal benediction
and a present of European horses ; it carried also a letter
from the Alan contingent of the Tatar army in China, a
force originally Christian—the Alans came from the central
Caucasus and were among the picked troops of the Great
Khans—and brought by Corvino into allegiance to Rome.
In response to this embassy the Pope sent a legation of four
Franciscans to Cambaluc ; one of the four was Marignolli,
who has left an account of the journey.    The envoys left
Avignon in 1338 and returned in 1353 ; they went by the
Crimea and Central Asia to China, and came back by India
and Persia, visiting all the mission communities near their
route.   In China they spent four years, enjoying the most
generous hospitality from the Great Khan, who was delighted
with the Frankish *destriers* presented to him, and humbly
received the Papal benediction given by Marignolli with
cross, candles, incense and chanting of the Nicene creed in
the palace itself.

The first half of the fourteenth century which saw Catholic
missionaries in Cathay saw also Italian traders arrive there
in the ordinary course of business.   The Polos had indeed
been merchants by profession, but in China they had played
the part only of diplomats and civil servants.   The first
mention of Latin merchants in China in a private capacity
occurs incidentally in Bishop Andrew of Zayton's letter of
1326, where he speaks of a quotation of Chinese currency
by ' the Genoese merchants.'   Marignolli, who visited
Zayton in about 1346, says that the Franciscan mission
there maintained a merchants' factory, and the inference
is that Genoese merchants coming by sea from Ormuz to

Zayton made an arrangement with the friars for the ware-housing of their goods in the great South China port. The presence of Genoese at Zayton is noted by the Arab traveller Ibn Batuta in about 1336, and is perhaps to be reckoned the most astonishing result of the commercial activity of Genoa in the early fourteenth century ; it is a fact which becomes the more significant in relation to the Genoese attempt in 1291 to sail to India round Africa.

In Pegolotti's *Libro di Divisamenti di Paesi*,[1] written some time between 1335 and 1343, there is an account of a trade route to China across the Central Asian steppes, starting from the port of Tana at the mouth of the Don. This route is ' perfectly safe, whether by day or by night, accord-ing to the report of merchants who have used it. . . . You may reckon that between Tana and Sarai the road is less safe than on any other part of the journey, and yet even in this part, if you are some sixty men in the company, you may go as safely as if you were in your own house. Any-one from Genoa or Venice wishing . . . to go to Cathay should carry linens with him and if he visit Organci [Urgenj] he will dispose of these well. In Organci he should purchase *somni* of silver, and with these he should proceed. . . . Whatever silver the merchants carry with them to Cathay the lord of Cathay takes from them and puts in his treasury and gives that paper money of theirs in exchange . . . and with this money you can readily buy silk and whatever other merchandise you desire to buy, and all the people of the country are bound to receive it, and you shall not pay a higher price for your goods because your money is of paper.'

Latin traders do not seem to have penetrated to China along this route before 1305, for Corvino in his letter from Cambaluc in that year writes that before the recent arrival of Arnold of Cologne there had been no Latin visitor to the Great Khan's capital since 1292—with the exception of a certain Lombard surgeon who had uttered appalling

[1] See extracts from Pegolotti in *Cathay and the Way thither*, ed. Yule (2nd ed., 1914) vol. III, pp. 137-73.

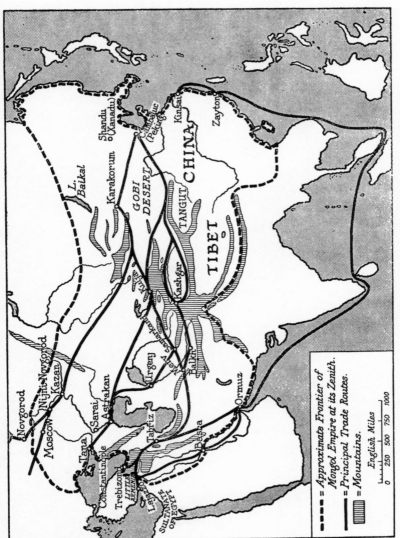

TRADE ROUTES OF THE MONGOL EMPIRE BETWEEN EUROPE AND CHINA

blasphemies about the Pope, to the dismay of the Catholic missionary. But Pegolotti implies that when he wrote the Tana-Cathay route was being regularly used by Italians ; he gives advice in his book, which is purely a commercial manual, on equipment for the journey, and notes on expenses and the approximate current prices of silk, damasks and *nachetti* of silk and gold in the Chinese marts.

There can be little doubt that the Latins' opening of direct commercial intercourse with China was due to their discovery that with the order established throughout Asia by the Mongol empire, by now grown out of its pristine ferocity and understanding that it was more profitable in the long run to tax caravans than to rob them outright— with this *Pax Tatarica* from the Sea of Azov to the Pacific, Chinese silks in spite of the costs of transport could compete with European in the European market. Silk for Pegolotti is evidently *the* merchandise of China. This revival of the China-Europe silk trade presents a feature which seems to have been absent from it in ancient times. There is no evidence that the Romans had any taste for Chinese patterned silk textiles ; the demand was mainly, if not entirely, for raw silk or plain white stuffs to be unravelled and re-woven into gauzes and dyed in the workshops of Syria. In the fourteenth century the Chinese silks that came to Europe seem to have been mostly damasks and brocades, and other patterned silks ; a few dating from this period have been preserved in Europe. One reason for this innovation in the character of the silk trade must have been the greater affinity of European to Asiatic feeling for textile design in the Middle Age than in antiquity.

The new silk trade from China to the Sea of Azov did not endure for very long. It required exceptionally favourable conditions for its maintenance, and these only continued for half a century at the most—and that interrupted by sudden disasters such as the massacre of Christians, including several Franciscan missionaries and a Genoese merchant, by a Moslem khan at Almalik (Kulja) in 1339. With the expulsion of the Mongols from China in 1368 and the war

carried on against them by the Chinese in Mongolia itself,
and with a recrudescence of tribal anarchy in Central Asia
at the same time, the trade disappeared, as far as the Black
Sea ports and the West European market were concerned.
To the towns of the Golden Horde on the Volga, however,
it appears that Chinese silks continued to be brought, for
the ways from Kulja to Sarai and Bolgar were hardly more
dangerous than those from the Black Sea and the Baltic.
A great commerce certainly continued between China and
the cities of Central Asia, for while Clavijo was at Samarkand
at the beginning of the fifteenth century a caravan of 800
camels arrived there from China, and Clavijo mentions silks
and satins as the chief merchandise of the Chinese traders.

The most historically important commercial development
due to the Mongol empire was not the temporary revival
of the China-Europe silk trade, but the great increase of
the Indies-Europe spice trade.   The cessation of the renewed
silk traffic from China made little difference to the economy
of Europe, since Europe produced silk for itself.   But the
spices which became more and more an essential for European cookery could not be obtained except from India and
Indonesia,[1] and must come through either Persia or Egypt ;
this indispensable and naturally monopolist trade came to
be the chief bone of contention in the politics of the Levant,
and was the most powerful single factor in stimulating the
European expansion of the fifteenth century.   The Tatar
ascendency in Persia, before the conversion of the Ilkhanate
to Islam, allowed Italian traders to go direct to India and
cut prices against the Egyptians who were wont to raise
them 300 per cent as middlemen between India and Europe ;
as a result Europeans knew where spices were produced and
at what cost, so that when they were again cut off from the
Indian market by a hostile Islam and by incessant wars in the
Levant they were well aware of the opportunities awaiting
any power that could find a new route to 'the Indies where
the spices grow.'   India proper and the Malay Archipelago

[1] China produced ginger and cinnamon, but both these came also
from India ;  China acquired no European fame as a spice land.

rather than China were the magnets that drew European mercantile ambitions in the Great Age of Discovery.

Nevertheless, China was inevitably involved in the European movement to find a new way to the Indies, for China and India were already united in one continuous maritime trade area ; once found, the all-sea route from Europe to India led to China also, and Columbus in aiming westward at Asia intended to reach China first and then go on to Indonesia.[1] And further, even though China had not regained the economic importance it had had, as the sole source of silk, for European antiquity, yet the accounts of China given by the European travellers in the time of the Mongol empire had a profound psychological effect in shifting the point of balance in the Latin Christian conception of *Weltpolilik*. In this respect the fourteenth century marks an advance not only over the early Middle Age but also over the Classical Age. It is usual to make the voyage of Columbus to America the point of division between the ' Mediterranean ' and ' Oceanic ' eras. But the mental transition from the outlook that accounted all other seas as secondary to the Mediterranean to a point of view already ' oceanic ' began two centuries before Columbus, and it was the outcome of the discovery, with the facilities of the *Pax Tatarica*, of the vast extent, population and wealth of the Asiatic lands beyond Syria and of the range and volume of maritime traffic in the Indian and Pacific Oceans. In the early Greek conception Europe, Asia and Africa had surrounded a central Mediterranean Sea, the Roman empire had been built round that sea as its centre of gravity, and from the seventh century Christendom and Islam had divided the Mediterranean world between them. Even after the great extent of Asia had become known to the Classical geographers, and India and China had begun to provide Rome with gems, spices and silk, the lands east of the Euphrates seemed only a fringe as compared in importance to the *Romanus orbis*. In the twelfth century European knowledge of Asia and Africa beyond the Mediter-

[1] See Chap. VII.

ranean littoral was meagre in the extreme, and most maps arranged the three continents with Jerusalem at the centre and the Mediterranean stretching half-way through the land-mass from east to west. But after the Mongol conquests Asia was explored from end to end and made known in shape and condition with a high degree of accuracy ; the result was a decisive breach in the Mediterranean-centred attitude of the Latin mind and a new sense of being cooped up in a corner of the world, in the margin instead of in the middle of human affairs. Travel had revealed in Further Asia an empire not only equalling but exceeding the measure of Europe in population, wealth, luxury and the greatness of its cities.

It was the travel to China more than that to any other part of Asia which captured the imagination and altered the mental perspective of Latin Europe. Most of the Latin travellers of the period visited Persia and India as well as China, but it is for China that they reserve their superlatives of description. The earliest accounts of China, indeed, aroused nothing but incredulity, so contrary were they to European preconceptions and so like fairy tales. A tradition relates that when Marco Polo was dying some of his friends implored him to save his reputation for veracity by cutting out from his book whatever went beyond the facts, to which he replied that he had not told half of what he had really seen. Similarly Andrew, Bishop of Zayton, writes in a letter from Cathay [1] that ' as to the wealth and splendour of this Court and its Emperor, the size of his dominions, the multitude of his subjects, the number of his cities, the peace and order of his realm, he will attempt no description, for it would seem incredible.'

But the unanimous testimony of travellers at last convinced Europe of the reality of this populous and magnificent Cathay. The size and splendour of the Chinese cities were asserted by all the narratives, and in the account of Friar Odoric of Pordenone comparisons with Italy are given to point the description. In Manzi or South China, called

[1] Summary of letter in Beazley, *op. cit.*, III, p. 179.

by Marco Polo the 'richest country in the world,' Odoric declares there were 2,000 cities 'so large that neither Treviso nor Vicenza could be named with any one of them' ; Canton, he says, was three times as large as Venice, and Zayton twice as big as Bologna. But these places were small compared with Hangchow, the old Sung capital, the *Quinsai* of Marco Polo, *Cansaia* of Odoric and *Campsay* of Marignolli, the greatest city at that time in China and, almost certainly, in the whole world. Marignolli calls it 'the most marvellous city that now exists or perhaps ever did exist' ; Marco Polo says that it had a circuit of 100 miles and 12,000 stone bridges over its network of canals, and Odoric adds that each of the great suburbs outside its twelve gates was larger than Venice or Padua. The size of Hangchow was only less remarkable than its abounding wealth and delicate luxury.

'In that country,' says Odoric, 'the number of people is so great that among us here it would be deemed incredible ; in many parts I have seen the population more dense than the crowds you see at Venice on Ascension Day. And the land has great store of bread, wine, rice, flesh and fish of all kinds.' The stone-paved roads and streets are spoken of with enthusiasm, while the quantity of shipping on the rivers and in the ports of China struck the travellers with amazement ; 'indeed,' says Odoric, 'it is something hard to believe when you hear of, or even see, the vast scale of the shipping in these parts.' Marignolli calls Zayton *portus maris mirabilis, civitas nobis incredibilis* ; his language finds support in the estimate of the Moorish traveller Ibn Batuta that Zayton was the greatest of the five chief ports of the world he had visited, the other four being Calicut and Kulam in India, Soldaia in the Crimea, and Alexandria.[1]

---

[1] Ibn Batuta knew Constantinople, but not the Italian ports. He and the Italian travellers between them, however, may be considered to have known all the ports of the world which could possibly claim primacy at that time. Zayton was roughly identical in situation with the modern Amoy, though its precise location has been the subject of much controversy.

All travellers in the Far East in this period tell of the ' great ships of Zayton,' the huge ocean-going junks with which the Chinese traded to Java, Malaya and India ; the largest had fifty or sixty cabins apiece, four or even six masts, double planks and watertight compartments, towed two or three large boats and carried some ten small ones, had crews of 200 or 300 and took as many passengers, grew vegetables on board and carried as much as 6,000 baskets of pepper in one cargo.

The Polos, indeed, before Columbus, may be said to have discovered a New World for mediaeval Europe. The discovery had a profound effect on European habits of thought. The revolution in geographical conceptions coincides with the appearance of the first scientific maps for practical use, the Italian and Catalan *portolani* ; the new knowledge is assimilated to an intellectual system worked out in terms of the mariners' chart. All that is known is clearly defined, and all the interrelations of place shown at once to the eye with a firm precision and certainty that urge on by the very quality of the lines to the conquest of the unknown. The thoughts of the new age extend beyond Europe and the Mediterranean lands. In 1428 Prince Pedro, a brother of Henry the Navigator, brought back to Portugal from a visit to Venice a copy of Marco Polo's book and a map ' with all the parts of the earth described, whereby Prince Henry was much furthered.' Within a hundred years of this one of the ships of Magellan will have circumnavigated the globe.

One other sequel to the contact between China and Europe promoted by the Mongol empire demands attention. About a decade after Prince Pedro brought his Marco Polo to Portugal printing with movable type began in Europe, and there is good reason to believe that this innovation owes something to the report of a similar process used on a large scale for some time previously in the Far East.

Paper is recorded to have been first made in China in A.D. 105, and block-printing dates at least from the ninth century ; the oldest extant Chinese printed book is a copy of a Buddhist *sutra* dated 868. In 953 an edition of the Classics was printed from blocks. In the middle of the eleventh century a method of printing with movable earthenware type was invented by a certain Pi Shêng. In the Yüan period wooden type was substituted for earthenware, but the process was not widely used. The great development of movable-type printing only took place at the beginning of the fifteenth century, and then not in China, the land of its invention, but in Korea. The development was due to the intense desire of the vigorous new dynasty ruling Korea from 1392 to introduce Chinese literary culture among the people and recivilize a country which had been terribly ravaged by the Mongols. King T'ai Tsung, who reigned from 1401 to 1419 and had been the guiding spirit of the administration even before his accession, was a devotee of Chinese learning and had a passionate enthusiasm for education ; desiring to multiply books as rapidly as possible, he took up and improved the Chinese method of movable-type printing. A Government ' Department of Books ' was set up, and began printing in 1403 ; during the next thirty years large numbers of books were turned out by this royally endowed press.

The Korean type was of metal, and the technique was very similar to that of the earliest European typography. To quote from Mr. T. F. Carter's admirable work on the subject [1] : ' The type mould was the key to the invention of typographic printing. And it was the type mould that the Koreans developed. That is the significance of Korean printing.'

By the fifteenth century Europe produced paper, the primary condition of successful printing, and had a method of block-printing, which does not, however, appear to have been used for printing books. China had already contributed to this equipment. The art of paper-making had been introduced into Europe from Moslem lands after these had first borrowed it from China—through Chinese artisans brought as captives to Samarkand by the Arabs in the eighth

[1] *The Invention of Printing in China and its spread Westward* (1925).

century.  Chinese block-printing was made known to
Europe as result of the Mongol conquests, especially through
the Chinese printed paper currency which aroused so much
interest, through playing-cards introduced into Europe by
the Tatars, and through religious image-prints made by the
Buddhists and probably also by the Nestorians.  The early
European printing of playing-cards and religious drawings
—the latter with a technique closely resembling the earlier
Central Asian—suggests Asiatic models ; Carter says that
the influence ' rests on such strong circumstantial evidence
as to be accepted with a reasonable degree of certainty.'

But it is the beginning of typography in about 1440 that
constitutes the real 'invention of printing' in European
history.  It was not preceded by any industry of book-
production by block-printing ; it appears as a developed
process and at once takes possession of the field.  Carter,
however, does not regard it as traceable to the work of the
Korean typographers ;  he considers the latter ' to be a
collateral branch, as it were—cousins rather than ancestors
of the inventor of European typography.'  He makes the
further comment that ' it seems a strange coincidence if
entirely without connection the Koreans began printing
with metal type just half a century before Gutenberg's
invention.  Yet there is no evidence of such connection.
And intercourse between Europe and the Far East during
that half-century was, so far as we now know, almost non-
existent.'

We may agree that it seems a strange coincidence that
the process should appear in Europe quite independently
soon after it had been adopted by the government of Korea
as the method for an increased output of books, and yet
may question the assertion that there was no likely channel
by which an account of the Korean industry could have
reached Europe.  By 1400 the former Mongol empire had
indeed broken up, but several of the hordes formed from
its dissolution were still powerful and wealthy, and there are
many indications that long-distance caravan trade in Central
Asia was still carried on.  A trade in these wild regions was

difficult to start, but once started also difficult to obliterate. It is true that Italians could no longer penetrate along the Central Asian trade routes, but that was largely because they were Christians, and subject not only to brigandage but also to persecution by Tatar Moslem converts. And in times of confusion in Central Asia the nomads themselves, born and bred to the life of the steppe, to its privations and its warfare, were best suited to form caravans. The narrative of Clavijo shows that Samarkand in the time of Timur was the centre of a far-reaching network of routes ; in 1404 there came to Samarkand a caravan of 800 camels from China with silk, gems, musk and rhubarb, envoys from a tribe living apparently in eastern Siberia bringing falcons, sables and marten-skins to Timur, and Russian merchants with linen and furs. And the trade lines thus indicated link up with another to the west, that of the German Hansa operating through Novgorod, a city which had escaped the Mongol conquest thanks to its protecting marshes, and now extended its commercial activity eastward to and beyond the Urals in quest of the most prized of all furs, the Siberian sable. On the upper and middle Volga was a growing population due largely to migration from southern tracts, which were more exposed to the truculence of the nomads ; here the new Russian power of Moscow confronted the half-settled population of the Bolgar branch of the Golden Horde, which formed from 1438 the independent khanate of Kazan ; here Nijni-novgorod was already becoming a notable mart, and commerce was growing rather than declining. At Nijni-novgorod or Kazan a German Hansa merchant may well have heard from some far-travelled silk or fur trader [1] of a country in the Far East [2] where

[1] Or perhaps an escaped Russian slave ; there were still many in the Tatar khanates, and, as we have seen, these unfortunates often travelled by compulsion where their compatriots did not go voluntarily Schiltberger in the retinue of the Tatar chief Chekre accompanied expeditions to Sibir (West Siberia) and Bolgar in this period.

[2] Korea at this time was very prosperous and provided a market where Chinese goods could be purchased by the Mongols when the prolonged Chinese-Mongol wars interfered with the Chinese trade.

books were made with movable metal type ; just as Clavijo was told at Samarkand some truth and many fables about China by a Tatar caravan convoy who had spent six months in Peking.   The state printing of Korea was not a thing done in a corner, and it was just the kind of marvel which might be related in caravanserai gossip.   Such an idea, passed on by the Hansa merchant, would find fertile soil in Germany.   There is no stimulus to invention like the knowledge that the thing has been successfully done, even where the exact method is not revealed.

All this of course is mere guesswork ; it is not proof.   But we can say with some confidence that there was no impassable barrier between the Volga and Mongolia, and that the conditions in Central Asia from 1400 to 1440 were such that a suggestion from the Far East may be supposed to have reached Europe without an excessive strain on the probabilities of the case.

According to the article *Printing* in the latest (14th) edition of the *Encyclopaedia Britannica* [1] : ' There is no certainty as to the actual date of the European invention of printing from movable type, which was independent of the discovery of the principle by the Chinese, but it is assumed that it took place about 1440. . . . Just as there is no actual certainty as to the date of the European invention of printing from movable type, so it is also doubted who the inventor really was and where the invention took place.'

But surely we have a right to ask how, if it is not certainly known when, where or by whom the invention was made in Europe, it can be so categorically asserted that it was independent of the earlier and conspicuously used Chinese-Korean process.   And it may even be suggested that since Korean typography underwent so remarkable a development just before the appearance of the process in Europe, and since there were possible lines of news transmission between the Far East and Germany, the burden of proof really lies on those who assert the complete independence of the European invention.

[1] By J. R. Riddell and J. C. Oswald.

# CHAPTER VI

## The Way round Africa

IN May of 1291, the year in which Acre, the last stronghold of the Crusaders in Syria, was recovered by
Islam, and while Marco Polo was still in China, Ugolino
de Vivaldo with two galleys set out from Genoa in an
attempt to find a way to the Indies by the 'Ocean Sea'
(*ut per mare oceanum irent ad partes Indiae*). The aim was
primarily commercial (*mercimonia utilia inde deferentes*), but
religion was not neglected ; two Franciscan friars accompanied the expedition. It sailed out through the Straits
of Gibraltar and down the African coast past 'a place
called Gozora' (probably to be identified with Cape
Nun). Thereafter it vanished from European sight, and
no news of it was ever brought back.

Vivaldo's dream was at last brought to fulfilment, not,
however, by his fellow-countrymen of Genoa, but by the
Portuguese. In 1498–9 Vasco da Gama sailed from Lisbon
to Calicut and returned with abundant cargo of Malabar
pepper ; in 1500 his king, Manoel I, assumed the proud
title of 'Lord of the conquest, navigation and commerce
of India, Ethiopia, Arabia and Persia.'

The opening of the all-sea route to India was soon
followed by the attainment of Chinese waters. The capture
of Malacca in 1511 opened to the Portuguese the gates
of the Pacific, and China was reached three years later.
Now for the first time in history the ports of Asia from
the Red Sea eastward were visited by direct sea voyage
from Europe. Nor was the European achievement limited
to the way round Africa ; the voyage of Magellan put a
girdle round the Earth, and the Indies were attained by

sailing west. In 1492 Columbus, voyaging into the unknown Atlantic with a letter from the Spanish Sovereigns
to the Great Khan of Cathay, had made for Europe the
decisive [1] discovery of America ; Magellan found a way
round America as Vasco da Gama had found a way
round Africa, and later on in the sixteenth century
Spain made a contact with China *via* Mexico and the
Philippines.

The whole movement of maritime enterprise that brought
European ships to the shores of China in the days of the
Ming should be viewed as a sequel to the *Pax Tatarica*.
It is indeed clear that the voyage of Vivaldo was a part
of that great outburst of activity in travel which was the
response of the Italian cities to the revelation of Asia by
the Mongols. It is, however, difficult at first sight to dis-
cern the continuity between this period and the age of
Henry the Navigator and Columbus. More than a hundred
years elapse between the voyage of Vivaldo and the first
expeditions of the Navigator down the African coast ; in
the fifteenth century Atlantic exploration is organized no
longer by the Italian republics but by Portugal, and in
the 'nineties by Spain and England. But if we look closer
we see that the later movement grows in the beginning
from Italian initiative, and throughout its course shows
the inspiration of mediaeval Italy, the Italy that held the
capital of Catholic Christendom and had become wealthy

---

[1] The real significance of the voyage of 1492 lies in the fact that
it was immediately and continuously followed up, and led to the general
exploration and exploitation of the continent by Europeans. There
was certainly one, and were probably several, ' discoveries ' of America
before Columbus. The discovery by the Norsemen in the eleventh
century is universally admitted. Chinese voyagers seem to have
reached Alaska and British Columbia in the sixth century ; for a
brief discussion of the evidence see Beazley's *Dawn of Modern Geography*,
vol. I, pp. 492–503. For discoveries deduced from European mediaeval
maps (Brazil and the Antilia island group) see W. H. Babcock's *Legendary
Islands of the Atlantic*. There is also the ' authentic island ' of Bianco's
1448 map, given as 1,500 miles to the west of a point south of Cape
Verde. For yet another claim see Sofus Larsen, *The Discovery of America
twenty years before Columbus* (Copenhagen—London, 1925).

and adventurous and far-minded from the profits of the Crusades and from the commerce of the East. As a naval power Portugal was the adopted daughter of Genoa, and the rise of Lisbon to prosperity was largely due to its position on the route of Genoese and Venetian sea traffic with Flanders through the Straits of Gibraltar. In the arts of navigation and in geographical theory and erudition the Portuguese were the pupils of the Italians. Italy was the clearing-house for all knowledge regarding the further regions of Africa and Asia, and from Italy came the maps which formed the minds of the leaders of exploration. Italian names are inseparable from the Great Age of Discovery—Uso di Mare and Cadamosto sailing in the service of Prince Henry of Portugal, Toscanelli who first made a practical proposal for a Transatlantic way to the Indies, Columbus who first attempted it, Amerigo Vespucci who gave his name to two continents, and John Cabot who would have made London 'a greater market for spices than Alexandria.'[1] It was a Genoese who made the first effort since Hellenistic times to reach India by sailing round Africa ; it was a Genoese who officially discovered America. It was an Italian merchant who gave Europe its first real knowledge of China, and it was to be an Italian Jesuit who would open intercourse of thought between those sundered worlds.

The expedition of Vivaldo, supported also by the no less eminent Genoese house of Doria,[2] was a move in the intense struggle for commercial supremacy waged between Genoa and Venice in the period following the Greek Restoration at Constantinople in 1261. The conflict was above all for the control of the spice trade, the most lucrative part of the Asia-Europe traffic. As already mentioned, the bulk of the spice import to Europe, especially pepper,

---

[1] *Letter of Raimondo di Soncino, Milanese Minister to England, to the Duke of Milan.* Ed. A. W. Lawrence and Jean Young, *Narratives of the Discovery of America.*

[2] Tedisio Doria helped to equip the two galleys, but did not himself embark.

ginger and cinnamon, came by the Red Sea and through
Egypt, while a considerable amount, including most of
the very valuable clove and nutmeg supplies, came to the
Persian Gulf and took the caravan routes from Ormuz
through Tabriz to Trebizond or from Basra to the port
of Lajazzo in Little Armenia (Cilicia). The Red Sea and
Persian Gulf routes were controlled respectively by the
Mameluke kingdom of Egypt, which also ruled over most
of Syria, and by the Ilkhanate, the Tatar kingdom of
Persia, which included Mesopotamia under its sway. At
the time of the Greek Restoration at Constantinople the
Ilkhanate was a new creation, for it was only after the
capture of Baghdad and execution of the last Abbasid
Caliph in 1258 that Hulagu assumed the title of Ilkhan
and made his Persian province a distinct sub-state of the
Tatar realm.

Before 1261 the position of the Venetians in the Eastern
Mediterranean was unrivalled ; to the south their diplomacy
had secured for them almost a monopoly of trade in the
ports of Egypt, and to the north, as a result of the part
they had played in the Fourth Crusade, their mercantile
interests were supreme in the Aegean and the Black Sea.
Only in Cyprus and Little Armenia and the decaying
Christian states of Syria could the Genoese compete on
anything like equal terms with the Venetians. But the
Greek Restoration was disastrous to Venice throughout
the northern Levant, for her power had been bound up
with the fortunes of the Latin empire, and she was
now supplanted by the Genoese who had correctly gauged
the trend of events and had thrown in their lot with Michael
Palaeologus. On the Egyptian trade the Venetians maintained, and even strengthened, their hold, but in the
Black Sea the hegemony passed to Genoa.

Beyond the narrow waters of the Bosphorus vistas of
golden opportunity opened out before the Genoese. From
the Black Sea all the great trade routes of Russia, Central
Asia and Persia could be tapped, and close contact established with the two great western Tatar kingdoms, the

Western Kipchak and the Ilkhanate. Trebizond, the centre of an independent Greek state, was one of the two most important gateways from the Mediterranean maritime area to the Ilkhanate, which had its capital at Tabriz, and at Trebizond from 1261 to 1319 Genoese trade was without rival ; in about 1300 the Genoese acquired a quarter of their own in the city with extraterritorial rights. Nor were they content only to sail upon the Black Sea ; they invaded the land-locked Caspian with their ships. Ascending the Don from the Sea of Azov in small, light vessels and conveying them probably on ox-waggons over the narrow neck of land to the Volga near modern Stalingrad (Tsaritsyn), Genoese merchant-adventurers made their way by the Volga to the Caspian and across the Caspian to the coast of Persia itself.[1]

It was probably their feat in opening the Caspian to their seamanship that suggested to the Genoese a still more ambitious project, the brilliantly audacious idea of launching a fleet on the Indian Ocean in the service of the Ilkhanate. William Adam tells us in his *De modo exstirpandi Saracenos* that the Genoese made to the Ilkhan Arghun (1284–91) a proposal for an alliance whereby a Genoese fleet on the Indian Ocean was to seize Aden, blockade the Straits of Bab-el-Mandeb and divert Egypt's share of the Indian spice trade to Persian ports, to the great profit of the Ilkanate and Genoa and the ruin of Egypt and Venice. In recommending such a course the Genoese could rely on the permanent enmity of the Ilkhanate for Egypt as well as on the attractive prospect of pecuniary gain ; they had, moreover, friends at the court of Tabriz in two citizens of Genoa, Buscarello de Ghizolfi and Tommaso degli Anfossi, who were in the diplomatic service of Arghun. In the event, nevertheless, the scheme was not taken up by the Ilkhan ; he was, doubtless, unwilling to become so much dependent on foreign aid,

---

[1] Marco Polo, ch. 19 (French text, Paris, ed. 1824). Compare the raids into the Caspian by the Genoese in 1374 and by the Venetians in 1428.

and he may also have been influenced by Venetian intrigue.[1]

But, in spite of the fact that it was never translated into action, the plan has great historical significance in that it marks the birth of a new idea in the policies of European states, the idea of obtaining control of the spice trade at its source by means of naval power in the Indian Ocean. The Crusades had been a frontal attack on Islam in Syria and Egypt with only the dimmest of notions as to what lay beyond. If the Crusaders had conquered Egypt, they would indeed have found themselves on the shores of the Red Sea and would have been able to sail by direct voyage to India as the Romans had once done. But Egypt remained unsubdued, and after the disastrous failure of St. Louis in 1248 hopes for the speedy triumph of Christian arms dwindled away. The advance of the Mongols, however, suggested new possibilities—perhaps their conversion to Christianity or, failing that, a Christian-Mongol alliance against the Egyptian foe ; at the same time the increased facilities of travel in Western Asia under Mongol rule gave to Europe a clearer knowledge of the Indian Ocean and of the sources of oriental traffic. Hence emerges in the fertile brain of the Genoese merchant the new strategical conception of outflanking Egypt commercially, of finding a way round and taking Egypt in the rear. The eye of fancy saw Genoese galleys on the Sea of the Indies, defeating at one stroke the Moslem arch-enemy of Christendom and the iniquitous Venetian who had betrayed the Faith by his venal pacts with Cairo.

The Ilkhanate proved impervious to this ambition of Genoa. But the lure of the Indian Ocean, once it had taken hold on the imagination, was not easily weakened by disappointment. It was suggested that there might be another way round, a way to the right instead of to the left of Egypt, a way circuitous and leading past unknown lands, but one which had not to cross any land isthmus

[1] The Venetians at this time reached Tabriz from Lajazzo and Little Armenia.

and was not subject to the caprice of a Tatar king. There was a belief that it was possible to circumnavigate Africa. And if it were possible to do so, the conditions were all in favour of the Genoese as against their Venetian rivals. While in the Eastern Mediterranean Venice and Genoa clashed at every turn in a struggle for commercial empire, the less profitable Western Mediterranean was virtually a Genoese lake, and the Genoese alone of Italians were accustomed to sail outside the Straits of Gibraltar. Venice might dominate the markets of Egypt and obstruct Genoese diplomacy at the court of Tabriz, but a sea route round Africa would be beyond the range of her interference.

The way as far as the Canaries was already known to Genoa, for those islands, which had been known to the Carthaginians and Romans but had been forgotten by Europe in the early Middle Age, had been rediscovered by a Genoese expedition under Lancelot Malocello in about 1270. To the south beyond settled Morocco, where the Sahara reaches to the sea, the African coast was quite unknown, though camel caravans went overland from Morocco to the Sudan. But traditional geography, confirmed by contemporary rumour from Arab sources, affirmed that Africa was surrounded by the Ocean to the south, and on this doctrine the organizers of the expedition of 1291 relied.

The doctrine went back to the earliest speculations of the Ionian cosmologists, who conceived of Europe, Asia and Africa as one great, gulf-pierced land-mass, surrounded on all sides by the Ocean. Apart from such guesswork theory Herodotus believed that the circumnavigability of Africa had been proved by actual experiment ; according to him a voyage round Africa was made by Phoenician ships sent out for the purpose by Necho, king of Egypt from 610 to 594 B.C. The Phoenician explorers set out from the Red Sea and in the third year returned to Egypt through the Mediterranean, having renewed their supplies each year by landing on the coast and growing corn ' wherever they might be in Libya as they voyaged ' ; they asserted what Herodotus found incredible, ' namely that in sailing

round Libya they had the sun on the right.' Much doubt
has been cast on this story by modern criticism, but the
balance of probability is in its favour.[1]  Among later Greek
geographers some believed and some disbelieved in the
peninsular character of Africa, and finally the great authority
of Ptolemy was cast for a view which made the Indian
Ocean a closed sea with the coast of East Africa turning
east south of the Equator and joining on to the south-east
extremity of Asia beyond Java.  But the older tradition of
the circumfluent Ocean was transmitted to the Latin Middle
Age through Strabo and others, while the work of Ptolemy
for a long time suffered almost complete eclipse, an eclipse
which in this respect at any rate was all to the good.

In the thirteenth century there was a channel of information which served to confirm traditional belief.  The trade
carried on by Moorish caravans across the Sahara to the
lands of the Senegal and Niger, a trade in which Jews and
even, at times, Italians participated, seems to have brought
to Europe reports of an east-west coastline to the south
of the Western Sudan.  The West African forest zone was
indeed a barrier against penetration to the Gulf of Guinea
from the north, but the Senegal country (Bilad Ghana)
with its Atlantic shore appears in Idrisi's map made for
Roger II of Sicily in about 1150, and a knowledge of the
West African coast too correct to be mere coincidence is
shown by the famous Laurentian Portolano of 1351.  In
this map, says Beazley, 'the general shape of Africa, the
southern projection of the Dark Continent towards the
Cape, and especially the great line of the Gulf of Guinea,
are represented with such an approach to reality, that we
cannot believe the designer was merely guessing at the
truth.  In particular, the shore-line between our Sierra
Leone and Cameroons must have been here laid down
with some help from actual knowledge." [2]

[1] Herodotus, IV, 42.  An excellent summary of objections to the
story and answers to them is given by Cary and Warmington, *The
Ancient Explorers*, pp. 87-95.

[2] *Dawn of Modern Geography*, vol. III, p. 524.

The Laurentian Portolano is sixty years later in date than the Genoese attempt to sail round Africa, and may well have incorporated knowledge only acquired during that period. It is indeed very probable that the southward extension of East Africa was not known in 1291, for the fact seems to have been ascertained from Marco Polo or from Sorleone Vivaldo, who is said to have journeyed as far as Magadoxo in an endeavour to obtain news of the lost 1291 expedition. It is, on the other hand, likely that the Gulf of Guinea was known earlier, and that the long west-east Guinea coastline was assumed to continue in the same latitude to the Indian Ocean ; such an assumption would have made the project of circumnavigation much less formidable.

The voyage of Necho's Phoenicians is the only circumnavigation of Africa recorded as actually achieved before Vasco da Gama, and it was made not from west to east, but from east to west. We have, however, an account of one unsuccessful attempt made in Hellenistic times [1] with just the same aim as the Vivaldo voyage pursued, that of finding an all-sea route from Europe to India so as to avoid Egypt. Eudoxus, a merchant of Cyzicus on the Propontis, made two voyages from Egypt to India in the service of the Ptolemies towards the end of the second century B.C., but he fared so badly under the state monopoly of foreign trade enforced by the Egyptian government that he determined to find another route to the land of gems and spices. On returning from his second voyage to India he had been blown by a monsoon some way down the East African coast south of Guardafui, and had picked up a ship's prow, which, he was assured by sailors in Alexandria, belonged by its type to a vessel of Gades in Spain. This convinced him that it was possible to sail round Africa. So, having collected a cargo in the Mediterranean, he set sail from Gades (Cadiz), but was forced to turn back after reaching some point on the coast to the south of Morocco ; his ship ran aground and broke up, and, although the cargo

[1] Strabo, II, 98–102. Cary and Warmington, *op. cit.*, pp. 99–103.

was rescued and a smaller ship built out of the timbers, he decided to give up the idea of going all the way to India. But a fancied resemblance of a language of natives of the Atlantic coast with that spoken on the East African shore south of Guardafui—Eudoxus had made a list of words of the latter, according to Strabo—gave him hope that he was not far from the Indian Ocean. So, on his return to Gades, he fitted out another expedition to make the complete voyage. He sailed for a second time down the African coast and was never heard of again.

The disappearance of Eudoxus did not encourage further ventures in the same direction, and not long afterwards the Roman annexation of Egypt ended the intervention of an independent middleman power between Europe and the Red Sea. As we have seen, the greater part of Rome's immense oriental commerce in the first two centuries A.D. was conducted from the Egyptian Red Sea ports, and therefore in that age when the European Classical civilization reached its acme of power and prosperity there was no incentive to search for the Indies round Africa. But in the late Middle Age, when economic revival had created a new demand for the luxuries of the East, and when Egypt was held by a power no less greedy than that of the Ptolemies—and, in addition, hostile to Europeans from difference of religion—a situation such as had confronted Eudoxus of Cyzicus confronted the merchant of Genoa or Venice. Venice, however, succeeded in establishing a diplomatic ascendency at Cairo and securing for herself a virtual monopoly for the European distribution of Egyptian trade, while by diverting the Fourth Crusade from Egypt to Constantinople she obtained economic control of Byzantine waters. With such a position of privilege Venice was well content. But the Greek Restoration at Constantinople enabled Genoa to supplant Venice in the northern Levant, and in the elation of so sudden and sweeping a victory the Genoese dreamed also of breaking the Egyptian-Venetian monopoly on the main spice route. A direct

attack was not feasible, but an outflanking strategy promised
the desired result.  The first plan was to operate in alliance
with the Persian Ilkhanate, launching a Genoese fleet
from the Persian Gulf; the second was to sail round
Africa.  There can be no doubt that the second plan was
tried as an alternative after the failure of the first ; the
proposal to the Ilkhanate was made at some time during
the reign of Arghun, and the expedition of Vivaldo sailed
in the year of Arghun's death.

Vivaldo, like Eudoxus his predecessor, was swallowed
up by the unknown south.   His fate was likewise a deterrent
against further attempts.  And indeed the odds were
heavily against the success of an endeavour to reach India
by the Cape route while the African coast beyond Morocco
remained unexplored.  The condition of victory was that
the incentive of reaching India should be reinforced by
the attraction of nearer and more easily attained objectives
along the route, so that progress might be made by stages,
and that failure to achieve the ultimate aim might not
spell dead loss and utter discouragement.  It was in the
event by concentration on such nearer ends, on the trade
of Guinea and the finding of Prester John rather than on
the direct voyage to India, that the Portuguese did finally
reach India by the Cape route.

The fourteenth century saw no repetition of Vivaldo's
attempt.  But it witnessed an immense progress in geographical realism, and laid the solid foundation on which
the enduring structure of fifteenth-century achievement was
reared.  It created ' the first true maps.'  With the appearance from about 1300 of the *portolani* charts we enter on
a new chapter in the story of travel and exploration.  Never
before had there been so close a union between theoretical
geography and practical navigation as is shown by these
charts ; now for the first time it became possible for the
sailor really to think in terms of the map.  Materials of
experience and observation and bearings taken with the
compass were collected from every quarter and reduced
to order in maps which are the most notable manifestations

of European science in the age that produced them. The *portolani* exorcized the vagueness and confusion of ideas that still prevailed about even the most familiar regions of the world, and urged advance into the unknown by the very contrast between the minute and accurate detail of their known lands and the blank spaces beyond. Of the *portolani* it has been well said [1] : ' Nothing in the history of cartography is more significant ; at no point, perhaps, is there a more impressive advance in human knowledge than when we pass from the highest designs of the pre-portolan type—designs on the whole quite abreast of Ptolemy's—to that *Carte Pisane* with which opens the great series of the mediaeval *peripli*.'

While the new cartography was in full course of development Marino Sanuto the Elder in his *Secreta* [2] (partly written in 1306–7 and completed in 1321) vividly expressed the dissatisfaction and restlessness of a good European at being cooped up nautically in the Mediterranean, and revived in a different form the idea of European naval power in the Indian Ocean, which had been the essence of the Genoese proposal to Arghun.   Sanuto's scheme differs from the Genoese in that it goes back to the traditional Crusade policy, and contemplates not the outflanking but the conquest of Egypt.   Further, being himself a Venetian, Sanuto does not aim at the discomfiture of Venice.   But he was more than a patriotic Venetian ; he had a conscience as a Catholic which caused him grave misgivings as to the Venetian policy of friendship and trade with Moslem Egypt.   His plan was for a new Crusade, to be carried out by the united efforts of Latin Christendom and to be preceded by an economic blockade of Egypt for the purpose of reducing her strength.   Sanuto has great faith in the efficacy of a blockade on the ground that Egypt is dependent on Europe for essentials of her military and naval strength such as iron, ship-timber and pitch, and also for the Turkish

---

[1] Beazley, *op. cit.*, iii, p. 512.
[2] *Liber secretorum fidelium crucis super terrae sanctae recuperatione et conservatione.*

and Circassian slaves who were required to replenish the Mameluke army and were mostly brought to Egypt in Venetian vessels. Sanuto is well aware that a boycott of Egyptian commerce will not recommend itself easily to Venice, but if the Venetians can exercise self-control for a while, they will have their reward—the trade of the Indian Ocean, as well as the less corporeal satisfaction of having helped to recover the Holy Land for Christendom. During the period of the blockade Christians are to buy oriental commodities only from Persia, an arrangement in which Persia may be expected to acquiesce. The gradual assimilation of the Persian Tatars to Islam has by this time greatly diminished the hope of their conversion to Christianity, but they are still regarded as potential allies in the struggle with Egypt.

Sanuto's manifesto had no appreciable effect on the policies of the Christian nations. It produced no new Crusade. Egypt of the Mamelukes continued to receive the pepper of Malabar and sell it to the Venetians, who sold it to the rest of Europe. It was no longer possible to unite Europe for an assault on the Mameluke power ; the old crusading enthusiasm had died out and could not be rekindled. Only in Spain and Portugal, where the struggle between Christian and Saracen had continued for centuries, was religious zealotry still a vital force, and there it was still busy enough with its local crusading. But it was in that quarter that European expansion was soon to find its leaders ; the Atlantic seaboard of the Iberian Peninsula was to become the first base of a world-wide navigation, and the most decisive Crusade was to begin with Henry the Navigator.

The sea power of Portugal was the creation of Genoese in the Portuguese service. In 1317 King Diniz appointed a Genoese named Pezagno to be Admiral of Portugal, one of the terms of appointment being that he and his successors should maintain a number of not less than twenty Genoese captains and pilots in the royal navy. With their Genoese-led fleet the Portuguese made two expeditions to the

Canaries, one before 1336 and another in 1341 ; these were their first ventures into the Atlantic. The Azores were discovered before 1345, though we do not know certainly by whom. During the same period Lisbon grew to be one of the principal ports of Europe. The Genoese had long been accustomed to sail as far as Flanders by the Straits of Gibraltar, the Venetians participated in this commerce from 1317, and the Florentine commercial houses established branches in Lisbon. Through Lisbon, also, dates and ivory were exported to North-west Europe from Morocco.

Prince Henry, called in history ' the Navigator,' was the third son of King John I of Portugal by Philippa of Lancaster, daughter of John of Gaunt, who brought an English army to the aid of Portugal in the war of 1383–6 against Castile. In 1415 at the age of twenty-one Henry greatly distinguished himself at the Portuguese capture of Ceuta in Morocco, the event which first carried the war against the Moors into Africa, and in 1419 he was made governor of the province of Algarve in the extreme south of Portugal. He also received the office of Grand Master of the Lusitanian Order of Christ, a foundation which had inherited the properties, considerable in Portugal as elsewhere in Europe, of the dissolved Templars.

From the year of the capture of Ceuta Henry carried on, as a semi-private enterprise, exploration down the African coast. According to Zurara [1] : ' After the taking of Ceuta he always kept ships well armed against the infidel, both for war and also because he had a wish to know the land that lay beyond the isles of Canary and the cape called Bojador, for up to that time, neither by writings nor by the memory of man, was there any certain knowledge of the land beyond that cape. . . . And because the said Lord Infante wished to know the truth of this— since it seemed to him that if he or some other lord did not endeavour to gain that knowledge, no mariners or mer-

[1] Zurara, *Chronicle of Guinea*, ch. 7 (ed. Beazley and Prestage in Hakluyt Series, 1896).

chants would ever dare to attempt it, for it is clear that such would never trouble to sail to a place where there is not a sure and certain hope of profit—and seeing also that no other prince took any pains in the matter, he sent out his own ships to those parts. And to this he was stirred up by his zeal for the service of God and of King Edward his lord and brother, who then reigned. This was the first reason of his action.'

After this first reason for Henry's policy Zurara enumerates four others in the same chapter of his *Chronicle*. The second reason was that ' if there chanced to be in those lands some population of Christians, or some havens into which it might be possible to sail without peril, many kinds of merchandise might be brought to this realm [i.e. Portugal], . . . and also the products of this realm might be taken there, which traffic would bring great profit to our countrymen.' The third reason was to ascertain the extent of the Moorish (i.e. Moslem) power in Africa. The fourth, to find out if there were any Christian people in the said lands with whom an alliance against the Moors might be made. The fifth reason was ' to make increase in the faith of our Lord Jesus Christ and to bring to Him all the souls that should be saved.'

According to Diego Gomez, Henry obtained information from Moorish prisoners at the capture of Ceuta ' of the passage of traders from the coasts of Tunis to Timbuktu and to Cantor on the Gambia,' and this information ' led him to seek those lands by way of the sea.' This account probably reveals the mainspring of Henry's original enterprise, and shows it as a design parallel on a smaller scale to Vivaldo's, an attempt to outflank an intercepting land power by a sea route. The enemy of Christendom barred the way to Guinea by land just as he barred the Levant routes to India. And, as the sea road to Guinea was also the sea road to India, both ends were served by Prince Henry's expeditions, and the success of the endeavour to reach Guinea inevitably led the Portuguese on to attempt the passage to India. There can be no doubt, however, that in the beginning Henry's objective was purely African, and not at all Asiatic ; in the chapter of Zurara above quoted there is no suggestion of an intention to sail round Africa to the Indies.   Only as time went on, and after the formidable Cape Bojador had been passed, did Prince Henry's imagination enlarge its scope and reach out with the ambition of Eudoxus and Vivaldo ; in 1441 Zurara [1] represents him as desiring to have knowledge ' not only of that land [Senegambia] but also of the Indies and of the land of Prester John, if he could.'   Even so, the quest of the Indies was never more than an afterthought with Henry ; to the last his main attention was given to the African objective, and when he died in 1460 his captains had not penetrated farther than Sierra Leone.

The real contribution of the Navigator to European maritime expansion was the passing of the desolate and unproductive Sahara coast, which had hitherto set a limit to navigation and was by far the worst, as it was also the first, obstacle to be overcome in sailing round Africa. According to Zurara [2] it was said among sailors that ' beyond the cape [Bojador] there is no race of men or inhabited place ; the land is like the Libyan desert where there is neither water nor tree nor green herb ; the sea is so shallow that it has only a fathom depth a whole league from the shore, and the currents so terrible that no ship, having once passed the cape, can ever return.'

Once beyond the Sahara shore—the Senegal was reached in 1444—a forested and inhabited coastline unfolded itself endlessly, inviting continuous progress.   Progress, however, was not rapid, for the very opportunities of trade at the

---

[1] Ch. 16.   The land of Prester John in this context is Abyssinia, whence an embassy came to Lisbon in 1452.   Abyssinia was commonly included in the Indies, and Vignaud held that the Portuguese as late as 1474 (the year of the Martins-Toscanelli correspondence on routes to the Indies) meant by India nothing more than Abyssinia.   But the above quotation from Zurara refutes this view (see E. Prestage, *The Sea Route to India* in *Travel and Travellers of thr Middle Ages*, ed. A. P. Newton, 1926).

[2] Ch. 8.

mouths of the Senegal and Gambia acted as a diversion.[1]
Then in 1461, the year after Henry's death, De Sintra
sailed as far as Ashanti. In 1469 King Affonso V leased
the West African trade of Portugal to Fernam Gomez, a
citizen of Lisbon, for five years, in return for an annual
payment of 1,000 ducats and an undertaking to explore
annually 300 miles of new coast. Under this scheme the
coast was made known eastward to the Bight of Biafra and
then round to the south as far as a point two degrees below
the Equator.

During the years 1475–83 no further advance was made
along the coast, but within the area already opened up
commerce was extended and developed as a monopoly of
Portugal. In 1480 Portugal and Castile concluded the
Treaty of Alcaçovas, whereby Castile obtained recognition
of her claim to the Canaries but undertook not to send
ships to the south of them, and in 1482 the Portuguese
established the fortified settlement of St. George La Mina
on the Gold Coast. Of the Guinea trade in the fifteenth
century Cadamosto says that ' from no traffic in the world
could a like gain be had.' This harvest was now being
reaped by Portugal as a result of Henry's policy ; the road
to India, on the other hand, appeared to be barred by the
southward-stretching coastline beyond the Bight of Biafra.
The turn to the south dashed the hopes of those who expected a speedy penetration to the Sea of the Indies in
reliance on the view that Africa did not extend below the
Equator ; such a view was generally accepted in spite of
the more correct idea of the shape of Africa shown by the
Laurentian Portolano. The discovery, therefore, of the
southward projection of the continent by the voyages of
1471–5 led Portugal to call a halt for nearly a decade.
There was always a party at court which was opposed to
overseas ventures on the ground that the despatch of ships
and men to remote regions dangerously weakened Portu-

[1] Colonial schemes in the Madeiras and Azores, warlike bickerings
with Castile over the Canaries and debts incurred in his ventures also
distracted Henry from following up the West African discoveries.

gal's position in Europe, and the reverses of the war against Castile in 1475–8 gave point to their argument. Further, the treasury was empty after the Treaty of Alcantara, and a feudalism which left the Crown ' no estates except the high roads of Portugal ' provided little opportunity of replenishing it. Prudence urged that the Crown should make the most of the assured Guinea commerce and refrain from speculative exploration.

It was after the discovery of the southward extension of Africa to the east of the Gulf of Guinea that King Affonso V gave consideration for a while to a project suggested by the Florentine astronomer Toscanelli ' concerning a shorter way of going by sea to the land of spices than that which you are now making by Guinea.' [1] Toscanelli proposed to sail due west from Portugal to the coast of China. He communicated his idea to Fernam Martins, a Canon of Lisbon, who spoke of it to the King ; the latter asked for further details of the plan, and Toscanelli gave them, together with a map illustrating his geographical theories, in a letter a copy of which he afterwards sent to Columbus.

However, Affonso did not approve the plan, and it was left to Spain to try the westward voyage to the East. When Portuguese exploration was renewed it was along the African route. Affonso was succeeded in 1491 by John II, ' the Perfect,' who proceeded to strengthen and enrich the Crown by attacking the truculent feudal nobility of Portugal and confiscating their lands. In 1483 John sent out Diogo Cam with orders to go as far south as he could ; Cam discovered the mouth of the Congo, and on a second voyage in 1485 added a further stretch of coast. Finally, Bartholomew Diaz was sent out and succeeded in rounding the southern extremity of Africa (1488), turning back after he had satisfied himself of the northerly trend of the shore beyond the Cape, and returning to Lisbon to report. The Cape thereupon received from the King the name of *Good Hope*, ' for the promise it gave,' says Barros, ' of the find-

[1] From *The Letter to Martins*, tr. in Vignaud, *Toscanelli and Columbus*.

ing of India, so desired and for so many years sought
after.'

In the year after Bartholomew Diaz set sail from Lisbon,
and before he had yet doubled the Cape of Good Hope,
King John sent out Pedro Covilham and Alfonso de Payva
to travel to the Indies from the Mediterranean and bring
back information relevant to the Portuguese enterprise.
John had already despatched Antonio de Lisboa, a Franciscan friar, on the same mission, but the friar, being
ignorant of the Arabic language, had failed to penetrate
further than Jerusalem.   Covilham and Payva were both
accomplished speakers of Arabic.   Covilham had served
the King in diplomatic negotiations in Morocco ; on his
return to Portugal he found that John, ' desiring by all
means that his ships should find out the spiceries, had
determined to send by land certain men to discover as
much as they might.' [1]   Selected for this purpose, Covilham
and his companion were given instructions which clearly
reveal the guiding ideas of Portuguese policy in the 'eighties
of the fifteenth century.   They were ' to discover and learn
where Prete Janni [2] dwelt, and whether his territories reached
unto the sea ; and where the pepper and cinnamon grew,
and other sorts of spicery which were brought unto the
city of Venice from the countries of the Moors.' [3]   They
were further charged to find out whether it were possible
to sail round the southern end of Africa to India and to
gather any information they could about sailing in the
Indian Ocean.   A special map was prepared for the use
of the envoys by Calzadilla, Bishop of Viseu, and the doctor
masters Roderigo and Moyses, the latter a Jew ; the work
was done ' very secretly ' so that no rumour of it might
reach non-Portuguese ears.   Covilham was told that ' in
those seas [the Indian Ocean] there had been some knowledge of a passage into our western seas ; because the

[1] Alvarez in Purchas, vol. II, p. 1091.
[2] i.e. Prester John.
[3] i.e. Syria and Egypt.   Any Moslems were ' Moors ' for the Portuguese.

said doctors said they had found some memorial of that matter.' [1]

Covilham and Payva left Lisbon in May, 1487, and went to Aden via Naples, Rhodes, Alexandria and Cairo. At Aden they parted, Payva proceeding towards Abyssinia, while Covilham took ship to India, visited Cananore, Calicut and Goa, and then took ship again to Sofala, the most southerly of the Arab settlements in East Africa. Payva was murdered on his journey, but Covilham returned safely to Cairo, where he was met by two messengers from King John, the Rabbi Abraham of Beja and Joseph of Lamego, and sent home by the latter a report in which he declared ' that the ships which sailed down the coast of Guinea might be sure of reaching the termination of the continent by persisting in a course to the south, and that when they should arrive in the eastern ocean, their best direction must be to inquire for Sofala and the Island of the Moon [Madagascar]."

[1] This no doubt refers to an account similar to that in the legends of Fra Mauro's map of 1457–9. Fra Mauro preserves the tradition of two voyages from India past the southern end of Africa. He marks the southern cape with the name Diab, and says that an Indian ship in about 1420 was storm-driven to this point, and sailed westward 2,000 miles in forty days without touching land. Fra Mauro had also himself spoken with a person worthy of confidence who said he had sailed from India past Sofala to a place called Garbin on the west coast of Africa. The report of Covilham that the Portuguese might be certain of rounding Africa, a report made after a visit to Sofala, points to a tradition of such voyages in the Indian Ocean, and although the positive evidence is slight, there does not seem to be any good reason for denying the voyages mentioned by Fra Mauro. Arab navigation did not normally extend south of Corrientes, chiefly because the Arabs were afraid that the powerful southward currents along the coast would make return impossible. A similar idea about the currents beyond Cape Bojador was entertained by European sailors. But one or two Arab captains may have ventured south of Corrientes, and it may be suspected that they had heard of sea on the other side (i.e. to the west) of the gold-producing kingdom of Benomotapa (in Rhodesia), and thought of tapping the trade by a new route ; if they were Arabs from the north they would probably be in conflict with the monopoly of Sofala.

Having thus performed the main part of his mission, Covilham went to Ormuz in company with Rabbi Abraham, and then sent the latter back to Portugal with a further report on the commerce of the Persian Gulf. Returning to Aden, he made a journey to Mecca and then crossed again into Africa to carry out the task which had been set to Payva. In Abyssinia, however, his ability so commended itself to the Emperor that he was not allowed to leave the country, and he spent the rest of his life there, consoled for his exile by high office and wealth and an Abyssinian wife.

The travels of Covilham are of great historical import-aince, in that they gave to the Portuguese for the first time a clearly-defined objective in the East, and thus made possible the swift, sure strategy which established in a few years a Portuguese hegemony of the Indian Ocean. Covilham's precise information, methodically gathered for set questions, superseded all previous accounts of the nearer Indies and East Africa as a reference for Portuguese policy. When Bartholomew Diaz had rounded the Cape of Good Hope and Covilham had explored the Arab zone of navigation from Sofala to Ormuz and Malabar, there remained only a short gap as yet untraversed between two clearly-known areas of sea, and all was ready for the decisive voyage from Lisbon to India.

There was a delay in making the voyage owing to the need for Portugal to concentrate her strength and meet developments of the political situation nearer home. Spain, the realms of Castile and Aragon unified by the marriage of Ferdinand and Isabella, was now at war with the last of the Moorish states on Spanish soil, and received a great accession of strength by the conquest of Granada in 1492. In the same year Columbus made his first voyage to the west in the service of the Spanish sovereigns, and his discoveries at once raised points of dispute as to spheres of navigation between Spain or Portugal. Negotiations were opened, not without threats of war in the background, and at length resulted in the Treaty of Tordesillas, signed on June 7, 1494. By this treaty a meridian 370 leagues west

of the Cape Verde Islands was agreed on as a line of demarcation, the Portuguese and Spanish zones to lie respectively
east and west of it ; the Spanish were to be allowed to sail
unhindered through the Portuguese zone in order to reach
their own, but bound themselves to hand over to Portugal
any lands they might discover to the east of the line.   The
treaty was a victory of Portuguese diplomacy,[1] for it gave
Portugal the right of profiting by possible Spanish discoveries over a large portion of the Earth's surface as yet
entirely unexplored, but the bargain was such as to raise
doubts in Portugal as to whether Spain would keep to the
terms if her ships found some rich land in the Portuguese
zone.   To assert her claims in the event of Spanish evasion
of the treaty Portugal would require all her strength, and
could not at this point afford to dissipate it by an expedition into the Indian Ocean.   However, the second voyage
of Columbus did not result in any discovery of lands east
of the line of demarcation, so at last in 1497 King Manoel I,
who had succeeded John II in 1495, sent out four ships
under Vasco da Gama to sail to India.

[1] The Portuguese diplomacy at Tordesillas appears to have been
inspired by the beliefs (1) that there was continental land in the South
Atlantic which might lie, partly at least, east of the 370-league limit,
and (2) that Columbus had not reached the real Indies or anywhere
near them.   The Spanish representatives seem to have been sceptical
as to (1) and to have accepted Columbus' own claim as to (2).   On
both issues the Portuguese were in fact right and the Spanish wrong,
and hence Spain concluded a treaty which in the circumstances was
very unfavourable to herself.   The Spaniards, believing that they had
anticipated the Portuguese in reaching Asia, were willing to buy off
Portuguese interference with their Transatlantic route by a concession
which was not known to be of any value.   The Portuguese considered
that they had time enough to reach India before the Spanish could
get there, and meanwhile they wished to peg out a claim on the rumoured
but not definitely located land in the South Atlantic.   This alleged
land was probably the same as that marked on the edge of Bianco's
1448 map below Cape Verde with the inscription : ' Authentic island
distant 1,500 miles to the west.'   The evidence points to an accidental
discovery of South America before 1448, probably by a non-Portuguese
ship poaching in the Guinea trade.   See my article *The Discovery of
South America* in the *Nineteenth Century Review*, April, 1931.

A scheme had been devised whereby Portugal could shorten the route to India and at the same time explore a section of the still unknown part of her sphere of navigation in the Atlantic. The idea was to sail straight from Cape Verde to the Cape of Good Hope, a course which would cut out the long coasting round the Gulf of Guinea and might also reveal new lands in the South Atlantic between Africa and the Tordesillas line. Da Gama did not find any such land, but he was pressed by the trade winds quite close to the shores of South America, and the second Portuguese expedition to India, that of Cabral in 1500, was actually blown on to the Brazilian coast in following Da Gama's route. Two years before this Columbus on his third voyage had struck the delta of the Orinoco, thus making the official discovery of South America ; he had in his own words, as recorded by Las Casas, set his course south-west from the Cape Verde Islands, ' because he wished to test the idea of King John of Portugal who said that there was mainland [*tierra firme*] to the south.' It was because the Portuguese believed in the existence of continental land not very far from Africa in the South Atlantic, and on the strength of that belief had exacted from Spain a zone extending to a meridian 370 leagues [1] west of the Cape Verde Islands (contrary to the Papal Bull *Inter caetera* of May 4, 1493, which had only given them 100 leagues), that in the sixteenth century they were able to claim for their empire not only their conquests from West Africa to the Moluccas, but also Brazil.

Da Gama, although he did not find South America, successfully doubled the Cape of Good Hope, and sailed up the east coast of Africa until he came to the Arab settlements. At Malindi he obtained the services of an Indian

[1] Why 370 ? It seems at first sight a most arbitrary figure. But Bianco's ' island ' was 1,500 miles (= 375 leagues—four miles to the league as then reckoned) to the west of the meridian of Cape Verde. Three hundred and seventy leagues west of the Islands was probably the ' irreducible minimum ' of the Portuguese demand ; by it they hoped to get at least a slice of the supposed land. The Treaty of Tordesillas provided for a land frontier if the line cut land.

pilot, and striking out with the south-west monsoon crossed
to the Malabar coast.   He entered the harbour of Calicut
on May 20, 1498.

Thirteen years elapsed between the first arrival of the
Portuguese in Indian waters and their first meeting with
Chinese ships.   During those thirteen years the Portuguese
destroyed the naval power of the Arabs in the Indian
Ocean and excluded them entirely from the commerce of
South India.   War between the Portuguese and Arabs for
control of the Indian Ocean was inevitable from the beginning ; it was not to be expected that the interests which
held a monopoly of the traffic of the Indies should admit
interlopers to free competition with themselves except by
the decision of the sword, least of all that they should share
their realm with the enemies of Islam.   The trouble started
almost immediately on the arrival of Da Gama at Calicut ;
the Arab mercantile community in the city persuaded the
Hindu king, whose capital it was, to imprison Da Gama
and some of his men who had landed, on the ground that
they were pirates.   The king soon changed his mind and
released the prisoners, but, although actual hostilities were
on this occasion avoided, the experience led the Portuguese
to equip with heavy armaments the second squadron which
they sent to India.   The latter arrived at Calicut in the
summer of 1500 and obtained permission from the king to
land and trade ; those who went ashore, however, were
massacred by the Arabs without any serious effort on the
part of the king to protect them, and in retaliation Cabral,
who commanded the squadron, ordered the bombardment
of the city.

Calicut was one of the two principal centres of export
for the spice-producing countries, the other being Malacca.
Calicut was the outlet for the spices of South India, Malacca
for those of Malaya and Indonesia.   Each city was the
capital of a local despot levying dues and tolls on the
overseas trade, which was conducted by colonies of Arab
or semi-Arab traders linked up with Mecca, Ormuz and
Cairo.   The long-distance carrying trade from Malacca

westward was entirely in the hands of the Arabs, Hindu and Malay shipping being confined to local traffic. Chinese ships had ceased by the end of the fifteenth century to come farther west than Malacca.

The naval war between Portuguese and Arab was decided by two campaigns. In 1502 a merchant fleet of ocean-going dhows from the Red Sea in alliance with a local Malabar flotilla attacked Vasco da Gama, who had returned to India with the third squadron sent out from Portugal, and suffered a disastrous defeat. In 1508 a fleet specially prepared and sent out by the Sultan of Egypt and joined by the navy of Gujerat won a Pyrrhic victory over a detached Portuguese squadron, but was subsequently destroyed together with its ally by Almeida in the harbour of Diu. Before this a reinforcing fleet sent out from Portugal under Tristan da Cunha and Affonso d'Albuquerque had occupied Socotra and reduced Ormuz to subjection. The year 1509 saw the Portuguese undisputed masters of the Arabian Sea. Portugal took the place of Egypt as intermediary of commerce between India and Europe ; the Portuguese ships, all sailing under a royal monopoly, loaded in the intervals of warfare the cargoes that Cairo had been wont to send to Venice ; hostile Indian ports were bombarded or blockaded. It only remained for the Portuguese to acquire a permanent naval base in India, and this they did by the capture of Goa in 1510 ; they were aided in driving out the Moslem ruler by the Hindu population.

Up to 1509 the Portuguese had not sailed east of Ceylon, as they had been fully occupied with trading and fighting in the Arabian Sea. They had heard, however, of the great commercial prosperity of Malacca, and knew that it was the market for the spices which were not produced in India, notably cloves and nutmeg. Even after their elimination by the Portuguese from the ports of Malabar the Arab merchants continued to carry spices from Malacca to the Red Sea, keeping their dhows well out to sea to the south of Ceylon, but it was clearly only a question of time before the Portuguese would invade Malay as they had already invaded Indian waters. A plan for opening up commercial relations with Malacca was approved by King Manoel in 1508, and a squadron of six ships was sent out under Lopes de Sequiera with instructions to obtain a permit for trade from the Sultan of Malacca. Sequiera sailed first to Cochin in Malabar, assisted Almeida in destroying the Egyptian Red Sea fleet at Diu, and went on to Malacca with the spring monsoon of 1509.

Three years before the arrival of Sequiera, the Italian pseudo-Moslem traveller Ludovico di Varthema of Bologna visited Malacca on his way to and from the Spice Islands, and has left us an interesting account of the city as it was in the first decade of the sixteenth century. ' When we had arrived at the city of Melacha,' says Varthema in his *Itinerary*,[1] ' we were at once presented to the Sultan, who is a Moslem, as are all his subjects. The said city is on the mainland and pays tribute to the king of Cini,[2] who caused this place to be built about eighty years ago, because there is a good port there, which is the principal port of the main ocean. And indeed I believe that more ships come here than to any other place in the world ; in particular, all kinds of spices are brought here. . . . A great quantity of sandalwood and tin is found here.[3] . . . The people are olive-coloured, with long hair, and dressed after the fashion of Cairo. . . . One cannot walk about at night here, because people are killed like dogs, and the merchants who come sleep on their ships. The inhabitants are of the nation of Giavai [Java]. The king has a governor to administer justice for foreigners, but the people of the country take the law into their own hands, and they are the worst race that was ever created on earth.'

Varthema's remarks give a vivid picture of the half-

---

[1] The original Italian edition was printed at Rome in 1510. Ed. Jones and Badger (*Hakluyt Soc.*), 1863.

[2] i.e. China—but Varthema frequently confuses China and Siam ; he did not visit either.

[3] The tin was produced locally, as now ; sandalwood came from the islands east of Java.

savage town which provided a market for the commerce of two oceans. According to the *Commentaries of Albuquerque* [1] ' the Malaccans call the Indians people of the west, and the Javanese, Chinese, Gores [Japanese of the Lu-chu Islands] and all the other islanders of those parts, people of the east ; and Malacca is in the middle. . . . Every year there used to come to Malacca ships of Cambay [Gujerat], Chaul, Dabul, Calicut, Aden, Mecca, Shehr [in Arabia], Jeddah, Coromandel, Bengal, of the Chinese, Gores and Javanese, of Pegu and all those parts ; but those of Siam did not come to Malacca with their merchandise, because Siam was continually at war with the Malays.'

Malacca was not only the gateway of the Pacific and the storehouse of clove and nutmeg ; it was also the terminus of Chinese shipping and formally a vassal of the Chinese empire. In order to understand how this came to be so and to appreciate the situation in Malayan waters in 1509, we must take leave of the Portuguese for a while and go back in time some little distance to pick up the thread of Chinese history after the expulsion of the Mongols.

The first hundred years of the Ming dynasty (founded 1368) were a period of great vigour in maritime enterprise. We have already seen that in the time of the T'ang dynasty Chinese ships sailed as far as the Persian Gulf, and that under the Mongols the Chinese regularly traded to Malabar and Ceylon. Yung Lo, the third Ming emperor, carried Chinese sea power to its highest point in history. He made himself Emperor in 1402 by dethroning his nephew, the second Ming, who disappeared in the confusion of the usurper's capture of Nanking.

Conscious of his position as a usurper and fearing that his nephew might have escaped abroad,[2] Yung Lo sought to establish himself in the eyes both of his own subjects and of foreigners by a forceful naval diplomacy, which was

[1] III, 18.
[2] Ma Huan, *Ying-yai-shêng-lan*. Cf. G. Phillips, *Journal of the Royal Asiatic Society*, 1895, pp. 523 *seq.*

at the same time materially profitable. He sent out a series of powerfully armed expeditions to visit the various island and littoral states of the South China Sea and the Indian Ocean, present gifts at their courts and persuade them to send embassies with tribute to China in return. Yung Lo's idea of gathering tribute bears a strong family likeness to that entertained by the Han emperor, Wu Ti, whom we have seen pursuing a similar diplomacy in the second century B.C. From the weaker states tribute was really exacted, with the stronger there was in fact nothing more than an exchange of diplomatic courtesies and presents, but in any case the Chinese claimed to have received homage and tribute. Further, the diplomacy served as a sort of majestic commerce ministering to the elegance and luxury of the Ming court,[1] for the commodities sent as tribute or return presents were naturally the valuable specialities of the countries concerned. The expeditions were primarily pacific in intention, but they carried strong detachments of troops [2] who were available to punish insult or treachery towards the envoys. In Sumatra and Ceylon some hard fighting had to be done by the Chinese armada. In Ceylon King Wijayabahu VI had maltreated a Chinese mission bringing offerings to the Shrine of the Tooth of Buddha at Kandy ; in 1410 the Chinese deposed him by force and intrigue, and carried him a captive to China. His successor, invested as a vassal of the Ming, paid regular tribute to China until 1459. To the west of Ceylon the Chinese ambassadorial fleets paid calls as far as East Africa ; among the places they visited were Cochin, Quilon, Calicut, Ormuz, Aden

[1] Private trading was combined with diplomacy. At Aden ' during the stay of the embassy people who had rarities were permitted to offer them for sale. Cat's eyes of extraordinary size, rubies and other precious stones, large branches of coral, amber and attar of roses were among the articles purchased. Giraffes, lions, zebras, leopards, ostriches and white pigeons were also offered for sale.' Mahuan's *Account of Aden*. G. Phillips, *J.R.A.S.*, 1896, p. 348.

[2] The expedition of 1405, under the command of the eunuch Chêng Ho, consisted of 62 ships with 30,000 soldiers on board. Some of the junks, according to Ma Huan, were 440 feet long and 180 broad.

and Magadoxo.[1]   Both Aden and Magadoxo sent embassies to the Chinese court in 1427.

When Ceylon after 1459 discontinued the payment of tribute, no effort was made to reassert Chinese supremacy ; the energy of an earlier generation had dwindled and the attention of the Chinese government was otherwise engaged. The rise of the Kalmuk power in Central Asia and the renewal of the nomad menace on the northern frontiers had diverted the thoughts of Chinese statesmanship from remote sea avenues ; the Ming capital had been transferred in 1421 from Nanking to Peking, and maritime affairs came to be more and more neglected, the eye of state regarding foremost Mongolia and Manchuria. Yung Lo's forward policy in the Indian Ocean was abandoned, and, lacking official support and encouragement, Chinese private traders also beat a retreat ; during the second half of the fifteenth century they ceased to sail west of the Straits of Malacca.[2] Malacca itself, however, remained not only a port for Chinese shipping, but also a tributary of the empire. It had submitted to Yung Lo's first expedition in 1405, and its subjection was clearly of great importance, since the Chinese fleets sailing into the Indian Ocean had to pass through the Straits.

In the early years of the fifteenth century Malacca was just beginning to steal away the pre-eminence of Palembang (a Javanese foundation with a large Arab colony), which had been the chief city near the Straits in the fourteenth. According to local tradition preserved both in Varthema's *Itinerary* and in the *Commentaries of Albuquerque*, Malacca was only founded in about 1420, but there is no

[1] In what is now Italian Somaliland.

[2] According to Admiral G. A. Ballard the Arab ships beat the Chinese in rapidity of conveyance, and this may account partly at least for the failure of the latter to retain their Indian Ocean commerce. ' The junk is much handier than the dhow in beating to windward, but slower when running free ; and in seas where all commerce swung east and west with the regularity of a pendulum according to the time of year, the faster vessel off the wind had the advantage.' (*Rulers of the Indian Ocean*, p. 6.)

doubt that the town itself was much older, and it is probable that the latter date really refers to the assumption of
the title of Sultan by the Malacca kings.  In the local tradition Malacca was founded by a king of Palembang named
Parimiçura, who was driven out by the Javanese and fled
to Singapore, a town which had previously been founded
from Palembang and was then subject to Siam.  Parimiçura
seized Singapore and held it for five years, at the end of
which time he was driven out by the lord of Patani, and,
again taking to flight, founded a settlement on the west
coast of the Peninsula which grew into the city of Malacca.
Parimiçura is clearly the same as the Pei-li-mi-su-la who
in the Chinese record comes in person in 1411 to bring
tribute to the Ming court.  But when Malacca first paid
tribute in 1405 a king of another name is mentioned in
the Chinese account as ruling there, so that Parimiçura
could not have been the founder of the Malaccan kingdom.

In the native tradition as preserved in the *Commentaries
of Albuquerque* [1] tribute was first paid to China not by
Parimiçura, but by his successor Xaquendarxa, and the
episode is related as follows :  ' This king Xaquendarxa,
after having several sons, desired to go and see the king
of China, saying that he wished to see a king who had for
his vassals the Javanese and the Siamese and people of all
other known lands ;  so he set out from Malacca, taking
with him a present for the king of China, and occupied
three years in the journey.  He became the vassal of China,
bringing back with him a half seal in sign of vassalage,
and obtained permission to coin small money of pewter,
which money he ordered to be made as soon as he returned
to Malacca.'

In the latter part of the fifteenth century Malacca continued in its allegiance to China, but entered into sharp
conflict with the kingdom of Siam, which had formerly
held supremacy over the petty states of the Malay Peninsula.  In 1489 the Siamese made war on Malacca with a
fleet of 100 ships, but were completely defeated.  Thus

[1] III, 17.

when the Portuguese arrived in Malay waters Malacca had a bitter enemy in Siam, and further the reigning Sultan, though still acknowledging Chinese imperial suzerainty, had made himself exceedingly unpopular with the Chinese merchants by his arbitrary exactions. These enmities were to have the effect of isolating the Malacca Sultanate when it was attacked by Albuquerque. But on the eve of its fall Malacca appeared to be growing stronger and more prosperous than ever. According to the *Commentaries* ' when Affonso d'Albuquerque took it, the city and the suburbs contained about 100,000 inhabitants, and extended a good league's length along the sea.'

Sequiera on his arrival in 1509 presented his letter from the King of Portugal to the Sultan, and was granted permission to land and trade. But the Arab merchants, furious at the invasion of their last stronghold in the Indies, intrigued with the Sultan and persuaded him to allow a treacherous attack on the Europeans. Sequiera was warned in time, and escaped with his ships, but a number of Portuguese, who were caught ashore, were killed or thrown into prison. To obtain satisfaction for this incident Albuquerque, the Portuguese Captain-General of the Indies, himself came to Malacca in 1511 with a fleet of eighteen ships. Arriving in front of the city Albuquerque claimed the release of the Portuguese prisoners and addressed several other demands to the Sultan. The latter was disposed to negotiate, but his attitude was so unrepentant that Albuquerque ordered the burning of some houses ashore and of the Arab and Gujerati ships lying in the roadstead, as a demonstration. After this the prisoners were given up, but soon negotiations again broke down, and the Portuguese prepared to attack the city, which was defended by a numerous army equipped with cannon and war elephants.

Among the foreign ships lying off Malacca at the time of Albuquerque's arrival was a Chinese trading squadron of five large junks, which the Sultan of Malacca had just forcibly requisitioned to transport his troops for an expedition against the neighbouring kingdom of Aru in Sumatra.

When Albuquerque burnt the Arab ships in the port, he
spared the Chinese along with the other non-Moslem vessels, and when the Chinese captains learnt of his intention
to assault the city they secretly communicated with him,
offering the assistance of their ships and crews. Albuquerque
thanked them very much for their offer, but declined to
accept it, ostensibly because in case of failure he was unwilling to expose the Chinese to Malaccan vengeance, in
reality because he wished the Portuguese to have the sole
glory in the capture of the city. He did, however, take
the skiffs of the Chinese junks as extra boats for landing,
and ' begged that they would stay there a few more days
to see what end came to Malacca, and then carry news
to the king of China of all that might take place ; and he
would send them a galley in which they could be drawn
up close by the place of disembarkation, so that they could
see the great spirit with which the Portuguese would attack
the city, and their manner of fighting.'

Albuquerque delayed the attack until the day of St.
James the Apostle, ' for he trusted that through the prayers
and merits of the saint Our Lord would give him victory,
as He had done at Goa.' The first assault, however, was
indecisive ; after an initial success the Portuguese were
compelled to withdraw to their ships. While they were
preparing for a second onslaught the Chinese captains asked
leave to depart with their cargoes, as their monsoon season
had arrived. Albuquerque gave them presents and bade
them farewell, requesting them on their way back to China
to carry an envoy from him to Siam, which they did. The
envoy was a certain Duarte Fernandez, who had been one
of Sequiera's officers imprisoned in Malacca and had turned
his captivity to account by learning the Siamese language ;
he was instructed to announce to the Siamese the impend-
ing destruction of their enemies in Malacca, the desire of
the King of Portugal for friendship with the King of Siam,
and the intention of the Portuguese to extend to the Siamese
trading privileges in Malacca after they had captured it.
Fernandez was most favourably received at the Siamese

court, and paved the way for the subsequent embassy of Azevedo.

Meanwhile Albuquerque made his second assault, and succeeded in capturing Malacca. Just before the attack he exhorted his officers with a speech, which, as given in the *Commentaries*,[1] may not be strictly historical but admirably sums up the motives of his policy in the Indies. He urges on the Portuguese captains, some of whom were inclined to think there was no need for hostilities with Malacca, two reasons for them to exert themselves to the utmost in the coming battle. ' The first is the great service which we shall perform to Our Lord in casting the Moors out of this country, and quenching the fire of the sect of Mahomet so that it may never burst out again hereafter. . . . And the other reason is the service we shall render to the King Dom Manoel in taking this city, because it is the source of all the spiceries and drugs which the Moors carry every year hence to the Straits [of Bab-el-Mandeb] without our being able to prevent them . . . for I hold it certain that if we take this trade of Malacca away from them, Cairo and Mecca will be entirely ruined, and Venice will receive no spiceries unless her merchants go and buy them in Portugal.'

In the taking of Malacca no quarter was given by the Portuguese to the native Malay population, but the Hindu, Burmese and Javanese colonies were exempted from massacre and pillage. After the sack Albuquerque proceeded to build a strong fortress for a Portuguese garrison and a church dedicated to Our Lady of the Annunciation. Meanwhile the dispossessed Sultan fled to Pahang with a remnant of his army, and from Pahang sent his uncle as an envoy to his suzerain, the Emperor of China, appealing for aid against the Portuguese who had deprived him of his kingdom. But the merchants who had had dealings with Albuquerque at Malacca had already made reports to Peking in favour of the Portuguese, stressing at once their warlike prowess and their desire for friendly relations with

[1] III, 26.

China. So the Emperor took no action to help his vassal, but waited for the Portuguese to make a diplomatic approach to himself.

At Malacca Albuquerque received embassies from Siam, Champa and Java, sent out a squadron of three ships under Antonio d'Abreu to explore the Moluccas, made arrangements for the administration and defence of Portugal's new possession, and then at the end of the year 1511 sailed away to India with four ships, leaving the remaining eleven as a guard for the garrison under the command of Fernam Peres d'Andrade. Within a year of its capture and devastation Malacca under its new masters was attracting as much trade as ever, but this very prosperity brought upon it attacks by Malay monarchs who could not believe that it was tenable with such a small force as that stationed there. The King of Java in 1514 and the Sultan of Bintang in 1518 made war against the Portuguese with large fleets and armies ; both were defeated, but Bintang, as we shall see later, was able to do much harm to the Portuguese by intrigue at Peking.

Albuquerque did not before his departure from Malacca make any attempt on his own account to open diplomatic intercourse with China, though he despatched a second embassy to Siam. It seems he was well aware of the difficulty of establishing satisfactory relations with a power so intolerant of pretensions to equal status as the Ming empire, and felt that it was a task to be undertaken only under the direct authority of King Manoel. He therefore provided the King with full information, so far as he had been able to gather it, on Far Eastern affairs, and as a result of this and further advice a certain Thomas Pires was at length appointed as ambassador to the court of China. Andrade was ordered to escort him to Canton ; he mustered eight ships and set out from Malacca with the embassy on board on June 17, 1517.

Three years before the royal mission the Portuguese at Malacca had made an unofficial trading voyage to China. This, the first approach of Europeans coming to the Far

East by the all-sea route, is mentioned in a letter written by Andrew Corsalis to Duke Lorenzo de' Medici in 1515.[1] ' The merchants of the land of China,' he writes, ' also make voyages to Malacca across the Great Gulf to get cargoes of spices, and bring from their own country musk, rhubarb, pearls, tin, porcelain, and silk and wrought stuffs of all kinds, such as damasks, satins and brocades of extraordinary richness. For they are people of great skill, and on a par with ourselves [*di nostra qualita*], but of uglier aspect, with little bits of eyes. . . . I believe them to be pagans, though many allege that they hold our faith or some part of it.[2] During this last year some of our Portuguese made a voyage to China. They were not permitted to land, for they say it is against their custom to let foreigners enter their dwellings. But they sold their goods at a great gain, and they say there is as great profit in taking spices to China as in taking them to Portugal, for it is a cold country and they make great use of them. It will be five hundred leagues from Malacca to China, sailing north.'

[1] See Cordier, *L'arrivée des Portugais en Chine*, ext. from *T'oung pao*, XII, 1911.

[2] The reference is to Mahayana Buddhism, which seems to have been regarded by several early European observers of China as a distorted Christianity. The modifications which the Nestorian faith had undergone in Eastern Asia and the many striking resemblances between Catholic Christianity and the Mahayana make such an error easily comprehensible.

# CHAPTER VII

## *The Way by Mexico*

IN 1575 the Spanish, having crossed the Pacific from New Spain (Mexico) and established themselves in the Philippine Islands, made their first appearance in a Chinese port. Thus was accomplished the design, formed just over a century before by the Florentine astronomer Toscanelli, of reaching China by sailing westward from Europe, an aim first attempted by Columbus who set out from Spain in 1492 with a letter from the Spanish Sovereigns to the Great Khan of Cathay.

Although the main result of the voyage of Columbus was not the finding of a new route to Asia, but the revelation of the Americas, and although it was the Portuguese and not the Spanish who were the first to bring their ships to China, yet the Spanish maritime effort towards the west in the last decade of the fifteenth century has perhaps a greater relevance for the historical study of European relations with China than even the Portuguese voyages which we have considered. The success of the Portuguese in reaching India soon led them to add China to their mercantile sphere, but it was India and not China that was the specific objective of Portugal in the endeavour to circumnavigate Africa. That endeavour belongs to the history of European-Chinese relations because of its actual result, but, except in so far as there was a general purpose to open up all lands of Asia on the other side of Islam, there is no evidence that China figured in the Portuguese intention during the period of exploration round Africa. The all-important end was access to the sources of the spice trade, and these were in India and Indonesia, that is, on the hither side of China from the point of view of sailors voyaging round the Cape of Good Hope. For the Portuguese going round Africa India and Indonesia were both a nearer and a more profitable goal than China. But for Columbus sailing west China was the nearer, even if it was itself less alluring in his imagination than the islands which might be reached from it, and it was on the coast of China, included under the loose designation of the Indies, that he expected to arrive when he set sail from Palos on his memorable voyage.

As already pointed out in the last chapter, the Portuguese were disappointed in their hopes of speedily reaching India when they discovered by the voyages of 1471–5 the great southward extension of Africa beyond the west-east Guinea coast, and it is in the year 1474 that we hear of discussion at the Portuguese court on the alternative idea of reaching the Indies by sailing west. The adviser of Portugal in this matter was the Florentine astronomer Toscanelli, and though his advice was not followed by the Portuguese, it was to be the inspiration of Columbus. It was in Lisbon that Columbus heard of the scheme having been considered by the King of Portugal, which led him to write to Toscanelli and obtain a copy of the letter Toscanelli had written, explaining his theory, to Fernam Martins, a Canon of Lisbon and Portuguese courtier.

Neither the original letter to Martins, which was in Latin, nor the copy sent to Columbus have survived,[1] but we have the latter reproduced in three versions, one in Latin written on a blank page of a book belonging to Columbus, perhaps by Columbus himself, and presumably

---

[1] I assume throughout this chapter the authenticity of the Toscanelli correspondence, denied by Vignaud. Vignaud's able advocacy of his thesis has rendered an immense service to Columbian scholarship by showing up all the weaknesses of the traditional account of the enterprise, but it is hardly possible to maintain that he has proved the correspondence a forgery. For the two sides of the controversy see Vignaud, *Le vrai Christophe Colomb*, and De Lollis, *Cristoforo Colombo*.

a copy from the copy sent him,[1] the second in Italian in the *Historie del S.D. Fernando Colombo*, and the third in Spanish quoted in the *Historia* of Las Casas. These three versions present certain discrepancies on crucial points, and it is by no means certain that the Latin text represents the original in every case.[2] The letter to Martins and the copy sent to Columbus were each accompanied by a map illustrating the argument ; these have been lost altogether, but Las Casas says he had in his possession, among the papers of Columbus confided to him, the map sent by Toscanelli, and that ' Columbus had such faith in the letter and in the nautical map which the said Paulo, physician, had sent him that he did not doubt he should find those lands that were marked upon it.''[3]

In the opening lines of the letter to Martins Toscanelli writes (to translate from the Latin version) : ' Whereas I have spoken with you elsewhere about a shorter way of going by sea to the lands of spices [*cum tecum alias locutus sum de breviori via ad loca aromatum per maritimam navigationem*] than that which you are making by Guinea, and the Most Serene King now asks for some explanation from me, . . .' These clauses establish three points : first, that Toscanelli had discussed the matter with Martins at some time before 1474, the date of the letter ; second, that the King of Portugal had begun to take an interest in the idea ; and, third, that the goal in view was the region of spice production. On the first point the Spanish and Italian versions make Toscanelli assert that he had previously *often* spoken to Martins on the subject, and later on in the letter insert a clause, absent from the Latin text, to the effect that he

[1] The Latin text was discovered in the Seville Library in 1871 by Harrisse ; before that time only the Spanish and Italian versions were known.

[2] It appears to be a hasty transcript by a person with a very imperfect knowledge of Latin.

[3] Las Casas says that Columbus used Toscanelli's map as his road-map on the first voyage and that it was the map referred to in his consultation with Pinzon on September 25. In the *Journal*, however, no mention of Toscanalli's name is made in connection with this map.

had already explained the theory to Martins by word of
mouth ; while with regard to the objective of the Portuguese voyages the Italian has ' to India,' and the Spanish,
' to the Indies where the spices grow.'

After this opening Toscanelli goes on to say that he has
indicated on the map accompanying the letter the route
to be followed in order to reach ' the places most productive
of spices and gems,' and also adjacent localities, ' if they
[i.e. sailors following the route] should come by the winds
or by some chance where they did not think to come.'
He continues : ' It is said that only merchants stay in the
islands. [*Non considere autem in insulis nisi mercatores asseritur.*]
For so numerous there are those sailing with merchandise,
that there are not as many anywhere else in the world
as in the most noble port called Zaiton. For they say that
every year a hundred large ships laden with pepper are
brought into that port, apart from ships bearing other
spices. That country is very populous and very rich, with
a multitude of provinces and kingdoms and cities without
number, under one prince who is called the Great Kan,
which name in Latin means king of kings, whose seat and
residence are chiefly in the province of Katay.'

The reference to ' the islands ' is brought into this passage
quite without warning in the Latin text. What islands ?
The Latin text has so far only spoken of places (*loca*), and
not at all of islands as the objective. But in the Spanish
and Italian versions the islands appear as part of the
Asiatic goal, and the Spanish makes fairly clear what
islands are meant. The Italian says that on the map is
depicted ' the extremity of the west ' from Ireland to
Guinea, ' facing which directly westward lies depicted the
beginning of the Indies with the islands and places whither
you may go ' (*per fronte alle quali dritto per Ponente giace
dipinto il principio dell' Indie con le Isole e luoghi dove potete
andare*). In the Spanish this clause runs : ' opposite which
due west is the beginning of the Indies with the islands
and places whither you can deviate by the equinoctial
line ' (*en frente de las cuales derecho por Poniente esta pintado*

*el comienzo de las Indias con las islas y los lugares adonde podeis
desviar para la linea equinoccial*).

Since throughout the letter Toscanelli evidently draws
on Marco Polo for his assertions about the Indies, there
can be no doubt that these islands are the ones referred
to by Polo as dotted about in the Sea of Cin opposite Mangi
(South China), Cin (China) being the islanders' name for
Mangi.[1]  The islands, says Polo, numbered no fewer than
7,448 according to the testimony of experienced mariners
and fishermen ! They were independent of the Great
Khan, but ships traded to them from Quinsai and Zaiton ;
they abounded in gold, precious woods, pepper and all
kinds of spices, and great profits were made from the
commerce with them.  Marco Polo had not visited any of
these islands, but he did visit, and describes separately,
Java and Sumatra ;  the 7,448 islands of the Sea of Cin
may be taken, therefore, to include the Philippines, Borneo,
Celebes and the Moluccas, the Spice Islands *par excellence*.
Toscanelli's statement that there were only ' merchants '
in the islands appears to mean nothing more than that
the inhabitants of the islands all produced for export ;  or
perhaps *mercatores* was not the word used in Toscanelli's
original.  At any rate, it can be definitely asserted that
the islands Toscanelli has in mind are those mentioned
by Marco Polo.  He goes on to speak of the cargoes of
pepper brought to Zayton, and it is to be noted that in
here dwelling on the greatness of that port, it is not the
products of China that he stresses, but the goods brought
to China from Indonesia.  This point is of great importance for considering the problem of the real intention of
Columbus in 1492.

We are told, however, of Cathay, that ' this country is
worthy to be sought by the Latins, not only because thence
may be obtained vast gains of gold and silver and gems
of every kind and of spices that are never brought to us ;
but also because of the wise men, learned philosophers and
astrologers, by whose genius and arts that mighty and

[1] Marco Polo, 186–7 (ed. Paris Geog. Soc., 1824).

magnificent province is governed, and wars also are waged.'
There are statements about the splendour of Quinsai taken
from Marco Polo ; also the island of Cipangu (Japan) is
said to be marked on the map, and to be most fertile in
gold, pearls and gems, ' and they cover the temples and
the royal palaces with solid gold,' an assertion likewise
derived from Marco Polo.

Toscanelli refers to Kublai Khan's embassy of 1267 to
the Pope, and continues : ' In the time of [Pope] Eugenius
also a man [unus] came to Eugenius and spoke of their
great goodwill towards Christians. I had a long conversation with him, and he told me of many things, of the
greatness of the royal palaces and of the length and breadth
of the rivers, of the multitude of cities by the banks of the
rivers, and how on one river there are about two hundred
cities, and marble bridges of great length and breadth,
everywhere adorned with columns.'

This passage is not the least important part of Toscanelli's letter, for it affirms a visit to Pope Eugenius IV
(1431-7) made by someone from the Far East, who talked
to Toscanelli and gave him first-hand information about
China. The key to the allusion is to be found in Poggio's
narrative of the travels of Nicolo di Conti ; [1] Poggio says
that a man came to Florence from ' Upper India which is
towards the north,' alleging that he was sent to the Holy
Father, to obtain information on Western affairs, by the
patriarch of a Nestorian Christian kingdom twenty days'
journey from Cathay and under the dominion of the Great
Khan. Poggio conversed with him through an Armenian
interpreter who knew both Turkish and Latin, but seems
to have found the interpretation not quite adequate to
his curiosity. As speaking Turkish, the envoy must have
belonged to a Nestorian tribal community somewhere
north-west of China, some chiefry surviving from the
earlier Christian Turkish tribes, the Keraits and Onguts.
He had according to Poggio travelled through ' the country

[1] *Travels of Nicolo di Conti* in *India in the Fifteenth Century* (ed. Hakluyt)
p. 33.

of the northern Scythians, called at the present day Tartars, and that of the Parthians, to the Euphrates, and then, having embarked at Tripoli, he came to Venice and afterwards to Florence.' Finally he arrived in Rome and conversed with the Pope. He had evidently either been in China or knew it fairly well by hearsay. Vignaud argued [1] that Toscanelli's statement was suspect because 'Great Khan' was a Mongol title, and the Mongols in the fifteenth century no longer ruled in China; but if we remember that the envoy was a Turk talking about China through an Armenian interpreter to a man who knew from his Marco Polo that the monarch of China was properly called the Great Khan, there is no occasion for surprise at what is, strictly speaking, an anachronism.

For precise direction as to the voyage to be made to reach Asia Toscanelli tells Martins that 'from the city of Lisbon in a direct line westward to the most noble and very great city of Quinsay, there are twenty-six spaces marked in the chart, each one of them containing 250 miles. The distance is about a third part of the whole sphere [i.e. of the circumference of the Earth in the same latitude].'

The views on which this estimate is based are those of Marinus of Tyre, which Ptolemy records in order to criticize them and which have only been known in modern times through this criticism. Marinus drew two meridians to mark the limits of the then known world, one through the Fortunate Isles (the Canaries) reckoned as $2\frac{1}{2}$ degrees west of Cape St. Vincent, and the other through Sera, Sinae and Cattigara (Ch'ang-an, Lo-yang and Hanoi); these limits gave 225 degrees (or 15 hours in Marinus' measure) to the known world and left only 135 degrees (9 hours) to complete the circumference of the globe. Ptolemy gives an account of this system of Marinus, and then proceeds to demolish it on the ground that the distances given by Marinus are greatly exaggerated. Ptolemy himself assigns 180 degrees or just half the circumference

[1] *Toscanelli and Columbus*, pp. 68–70 and 285, note.

of the globe (still 50 degrees too much in reality) to the known world from the western meridian to the eastern, which is drawn through Sinae Metropolis known by Ptolemy to lie further east than Sera or Cattigara. But neither Marinus or Ptolemy makes the remainder from the known world estimate identical with the sea space to the west of Europe, for they bounded China to the east by unknown land, in this respect falling short of Pliny and Mela who definitely bounded the Seres on the east by the ocean.

Jacopo Angelo's translation of Ptolemy into Latin was done in about 1410, though it was not printed until 1475. The discovery of Ptolemy's work produced a curious situation in the Italian scientific circles to which it was available. The great astronomical and mathematical ability of Ptolemy earned an immense respect for all his assertions ; on the other hand, it was obvious that on matters of fact the fifteenth century possessed information which the great Greek geographer had not. As a result of the travels under the *Pax Tatarica* China and its eastern seaboard were fairly well known, and there were again current the exaggerated estimates of distance which had misled Marinus. In adjusting newly discovered facts to ancient learning it was natural, therefore, for scholars to revive the issue between Marinus and Ptolemy which the latter thought he had disposed of by his arguments. Perhaps after all Marinus had been right and Ptolemy wrong on the extent of the known world from west to east ; increased knowledge of remoter Asia enabled the new scholarship to judge between ancient authorities where they differed. Toscanelli must have taken such a view,[1] since

[1] Vignaud (*Toscanelli and Columbus*, p. 95, note) says that Toscanelli could not have accepted the theory of Marinus, ' because it was only a person ignorant of mathematics who could adopt such an idea, the error of which Ptolemy demonstrates in the very place where he records it.' But the issue between Ptolemy and Marinus was not really a mathematical one ; it turned on the empiric determination of distances. Toscanelli in the second letter to Columbus claims to have gathered information from merchants in oriental trade ; presumably he thought he could check Ptolemy from contemporary estimates.

we find him confidently adhering to the opinion of Marinus, and declaring the distance westward from Lisbon to Quinsay to be only a third of the total distance round the world. The nine hours allowed by Marinus for the unknown space are reduced to eight (i.e. a third of the twenty-four) on the ground that Marinus had not known the eastern limits of Asia, which had now been revealed by Marco Polo and others.

Such was the advice which Toscanelli gave in his letter to Martins dated June 25, 1474. The scheme was not taken up by the King of Portugal, who had asked Martins to obtain the statement of it from its author, and we may suggest some reasons why it was turned down after having first attracted attention. There was, to begin with, the war against Castile (1475–8), which distracted Portuguese statesmanship from overseas affairs, taxed all the energies and resources of the kingdom for three years, and left it in an exhausted condition. Moreover, when, in 1481, Affonso was succeeded by John II, the Portuguese throne was occupied by one who was an enthusiast for the Guinea route and within two years from his accession had founded Elmina and renewed the forward movement along the African coast.

But apart from these factors of diversion Toscanelli's scheme had weak points which must have made it vulnerable to criticism in Portugal. Toscanelli does not condescend to argue in support of his views ; his communication is pontifical in tone. But there were certainly men in Lisbon who, if they lacked the erudition of Toscanelli, nevertheless knew that his views, so confidently asserted, were disputed among scholars, and they could point out to the King that a voyage undertaken on the assumptions of Toscanelli's map would be a gamble on a doubtful theory rather than a reasonable experiment from a starting-point of ascertained fact. The Portuguese Crown at that time had but slender financial resources ; it could not afford reckless speculations.

Toscanelli's theory, however, commended itself strongly

to a certain obscure Italian resident in Lisbon, a Genoese of humble birth, slight education, no fortune and highly romantic temperament.  We need not here inquire whether Christopher Columbus first conceived the idea of sailing west to the Indies on hearing news of Toscanelli's proposal or whether he had already thought of it himself independently.  There is really not enough evidence for a decision on that point.  We only know that after hearing of Toscanelli's scheme he communicated with the Florentine scholar through a Florentine merchant of Lisbon and received in reply copies of the letter and map sent to Martins with the following covering note : ' To Christopher Columbus, Paul the physician, health.  I notice the high and great desire thou hast to journey thither where the spices grow, and as answer to thy letter I send thee a copy of another letter I wrote some time back to a friend and servant of the Most Serene King of Portugal, before the wars of Castile, in reply to another which by command of H.M. he wrote me on the said matter, and I send thee another such chart for navigating as is the one I sent him, by which thou shalt be satisfied of thy request.' [1]

In the years following this correspondence, which probably took place in about 1480, Columbus was engaged in his long struggle for royal patronage, ending in success and the voyage of 1492 in the service of Spain.  When we come to that voyage we reach one of the greatest events of all history, and one of which the story seems so simple and straightforward that there can hardly be anything in it to provide a problem for the historian.  Yet there are few episodes of history wherein first impressions are so deceptive as in this one.  Beneath a chain of events suggesting an easy explanation to the unwary we penetrate to a complicated battle of wits, a play of minds responding to obscure beliefs and precedents, influenced by diverse motives, and using the weapons of evasion and pretence.

According to what may be called the Columbus myth, that which was the orthodox history of the nineteenth

[1] See Vignaud, *Toscanelli and Columbus*, p. 320.

century and is still part of ' what every schoolboy knows,'
Columbus conceived the brilliant idea of reaching the
Indies by sailing west, had it confirmed by the authority
of Toscanelli, and then spent long years in trying to get
his idea taken up by stupid kings and courtiers.  It is the
picture of the poor inventor hawking round his invention
to unimaginative company directors, or of the young poet
or artist submitting his work of genius to one narrow-minded
critic after another and at last finding the discerning patron.
It is an appealing and edifying myth, but it is hardly
adequate as an historical account of the preliminaries to
1492.

Recent criticism has entirely demolished the conception
of Columbus as an original scientific thinker.  His powers
of logical reasoning were as inconsiderable as his knowledge
of Latin, and in geographical science he was behind, rather
than ahead, of his age.  As Professor A. P. Newton remarks :[1]
' It has now been proved that practically the only books
on cosmogony that were familiar to him were two—the
*Imago Mundi* of d'Ailly, published between 1480 and 1487,
and the *Historia rerum ubique gestarum* of Aeneas Silvius
[Pope Pius II], published at Venice in 1477. . . . In his
geographical ideas he was emphatically a man of the
Middle Ages, and an uncritical one at that.  He took his
arguments ready-made from old-fashioned, handy com-
pendia, but assumed an appearance of immense erudition
by quoting passage after passage from classical authors,
both Greek and Latin. . . . He refers incidentally to
d'Ailly as an authority supporting his view, but he does
not reveal the fact that almost every scrap of his classical
learning is lifted bodily out of the Cardinal's pages.'

In the period with which we are dealing the abstract
possibility of reaching Asia by sailing west, a corollary of
the sphericity of the Earth, was generally admitted ; the
whole question was one of distance.  The conditions of
navigation required something approaching certainty of
objective if caravels were to venture far out into the ocean,

[1] *Travel and Travellers of the Middle Ages*, pp. 15–17.

for these ships could carry only a limited amount of water and provisions and were very much at the mercy of calms and storms. Columbus believed with the utmost intensity of conviction that there was only a small sea space between Europe and the Indies, and was ready to stake everything on his belief. But he had really very slender grounds for his opinion, and there were rival theories in the field which on the evidence had claims as good as his. His conviction was that of a crank or fanatic rather than the reasoned conclusion of a scientific thinker. He deserves little credit intellectually for regarding as a certainty what any reasonable man would have doubted, nor would the royal councillors of Portugal and Spain have deserved any if they had been persuaded to a similar certainty.

But let us suppose that Columbus adducing his authorities, which are all well known to the more learned of his contemporaries, has persuaded a king that there is only a small sea space to the west of Europe and that a westward voyage to the Indies is practicable under the prevailing conditions of navigation. What then? All that remains for the king to do, having been thus persuaded of the nearness of Asia in the west, is to send out a ship of his own to sail there. There is no reason whatever why he should even give Columbus command of the vessel, much less make a contract with him by which he shall receive extraordinary powers and honours and a percentage of all profits if the voyage is successful. The most Columbus can hope for is that the king will show him a certain amount of gratitude for having given useful advice in a convincing way.

It is only necessary to look at the matter in this way to see the utter absurdity of the supposition that Columbus spent years of his life striving merely to persuade royalty to adopt his idea. Nothing would have been more disastrous for Columbus than to have had his idea adopted and himself left out. But there was no earthly reason why he should not be left out, if his idea were adopted. If he had once persuaded some magnate of the truth of his views,

Columbus was in no way indispensable for the carrying out of the project. The books he quoted were there for all to read, a practical scheme for the voyage had already been submitted by Toscanelli, and Columbus was not even a notably skilled mariner. *He* could not act on his belief, because he had no money, but anyone with the same belief and the resources for acting on it had not the slightest need to employ him or to make a bargain with him. Yet, when the expedition at last sails, Columbus is not merely in command of it, but has a contract with the Spanish Sovereigns which is likely to make him one of the most powerful and wealthy of their subjects. He is to be ennobled, to be made Admiral of the Ocean Sea, to be Viceroy and Governor-General of the lands he shall discover and acquire for the Spanish Crown, to receive ten per cent of all revenues resulting from the discoveries, and to transmit these privileges to his heirs.

What was it that induced Ferdinand and Isabella to make such a contract with an indigent Genoese adventurer ? Surely more than the conviction that Asia was not so far off as had formerly been supposed. It is clear that for some reason Columbus was regarded as indispensable for the success of the scheme. But he could only have been regarded as indispensable if he were believed to have a secret, to know something which no one else knew. As we have pointed out, this secret could not have been any general cosmographical theory based on well-known literary sources. Columbus must have succeeded in giving the impression that he had special information, that he knew just where to find land in the Atlantic.

It was to the interest of Columbus to pretend to have such a secret, whether he really had it or not. It was not to his interest that his patrons should believe what he himself believed, namely that Asia was near and that a ship going far enough could not fail to strike it. He must make himself indispensable for the enterprise, and he must make sure that he was not forestalled. He was in the position of a man who has found a mineral deposit and seeks to

make an agreement with a mining company in order to
work it ; he has to persuade the company of the reality
of the minerals without revealing their exact whereabouts,
his whole bargaining power lying in just that secret. And
so Columbus had to persuade his patrons that he could
guide them to profitable discoveries without stating just
what was to be discovered.

It is a fact that in the contract between the Spanish
Sovereigns and Columbus, the *Capitulations of Santa Fé*,
there is no mention whatever of the Indies, although there,
if anywhere, one would expect the aim of the expedition
to be clearly defined. The *Capitulations* merely deal with
islands and *tierra firme* to be discovered in the Ocean Sea
without any special reference to Asia. The form of the
agreement, therefore, is similar to that of the various grants
made by the Crown of Portugal during the fifteenth century
to the adventurers who searched for reported Atlantic
islands without any thought of reaching Asia. Thus in
1457 Fernam, Duke of Beja, nephew of King Affonso V,
received letters patent for islands he hoped to discover in
the Atlantic ; João Vogado in 1462 received a similar
grant for two islands he claimed to have located. In 1484
Fernam Dominguez de Arco was made governor of an
island he hoped to discover, and two years later Fernam
d'Ulmo received from John II letters patent conceding him
islands and continental land (*tierra firme*) he hoped to discover. The last of the above grants, made eight years
before the agreement with Columbus, is important because
it is the first to mention continental land as distinguished
from islands, and appears to reflect the growth of a belief
that land of such a character existed somewhere in the
Atlantic.

The absence of any reference to the Indies in the *Capitulations* led Vignaud to jump to the conclusion that there
was no idea at all at that time of reaching the Indies. But
the passport given by the Spanish Sovereigns to Columbus
does declare that Columbus is being sent *ad partes Indiae*,
and, according to the *Journal*, Columbus carried a letter`

from the Sovereigns to the Great Khan resident in Cathay.
The passport and the letter to the Great Khan may indeed
appear sufficient to establish the whole traditional view of
the voyage of 1492.  The matter, however, is not quite so
simple as that.  We have seen that the Sovereigns must
have believed Columbus to know something otherwise
unknown, and that this could not be in their belief merely
the theoretical nearness of the east coast of the Asiatic mainland.  But they may well have thought that the land or
lands the situation of which Columbus knew were nearer to
Asia than to Europe ;  indeed, Columbus must have let it
be understood that they were so, and as such were to be
included in the Indies, and also that they produced the
peculiar commodities of the Indies, which would make them
exceedingly desirable.  The lands to be found were of the
Indies.  But finding them was something quite distinct from
just sailing continuously westward until Asia was struck.
*That* was not what the Sovereigns expected Columbus to do,
for it was what anyone could be expected to do, provided
Asia were believed to be not too far off.  If the Sovereigns
thought Columbus might reach Asia, and therefore entrusted
him with a letter to the Great Khan, it must have been that
they considered it would be possible for him to go on to
Asia from the intermediate lands, not that they assumed
he would sail straight to China.

There is no need to suppose that Columbus really had
any secret beyond his conviction of the nearness of Asia.[1]
Our method of criticism requires us to distinguish between
the real intention of Columbus and his representation of it
to his patrons.  Once he had his contract he was safe ;  he
was confident of success, and if he could deliver the goods
he could claim his payment.  But he could never have
obtained his contract with the exceptional privileges it
conferred, had he let it be known that he intended nothing

[1] Apart from accepting the belief of Marinus of Tyre as to the eastward extension of Asia Columbus followed Alfragan in estimating the
Earth to be smaller than in the current theory, which was itself actually
an underestimate.

else than to sail due west from the Canaries with confidence that, if he did not first strike some island, he would certainly run into the mainland of Asia in approximately the actual position of America. Yet that *was* what he really intended, if we may trust the evidence of the *Journal* of the first voyage as reproduced by Las Casas.

Some writers have indeed held that Columbus did have special information of the position of the West Indian islands which he reached, and adduce the story current in the sixteenth century to the effect that he was given their bearings by a pilot who died in his house in Madeira, the last survivor of the crew of a ship which had been storm-driven on to one of them.[1] But the weight of the evidence is decidedly against the truth of this story. In favour of it is the fact that Las Casas, who was an admirer of Columbus and was in Hispaniola as early as 1502, accepts its authenticity, though he argues away the discredit to Columbus it involved on the ground that Columbus was divinely guided and that the dying pilot's communication was only one of the means by which God led him. The refutation of the story, however, is given by implication in the legal proceedings between the Crown and the heirs of Columbus after the discoverer's death. In that lawsuit the Crown lawyers used every argument to minimize the achievement of Columbus in order to weaken the embarrassing claims of Diego Colon ; in particular, witnesses were produced to magnify the part played by Martin Pinzon in the discovery of the New World. If there had been any real evidence for the story of the pilot who informed Columbus, we may be certain that it would have been brought forward in the lawsuit. As it was not, we can only conclude that the story was mere gossip ; it was just the sort of tale which would naturally result from the mystery surrounding the original proposals of Columbus and from the jealousy and enmity his career aroused. In his bargaining with the Spanish Sovereigns Columbus had pretended to the posses-

[1] For an able advocacy of the authenticity of the story see Vignaud, *Toscanelli and Columbus*, pp. 108–34.

sion of unique information ; rumour had its revenge by attributing the information to a deceased pilot, his debt to whom Columbus never acknowledged.

The *Journal* shows very clearly the determination of Columbus on his voyage to make straight for the Asiatic mainland. The three caravels sailed from Gomera in the Canaries on September 6.  On September 16 ' they began to meet with large patches of very green weed, which appeared to have been recently washed away from the land ; on which account they all believed themselves to be near some island, though not a mainland according to the opinion of the Admiral, who says,[1] " for I believe the mainland lies further on." ' Supposed signs of land continued on the 19th, but ' the Admiral was unwilling to remain here, beating about in search of land, but he held it for certain that there were islands to the north and south (which in fact was the case, and he was sailing in the midst of them).[2] His wish was to " keep on to the Indies, having such fair weather, for if it please God," the Admiral says, " we shall examine these parts on our return." ' At this time they were only a little way beyond the most westerly meridian of the Azores.  On the 25th Columbus had a conversation with Pinzon about islands marked, at about the point they had then reached, on the chart by which they were steering, and in the evening Pinzon thought he saw land, but next day they found no trace of it.  On October 3 ' the Admiral believed they had passed the islands marked in his chart. Here the Admiral says that he had been unwilling to stay beating up and down the week before, when they had so many signs of land, though he knew there were islands in that quarter, because his will was to proceed onward to the Indies, and he thought it would be unwise to linger on the way.' Finally, on October 6, when Pinzon recommended

[1] Las Casas gives a summary of the diary, but now and then quotes the actual words of it, introduced by ' the Admiral says.'

[2] There are no islands in the Atlantic anywhere near Columbus's position on this date.  But a belief in the existence of such islands persisted through the sixteenth century and even later.

that the course be changed to south-west, Columbus was
unwilling because ' he saw that if they made any mistake
they could not touch land so soon, and that it was better
to go at once to the mainland, and then to the islands.'

These extracts bear witness to Columbus's resolve not to
deviate from a straight course to Asia on his outward voyage.
Yet they appear at first sight to be inconsistent with his
behaviour after he had run into the Bahamas. For if his
one desire was to reach the mainland of Asia, how is it
that, after arriving in the West Indies, he seems to have lost
all interest in Cathay and the Great Khan, and never until
1502 made any determined effort to push on to the west of
Cuba ? Why, after having so steadfastly refused to turn
aside from his course to look for alleged islands, was he so
easily diverted by islands once he had run into them ?
Why, in spite of his assertion, in his letter describing the
first voyage,[1] to the effect that Hispaniola was well situated
for trade with the dominions of the Great Khan, did he
make no serious attempt to find those dominions on his
second voyage ? And why on the third did he forget about
Asia altogether, and, instead of aiming further west than
his previous discoveries, sail south-west of the Cape Verde
Islands to find King John of Portugal's alleged continent ?

The solution of the puzzle seems to be that Columbus
sailed due west in order to strike Asia in as short a time as
possible, but that the mainland of Asia was for him not
the end, but the means. Columbus's end was exactly what
he declared it to be in correspondence with Toscanelli, ' to
sail thither where the spices grow.' In his exploration of
the Antilles his thoughts are always of spices and gold. But
Marco Polo, whom Columbus had read quite apart from
Toscanelli's extracts in the letter to Martins, had said that
spices and gold were brought to China from the 7,448
islands of the Sea of Cin, and Behaim's globe, which
undoubtedly corresponds closely to the geographical conceptions of Columbus, shows these islands, large and small,

[1] *Select Documents illustrating the four Voyages of Columbus*, ed. Hakluyt
Soc., 1930, vol. I, p. 12.

scattered about in the ocean to the east of Asia, both above and below the Equator. It would be no use for a ship starting from the European side of the Atlantic to search for them, for maps could not be trusted to give their position exactly, and there was always the risk that a caravel would run out of food and water while cruising in unknown waters. The obvious course was to sail due west and strike Asia ; a ship might miss the islands, but the continent was too large a target. As the Chinese traded with the islands, it would be easy to obtain information about them in Chinese ports, and further plans could be made accordingly.

But if on the direct course to the west it so happened that islands were struck, the attainment of the Asiatic mainland would be superfluous, at any rate for the time being. The first task would be to explore the spice and gold archipelago and annex as much of it as possible. And this brings us to a further motive governing the actions of Columbus. By his contract he was to be viceroy and governor-general of the lands he should " discover and acquire." For the acquiring he had three small ships and a handful of men. But he could hardly hope to make annexations for Spain from the realm of the Great Khan, who was reputed to be one of the most powerful princes in the world. If he dreamed of making conquests at the expense of a warlike infidel power, he might as well have sailed with his little band to Morocco or Turkey. It cannot have been within the empire of the Great Khan that Columbus hoped to " discover and acquire " the lands of which he would be viceroy and governor-general, but in the islands of the Sea of Cin, which according to Marco Polo were not under the rule of the Great Khan. Surely of those 7,448 islands one might be acquired even with but three caravels ! Even if it were no bigger than Madeira, yet if it produced pepper, cloves and nutmegs it would be a rich prize for the Spanish Sovereigns and for the discoverer. Columbus was clearly resolved to take possession of any island where the inhabitants did not appear too formidable. In the *Letter* of the first voyage he says : " In thirty-three days I passed from the Canary Islands to the Indies with the fleet which the most illustrious King and Queen, our sovereigns, gave to me. And there I found very many islands filled with people innumerable, and I have taken possession of them all for Their Highnesses, by proclamation made and with the royal standard unfurled, and no opposition was offered to me." While it must be admitted that the annexation ceremonies were rather empty formalities as far as the natives of the West Indies were concerned, seeing that in their ignorance of Spanish they must have been quite unaware that they were being annexed, there is no doubt that the discoverers could have overcome any resistance which might have been offered by the population of Guanahani. It is, on the other hand, very doubtful whether, if Columbus had arrived at Canton or some other Chinese port, he would have been at pains to inform the local officials that he took possession of the place for the Spanish Sovereigns !

In China Columbus could not have hoped for annexations, but only for trade. It was not necessary to go to China for trade in the commodities most desired, since the source of these was in the islands of the ocean between China and Europe. And, even if China had been supposed to offer richer opportunities of commerce than the islands, the outlook of Columbus was not that of a merchant. He wanted lands he could annex, because his ambition was to be a lord and ruler, not merely a merchant, however wealthy. By birth a Genoese, he had become more Spanish than the Spanish in his regard for feudal values. He desired to present the Spanish Sovereigns not with permits to trade but with new dominions ; for himself he sought, not cargoes obtained by haggling under the supervision of petty officials in Asiatic ports, but princely power and dignity. From his humble origin he aspired to climb higher than the *hidalgos* ; with the hereditary viceroyalty of a territory in the Indies he would be one of the chief men of Spain and a figure of importance in the affairs of nations. Wealth he craved also, but for the maintenance of rank, not as a substitute for it. All his inclinations, therefore, led him to make the insular Indies rather than the Chinese empire his ultimate objective.

In bringing mainland (*tierra firme*) as well as islands within the scope of the *Capitulations of Santa Fé* Columbus no doubt had in mind the Portuguese settlements in Guinea, notably La Mina da Ouro, which in the ten years since its foundation had become famous. If he should by chance acquire a gold mine on a mainland coast either of Asia or of some new continent, which he might possibly discover, he did not intend to be deprived of his gain on the ground that it was on the mainland and not an island. We have seen that Fernam d'Ulmo was careful to bracket together continental and insular in his agreement for proposed discoveries in 1486. It was a wise precaution in drawing up a legal document, and the phrase as used by Columbus does not imply either that he expected to discover a new continent or that he proposed to conquer one with the crews of three caravels.

In a recent study on Columbus, Mr. Cecil Jane's introduction to the new Hakluyt edition of Columbus documents, a theory is expounded which makes Columbus aim not at any known or half-known land, but at the completely unknown part of the southern hemisphere. Mr. Jane points out the inadequacy of Columbus's armament for acquiring lands in the empire of the Great Khan, and agrees with the conclusion reached above, that Columbus meant to use China, had he reached it, as a stepping stone to a further purpose. But for Mr. Jane this further purpose goes altogether beyond the world as then known ; indeed it does not seem correct to call it a purpose at all. Mr. Jane writes [1] : ' It may, perhaps, be suggested with some confidence that Columbus himself was without any clear conception of that which he hoped to discover and gain, that his objective was altogether vague and that his purpose, when he set out on his first voyage, was not to reach any

[1] *Select Documents illustrating the four Voyages of Columbus* (Hakluyt Soc. ed. 1930), Introduction, p. cvi.

very definite point. It was to perform a mission, the precise nature of which he did not know, although he might suspect that which would in due course be made known to him.'

Mr. Jane's conception of Columbus as a half-crazy religious visionary, who did not know where he was going but trusted to divine inspiration, marks the extreme point of reaction from the great scientific Columbus of the old myth. But the new conception appears to exaggerate the wildness of Columbus's imagination in 1492. The hopeful enthusiast of the first voyage must be distinguished from the disappointed and embittered man of later years ; it was in those later years that Columbus, harassed by enemies, began to take refuge in apocalyptic extravagances. The *Journal* of 1492, in spite of its poetic flavour, is beyond question the work of a sane and sober mind ; in it Columbus often unreasonably jumps to conclusions and often shows himself confused in his geographical conceptions, yet there is no sign of the mystical megalomania with which Mr. Jane credits him. There is nothing to suggest that the islands of the Indies would not have been a sufficient goal for his ambition.

Mr. Jane interprets Columbus's secret-knowledge pose in his bargaining with the Spanish Sovereigns to mean that he really had no idea of what he was going to find, and so could not have explained his project even if he had wanted to. Nevertheless, he seems, according to Mr. Jane, to have expected to discover a new continent. ' That it was with him no question of some island which he might discover is proved by the inclusion of the term *tierra firme* [in the *Capitulations*]. It is, indeed, sufficiently clear that Columbus believed that he would discover and that he would be able to gain something of extreme importance, and this something was neither the eastern shore of Asia nor the islands which figured vaguely on maps of the Atlantic Ocean. His objective, then, becomes uncertain.' [1]

Mr. Jane is very contemptuous of mere islands, but it is

not at all clear that Columbus shared his contempt. Even a small island might be of extreme value if its products were as rich as those of the Indian islands were supposed to be. A continent, on the other hand, would be rather unmanageable for three caravels. Whatever disappointment Columbus suffered in the West Indies was due to the absence of the anticipated gold and spices, not to the fact that he had only found islands. And when in 1498— according to Las Casas who quotes from his diary—he sailed south-west from the Cape Verde Islands to test the King of Portugal's theory that there was *tierra firme* to the south, he seems to have been quite sceptical as to the reality of the alleged continent. When he first sighted the mainland coast of South America he thought he had discovered new islands, and even after finding the Gulf of Paria full of fresh water from the outpouring of the Orinoco he was slow to be convinced that he had found a continent. At last he records in his diary with a note of astonishment : ' I believe this to be a very great mainland of which nothing has hitherto been known.' There is no suggestion here that Columbus has found what he had been hoping to find from the beginning.

Mr. Jane rightly stresses [1] the tendency of Columbus to turn to the south in his voyages and also the fact that, in his notes on the *Imago mundi* and other works, he shows special interest in all references to lands south of the Equator. But this line of argument does not lead where Mr. Jane wishes it to. For if we turn away from the Chinese objective towards the south we do not come, even below the Tropic of Capricorn, into waters then considered to be entirely unknown. If we refer to the famous globe of Behaim we find that the south-east extremity of Asia corresponding to the Malay Peninsula is brought down not only over the Equator but even over the Capricorn, and that the great Indies archipelago with many of its islands labelled is spread over the whole tropic and into both temperate zones. The archipelago was certainly supposed to lie mainly in the

[1] *Op. cit.*, pp. cxiv–cxviii.

tropics ; Indonesia does in reality extend on both sides of the Equator. As Columbus first crossed the Atlantic on a line above the tropics, all the region ' where the spices grow ' lay to the south of him. No wonder he was drawn southward after making his landfall to the west of the ocean !

The view taken of the enterprise of Columbus in this chapter may be summed up as follows :

(1) The main objective of Columbus was the archipelago of the Indies lying to the east of southern Asia—the Spice Islands in the wide sense of the word, corresponding to the islands of the Sea of Cin mentioned by Marco Polo and to the islands marked on Behaim's globe on the Asiatic side of the Atlantic. Among these islands Columbus hoped to acquire a new dominion for Spain, more valuable than, but similar in kind to, the island groups already annexed by European maritime expansion—the Madeiras, the Canaries, the Cape Verdes and the Azores.

(2) The intention of Columbus was to sail due west from the Canaries, the Spanish possession furthest to the south-west, until he either struck one of the islands or ran into the mainland of Asia somewhere in the dominions of the Great Khan of Cathay. Striking an island would be a matter of luck, but, if the islands were missed, the reaching of Asia was for Columbus an absolute certainty, since his cosmographical theory, formed from Alfragan and Marinus of Tyre, required Asia to be quite near across the Ocean Sea. From Cathay the islands could easily be located. Columbus, therefore, had no doubts as to the success of his enterprise.

(3) Columbus's proposals first to Portugal and afterwards to Spain were not made on grounds of cosmographical theory, but on a claim to secret information such as later on made the fortune of Sebastian Cabot. Columbus admitted that his enterprise would take him in the direction of the Indies and that he might reach Cathay, for which contingency he obtained an ambassadorial commission from the Spanish Sovereigns ; but he did not strive to persuade his patrons of the nearness of Asia, since that would have

been directly contrary to his interests. By making a mystery of his project and representing himself as indispensable for its execution he obtained a grant of money for his expedition and extraordinary privileges in the lands he should ' discover and acquire.'

If these propositions are accepted, it follows, as from the old orthodox interpretation, that the enterprise of Columbus must be reckoned as a part of the movement of European maritime expansion directed towards the sources of the spice trade and beginning with the voyage of Vivaldo in 1291. The Spice Islands which Columbus sought in 1492 were actually reached by D'Abreu in 1512, and the lucrative clove and nutmeg monopoly, held first by the Portuguese and afterwards by the Dutch, realized Columbus's dream of vast wealth from small islands. The country of the Great Khan, or rather of his Ming successor, to whom Columbus never delivered the letter of the Spanish Sovereigns, was reached by the Portuguese in 1514. Columbus sailed west relying on a theory which was grossly in error both as to the size of the earth and the extent of Asia. The result of his voyage was an official and decisive discovery of America. For that discovery his theory of the nearness of Asia was essential, since it was only on such a theory that anyone would have struck out due west across the Atlantic as Columbus did.

It is clear that any one of the voyages made in the fifteenth century for the rediscovery of the Antilias and ' Brazil ' would have found America if it had gone far enough. There can be little doubt that both the Antilias and Brazil, as represented in certain mediaeval maps, correspond to accidental landfalls in America. The Antilia group (Antilia, Salvagio, Reylla and I. in Mar), described in Beccario 1435 as ' newly reported ' (*insulle a novo rep'te*) demands identification with Florida, Cuba, Jamaica and one of the Bahamas ; Brazil by its shape suggests too strongly for coincidence Newfoundland and the lands round the Gulf of St. Lawrence.[1] But the deliberate rediscovery of

[1] See W. H. Babcock, *Legendary Islands of the Atlantic*.

these places proved no easy matter, and the Antilias and Brazil eluded the mariners who sought them on the strength of tradition. Some time after 1452 Diogo de Teive, a Portuguese noble and the discoverer of Flores, sailed 150 leagues south-west of Fayal in search of Antilia. Two brothers of the Azores, João and Alvara da Fonte, spent their entire fortunes in searching westward for these islands. Vincente Diaz, financed by a wealthy Genoese merchant of Terceira, made three or four expeditions into the Atlantic with similar aim. In 1480 Thomas Lloyd of Bristol set out to reach Brazil, but had to return baffled.[1]

All these expeditions were failures for two reasons. First, because the bearings of the original discoveries were not correctly known ; the ordinary mariners of the late Middle Age were quite incompetent in the determination of longitude, and there was a general tendency to underestimate sea distances,[2] just as there was to overestimate land distances. Secondly, all the expeditions of rediscovery were tied to their bases and had to allow ample time for return in case they failed to find land. There is no need to reproach these navigators with timidity ; they were bold enough to venture on such voyages at all. But America was always a little too far for them to reach. Whatever chance they might have had of success they lost by cruising up and down as soon as they thought they were near the land they were seeking. They had no idea that they might be approaching the eastern coast of Asia ; they were confronted in their belief by an almost limitless expanse of ocean in which there were islands but no known line of continental shore. Columbus, on the other hand, believing in the proximity of Asia, struck out in a straight line for a land mass he could not miss.

[1] There is a list of these voyages given by Harrisse in his *Discovery of North America*.

[2] For example the Azores are generally marked on maps disproportionately near to Europe. One reason for the reduction of sea distances on maps was the costliness of parchment ; cartographers could nòt afford great expanses of empty sea, and as maps reacted on geographical belief, this may have had its effect on the tradition. But in any case there was only dead reckoning to rely on for sea distances.

From the very first there was in Spain an inclination to doubt whether the lands discovered by Columbus were anywhere near Asia or formed part of the Indies of the Spices. By 1502 leading geographers had certainly realized that they were not, for the world-chart of Nicolo de Canerio, made in that year, shows parts both of North and South America but does not identify them with any of the lands reported by Marco Polo. Gradually the Americas took shape from successive exploring voyages, and it was known that they formed a continuous land mass stretching from the far north to the far south.

For many years the Spanish discoveries and acquisitions in America proved remarkably unprofitable. There were a great many voyages, but very little of commercial value was found. The harvest of gold and spices was insignificant; there seemed to be only forested coasts inhabited by indigent savages. Nor did success attend the wanderings of Ponce de Leon in Florida in search of the fountain of perpetual youth. The tale of much early American exploration is summed up by Gomara in his *Historia de las Indias* : ' As most of those who made these discoveries were ruined thereby, there is no recollection left of any of them, so far as I know ; least of all, of those who sailed northward, coasting the Bacallaos region and Labrador.'

In the period after the early hopes had been dashed and before the riches of Mexico and Peru had been revealed, the harvest of Spain from overseas presented a sorry contrast to that of Portugal. While the Portuguese squadrons returned to Lisbon year after year laden with rich cargoes from Malabar or Malacca, the Spanish expeditions either resulted in financial loss or made a bare profit from odds and ends of trade. With this state of affairs Spain naturally returned to the idea of reaching the real Indies, and for several years the Spanish were so little grateful for the existence of America that their one desire was to find a way round it.

In 1517, the year before Grijalva discovered the gold abundance of Mexico, a disgruntled Portuguese noble came

to Seville and offered his services to the court of Spain.
Ferdinand Magellan had been in the service of King Manoel
I of Portugal from 1495 to 1514 ; he had been with Sequiera
on the first Portuguese visit to Malacca, with Albuquerque
at its capture, and with Antonio d'Abreu on the expedition
which explored the Moluccas in 1512. He thus had special
knowledge of the East Indies. Having fallen out of favour
with King Manoel, Magellan formally renounced his
nationality and, coming to Spain, proposed to take possession
of the Moluccas for Charles V on the plea that they legally
belonged to Spain under the Treaty of Tordesillas. When
that treaty had been concluded in 1494 the line of demarcation between the Spanish and Portuguese zones of navigation had been drawn along a meridian 370 leagues west of
the Cape Verde Islands. It was now assumed that the
Treaty implied the continuation of the same meridian right
round the Earth, and as the Treaty had not specified from
which one of the Cape Verde Islands the meridian was
to be reckoned, and as Indonesian longitudes were still very
uncertain, the *de jure* ownership of the Moluccas certainly
appeared open to dispute.

Magellan set out in 1519 with five ships and followed the
coast of South America southward until he found the
strait which bears his name. Beyond the strait he came
into the ' Great South Sea,' on which he bestowed the happy
epithet of ' the Pacific.' For ninety-eight [1] days Magellan
sailed north-west in the great ocean between America and
Asia without sighting any land except two uninhabited
atolls [2] ; the crews were ravaged with scurvy and reduced
to eating ox-hides, sawdust and rats. Then the Ladrone
Islands were reached, and from the Ladrones the Philippines,

[1] Columbus was 33 days at sea between the Canaries and Guanahani,
Da Gama 93 in cutting across from Cape Verde to the Cape of Good
Hope. But Columbus took off from a Spanish colony and Da Gama
from a well-known coast, whereas Magellan had followed an unknown
shore all the way from the Plata estuary before making his great open
sea leap.

[2] Actually he passed through the midst of Polynesia. The fact gives
point to apprehensions of early explorers searching for oceanic islands.

named by Magellan the St. Lazarus Islands. Here at last
he was in Asiatic waters, close to the Spice Islands and to
China. He had no intention of going to China, but he
was within the range of Chinese shipping, for junks from
Canton and other ports traded throughout the Philippines.

Having become involved in a war between local chiefs in
the Philippines, Magellan lost his life in a fight on the
island of Matan, but one of his ships, the *Vittoria*, loaded a
spice cargo at Tidore and sailed back to Spain round the
Cape of Good Hope, thus accomplishing the first circumnavigation of the Earth. The *Vittoria* returned with thirty-
two survivors after an absence of just under three years.

The voyage of Magellan was followed up by others round
South America, but they were not profitable owing to the
vast distances between ports of call and the hostility of the
Portuguese, who had established themselves in the Moluccas
and were determined to expel all intruders. The conquest
of Mexico, however, had given the Spanish a port on the
Pacific, and this promised a shorter and better way to the
East Indies. Now that America had turned out after all so
immensely profitable, the desire of the Spanish to invade the
Spice Islands was less keen than it had been in 1518, but
they were loath to abandon an enterprise on which they
had once embarked, so Ruy Lopez de Villalobos was sent
out from New Spain (Mexico) with a fleet in 1545 ; he
reached the Moluccas, but was attacked by the Portuguese
and all his ships destroyed or captured.

After this reverse the Spanish made no further effort for
nearly twenty years, but in 1564 by command of Philip II
another fleet was sent out from New Spain under Miguel
Lopez de Legazpi, who came of a family of Spanish colonists
in Mexico. There were dissensions among the officers of
the fleet, some favouring the Moluccas as the goal of the
expedition, others New Guinea, and others the Luzon
Islands (i.e. the Philippines) ; accordingly Legazpi was
given sealed orders which he was not to open until he was
300 leagues out to sea. When he opened them he found
that he was to go and annex the Luzon Islands. The

Spanish policy this time was to avoid conflict with the Portuguese and establish the Spanish power to the north of the area of direct Portuguese domination. A start was made in the island of Zebu, which was subdued, and the whole archipelago renamed the Philippines after Philip II. Then in 1571 the Spanish captured the town of Manila in Luzon itself, and made it their headquarters.

Most of the petty kingdoms of the Philippines had rendered homage to China in the early fifteenth century, but Chinese imperial authority had long since lapsed, and with the decline of the Ming power the South China Sea had become infested with Chinese pirates who operated often in fleets and carried on a regular warfare with the imperial navy. It was by the assistance they gave to the Chinese authorities in repressing Chinese piracy that the Portuguese atoned in part for the piracies some of their own number had committed, and earned the permission to settle at Macao. It was a similar co-operation of the Spanish at Manila with the Chinese government forces which gave them their first opportunity of entry into China. In 1574 the corsair Limahon attacked Manila with a fleet of 72 vessels, but after a hard-fought battle the Spanish garrison was victorious, and Limahon retreated into the north of Luzon. The Spanish followed him, burned his fleet and surrounded him on land. In the course of these operations, they were at one point about to attack a Chinese ship which approached them, thinking it to be one of the pirate vessels, when they found that it was the ship of a Chinese admiral in pursuit of Limahon. The admiral was pleased to find that his work was being so effectively done for him, and had a conference with Legazpi, who availed himself of the good offices of the admiral to send envoys to the provincial governor of Fukien.

Two Augustine friars were selected as envoys, one of them Martin de Rada, a native of Navarre, and the other Geronimo Marin, Mexican-born like Legazpi himself. Rada had already acquired a knowledge of Chinese in Manila, and was filled with such ardour to preach the gospel in China that he had contemplated getting himself taken there as a slave. The friars spent two months in China on their visit ; as they were sent by Legazpi, who was governor of the Philippines, and not by the King of Spain himself, they did not constitute an embassy to be sent on to Peking, but were given a friendly reception by the governor of Fukien, who sent them back to Manila with rich presents for Legazpi, urging him to complete the good work of destroying Limahon and his corsair band. The friars' request to be allowed to preach Christianity was referred to the Emperor.

From 1571 Manila, the colony of the Spanish coming from the east, and Macao, the colony of the Portuguese coming from the west, faced each other across the South China Sea. The tides of European enterprise spreading west and east had met on the other side of the world at the very gates of China. In 1581 the crowns of Spain and Portugal were united, and three years later Geronimo Roman, the Philippines factor at Macao, wrote : ' With five thousand Spaniards, at the most, the conquest of this country [China] might be made, or at least of the maritime provinces.'

# CHAPTER VIII

## China Besieged

DURING the period from the first penetration of the Portuguese to the coasts of China in 1514 to the close of the eighteenth century the nations of Europe drew a cordon around China both by sea and land, so that at the end of the period the country bore a resemblance to a walled city in a state of siege, a siege wherein the invaders coming from afar have occupied the open country but are not yet strong enough to storm the walls, while the defenders make no serious attempt to drive them away. In the centre of the city the Son of Heaven continued to reign in ceremonious majesty, and refused to accept any other ruler of men as an equal ; as the European envoys to Peking generally refused to acknowledge in any way the supremacy claimed, China remained outside the world of diplomatic intercourse formed by the European states and (including also its outer ring) such Asiatic powers as the Ottoman empire. Commerce was allowed to be carried on at certain of the gates of the walled city that was China, but unofficially and not by treaty, and it was subject to harassing restrictions. A few Europeans were able to enter within the walls and reside in the country. They were the Catholic missionaries. But even their tenure was precarious. As time went on, China withdrew herself more and more into seclusion and endeavoured to reduce the dangerous contacts with the outer world. Japan in a situation similar to that of China, and also influenced by the example of her great neighbour, likewise walled herself in and, after a period of extensive intercourse with European nations with untoward results, adopted a policy of the most rigorous isolation, leaving only a narrow postern-gate open for trade with the Dutch.

Nevertheless, in spite of all difficulties and obstructions, the sum-total of trade in these years between Europe and China and Japan was very considerable. And there was further, partly through the material commerce and partly through the Catholic missions, an exchange in aesthetic styles and philosophical ideas, an exchange in which, strange to say, the balance of influence was against the invaders. Influences passed both ways, but for a while in the eighteenth century China was a greater power culturally in Paris than was Europe in Peking. That was a sort of Indian summer of the antique culture of China. Destined in the nineteenth century and after to be violently invaded, overwhelmed and radically transformed by the progressing civilization of the West, Old China in the eighteenth reached out and cast a spell over its future conqueror, leaving indelible traces in the cultural tradition of Europe.

But in 1514, when the Portuguese first reached China from Malacca, there was no thought except for material commerce and for an arrangement with the Ming emperor to secure this. To make such an arrangement Thomas Pires was sent from Lisbon as ambassador of the King of Portugal and carried to Canton in 1517 with the escort of a pepper-laden Portuguese squadron by Fernam d'Andrade, the admiral at Malacca. The squadron was well received by the Chinese, put ashore the ambassador and his suite, sold its cargoes, and sailed away, while the Canton officials applied to Peking for permission to send on the embassy to the capital.

The situation seemed full of promise for the Portuguese. The Canton mercantile interest was strongly in their favour because their benevolence towards Chinese commerce at Malacca contrasted so favourably with the tyrannical exactions of the late Sultan. On the strength of the Canton merchants' reports the Ming court had already rejected the appeal of the dispossessed Sultan of Malacca for Chinese aid. But another Malay Sultan, he of Bintang, was intriguing more effectively against the Portuguese. He informed the Chinese government of the procedure of the Portuguese in the Moluccas, and maintained that their first peaceful visits to newly discovered lands were only for espionage preparatory to attempts at conquest or spoliation. With these reports Peking was doubtful as to what policy to pursue, and it was not until the end of 1519 that the order came to Canton for Pires to be brought to the capital. Meanwhile, however, events occurred which fully confirmed the hostile accounts of Portuguese intentions given by the Malays. Simon d'Andrade, the brother of Fernam but a man of totally different character, had obtained a licence from the King of Portugal to trade with China, and had come to Canton with a squadron ; there he ruined the good relations which had so far been established. In his dealings with the Chinese officials he was as arrogant and tactless as his brother had been courteous and conciliatory, and he crowned his misdeeds by committing acts of piracy and outrage along the Chinese coast. He was at length surrounded and attacked by a Chinese fleet, and only a storm which scattered the ships enabled him to escape and return to Malacca.

With Simon d'Andrade playing the corsair in the China Seas it was hardly to be expected that the Portuguese embassy would be favourably received at Peking. The unfortunate Pires and his companions were accused of being spies, sent back to Canton and imprisoned there. To make the rupture complete the Ming emperor ordered the Portuguese to restore the former reigning dynasty of Malacca.

After this disastrous failure in the attempt to open diplomatic intercourse Portuguese relations with China remained unofficial ; nevertheless, trade grew and flourished, and by the end of the century the Portuguese had a settlement near Canton that was virtually a fortress. This curious state of affairs proceeded naturally from the attitude taken up by the imperial court towards all foreign powers. The Son of Heaven was always in the position of pretending to an authority which he could not enforce ; his officials solved his difficulties for him by drawing a fine distinction between the formal and the informal. The new race of sea barbarians who had appeared on the horizon of the empire could not be admitted to imperial favour after they had shown so much truculence of disposition, nor could they be allowed to penetrate into the interior of China, but, as long as there was profit to be obtained from dealings with them, they might be tolerated in certain ports. The Chinese merchants desired trade, the provincial authorities for a consideration permitted it, and the officials of the central government, also for a consideration, affected not to notice it, as long as there was no question of diplomatic recognition.

So the Portuguese carried on trade in Chinese ports and even obtained warehouses and places of residence for their factors. The first settlements were at Ch'üan-chow in Fukien and at Ningpo, but from both places they were expelled—from the latter in 1545 and from the former in 1549—as a result of trouble with the inhabitants and of piracies committed by Portuguese ships. For a while after 1549 there seems to have been a diminution of the commerce, but its renewal was desired by both sides, and the Portuguese atoned for their sins by a suitable payment. If the Portuguese ships by their sailing power and armaments were notably formidable as pirates, they were no less effective for the work of suppressing the far more numerous Chinese pirate junks which infested the maritime trade routes, and for services rendered in this respect to the long-suffering Chinese navy of Kwang-tung province the Portuguese received informal permission in 1557 to rent land and carry on trade at Macao close to Canton. Macao, which has remained in the hands of the Portuguese to the present day, was to be for more than two centuries the most important link between China and the outside world, for even after the ruin of the Portuguese power in the Indies the conservative Chinese officialdom took the view that the Portuguese as the first comers from Europe had more claim to consideration than the later arriving English and Dutch.

Macao remained formally Chinese territory until 1847, when Portugal declared it annexed, the *fait accompli* being recognized by China by treaty in 1889.

Macao in the sixteenth century became the emporium not only for the commerce between Portugal and China, but also for that between Portugal and Japan and for a great part of that between China and Japan.

Japan appears to have been first reached by the Portuguese in 1542, and soon a flourishing trade sprang up with the various quasi-independent feudal rulers of Kyushu. The Japanese state had at the time of the Portuguese discovery reached the furthest point of the process of feudal disintegration which had set in after the death of Ashikaga Yoshimitsu in 1408. The tide was soon to turn, and the forces of recentralization were already at work, but for some time yet Japan was to be no more than an aggregate of many virtually independent, warring principalities. Such political conditions were far more favourable for Portuguese commercial penetration than the vast unified, if somewhat loosely administered, empire of China, for the feudal lords competed with one another to attract the lucrative foreign commerce to their ports. The situation also enabled the Portuguese to become middlemen for the commerce between China and Japan ; the feudal anarchy in Japan had led to an immense growth of Japanese piracy which not only preyed on shipping in the China Seas but also committed frightful ravages on the coasts of China itself. This lawless violence had almost put an end to direct commerce between China and Japan, and gave a great advantage to the Portuguese, whose vessels were too powerfully armed to be taken by corsairs whether Chinese or Japanese.

Later on in the sixteenth century, when Japan had been reunified politically and piracy suppressed from the Japanese side, events still favoured the Portuguese commercial interests, for Hideyoshi, having made himself supreme ruler of Japan, plunged his country into war with China, which again interrupted trade to the profit of the neutral Portuguese. Especially lucrative for the latter was the traffic in

240 EUROPE & CHINA

silk to Japan, the Chinese product being then preferred to the native by the Japanese nobles.

Until the Dutch penetrated into the Far East in the last years of the sixteenth century the only European rivals of the Portuguese in the China Seas were the Spanish established in the Philippines. Until 1581 this rivalry was one between the subjects of separate states, but in that year the crowns of Spain and Portugal were united; even so, there was always antagonism between Macao and Manila, and the commercial privileges guaranteed by Spain to Portugal at the time of the union were constantly encroached on by the Spanish.

As we have seen, the Spanish established themselves at Manila in 1571 and entered into communication with the provincial authorities of Fukien three years later. In their attempt to open up diplomatic intercourse with the Ming court the Spanish were no more successful than the Portuguese, and they did not obtain any foothold on the Chinese mainland, but Manila soon became a great resort of Chinese shipping and received a large Chinese population. There had been many Chinese in Luzon before the Spanish arrived, and with the suppression of local wars by the strong Spanish rule Chinese commerce and immigration rapidly increased. Junks came to Manila from the ports of Fukien, from Foochow, Amoy and Ch'üan-chow, laden with Chinese products, which were re-shipped from Manila across the Pacific. This trade soon attained great dimensions and brought prosperity to the Philippines, but it was an anomaly in the Spanish colonial system, and seriously upset its economy.

The theory of the Spanish empire was that the colonies should have direct trade only with the mother country and not with foreign states or with one another. But almost all the transit between Spain and the Philippines was via Mexico, since the long and dangerous all-sea route round South America was little used. Thus Mexico had a middle-man's position for commerce between China and Spain, and, what was more, the Spanish officials and colonists of

Mexico and Peru took to buying from Manila not only peculiarly oriental goods but also commodities which were produced in Spain but could be obtained more cheaply from Asia. As Spanish America produced little that could be exported to Asia with the exception of the precious metals which were its main wealth, the Chinese and other imports through Manila to America were paid for almost entirely with silver, and it was in this way that the Mexican dollar became the favourite currency of Chinese ports. This economic process was not at all to the liking of the royal government at Madrid ; the diversion of great quantities of American silver to Asia and the prosperity of the colonies at the expense of the mother country were contrary to all the principles of Spanish imperialism. Unfortunately for the policy of Madrid, administrative decrees were powerless to prevent the tendencies which were so much deplored ; the self-interest of the colonists and the venality of the administration conspired to defeat their enforcement, and silver of the American mines continued to be bartered from Callao and Acapulco for Asiatic textiles of cotton and silk, for spices and porcelain, cheating the treasury of Their Catholic Majesties who were so earnestly endeavouring to impose Spanish hegemony and the Holy Inquisition on the rest of Europe.

From the sixteenth century date several European accounts of China which take up the tale of the mediaeval travellers to Cathay. Among them two of the most noteworthy are the work of Portuguese who suffered imprisonment in China but derived from the circumstances of their captivity a wider knowledge of the country than was possible for traders who knew only the wharves of a Chinese port. One of these accounts is anonymous and represents the narrative of a man six years a prisoner in China, preserved by the Jesuit college of Malacca and included as an appendix in Alvarez's *Historia de Ethiopia* (edition of 1561) ; the other is the story of a certain Galeoti Pereyra, reproduced from an English translation in Eden's *Historye of Travaile in the West and East Indies*. More full and detailed than either of these accounts is that of Juan Gonsalez de Mendoza, an Augustine friar, a native of Toledo, who was a member of an abortive Spanish embassy to China in 1584 ; it is made up from a collation of the reports of various Augustine and Franciscan friars who had attempted to penetrate into China. Mendoza's work was published in Rome in 1585, and an English translation by R. Parke was printed in 1588 under the title of *The Historie of the great and mightie kingdome of China and the situation thereof : Togither with the great riches, huge citties, politike gouernement and rare inuentions in the same.*[1]

In these notices the main features of contemporary China are portrayed with great vividness and accuracy. Some of the traits belong to the enduring core of Chinese traditional culture ; others are more special to the century, the time of the autumnal splendour of the Ming dynasty. Mendoza's book reaches the very essentials of the life of Old China, and its publication may be taken to mark the date from which an adequate outline knowledge of China and its institutions was available for the learned world of Europe.

The anonymous account and Pereyra's narrative have a special value in that both authors derived most of their impressions while captive in the country and therefore seeing it under conditions most unlikely to leave a pleasant memory ; the praise they have for many things Chinese is for this reason the more impressive. No doubt their field of vision was limited by their situation, and so much is admitted by the anonymous one who says : ' I have heard much of the grandeur of these kingdoms [i.e. provinces of China], and seen somewhat (though little), which to those who have no knowledge of China would scarcely appear true ; wherefore I speak only of those things which are most common among the people, leaving the rest to time, which will discover them.'

All three authors have something to say of the Chinese

[1] See Hakluyt Society ed. 1853. In quoting from Pereyra and Mendoza I have used the English of the Elizabethan translations, but with modernized spelling.

political system. Thus the anonymous : ' The governors of provinces and those who hold any command are chosen for their learning and great prudence, without regard to anything else, and if the sons are as able as their fathers they succeed them in their offices ; otherwise they are not admitted by the king into his service. The special governors of the towns are obliged to sit to hear and do justice to all every morning until midday and after having dined until sunset. . . . The officers are waited on with much veneration ; all who speak to them do so with genuflexions, and every request must be made in writing. . . . No man governs in his native place where he has relatives, that he may do justice to all without respect of persons.' Similarly Pereyra : ' Such *Louteas* that do serve their prince in weighty matters for justice are created after trial made of their learning ; but the others, which serve in smaller affairs, as captains, constables, sergeants by land and sea, receivers and suchlike, whereof there be in every city, as also in this, very many, are made for favour. The chief *Louteas* are served kneeling.' A more detailed notice is given by Mendoza, who describes the competitive examination system, the degrees of rank, and the method of appointing officials, remarking on the rule of exile in office : ' The principal matter that they do advertise themselves is that the viceroy, governor or counsellor be not a natural of the country that he is provided for ; and that for to prevent the inconvenience that might happen in the executing of good justice, which many times chanceth, either for the love of his friends and kinsfolk, or else for the hate he hath to his enemies.'

The tribute paid by our authors to the administration of justice in sixteenth-century China is astonishing in contrast to the reputation of Chinese justice in recent times, but coming as it does from men who had been on the wrong side of the Chinese law it cannot be lightly disregarded. The anonymous ex-captive tells us : ' The sentences which the officers pronounce are conformable to the laws of the kingdom ; they judge according to the truth of the matter, which they inquire into themselves, without

taking account of what the parties say ; and so they are
very correct in affairs of justice, for fear of the visitation
[of commissioners on tour from Peking], which they say is
made every six months.'  Pereyra is even more emphatic :
' There is placed in each shire [i.e. province] a *Tutan*, as
you would say a governor, and a *Chian*, that is a visitor
as it were, whose office is to go in circuit and see justice
exactly done.  By these means so uprightly are things
ordered there that it may be worthily accounted one of
the best governed provinces [i.e countries] in all the world.'

Mendoza gives a full account of legal procedure in which
he declares : ' The king doth pay them all [the magistrates]
sufficient wages, for that it is forbidden upon great penalties
to take bribes or any other thing of any client. . . .  These
judges are straitly charged and commanded by the king's
authority that they must go fasting into the hall of audience
or judgement hall without drinking of any wine, and that
they must give no sentence with wine ; and that is such
a custom amongst them, that whosoever doth break it is
severely punished. . . .  In matters of great importance,
and such as do touch grave personages, the judge will not
trust the scrivener or notary to write any information ; but
they with their own hand will write the declaration of any
witness, and will consider very much of that which is
declared.  This great diligence is the occasion that few
times there is any that doth complain of any ill justice
done, the which is a great and notable virtue, and ought
to be imitated of all good justices, for to avoid many in-
conveniences which do happen for the not using the same,
the which these Gentiles have great care to perform.'

There is no endeavour in these accounts to minimize
the cruelties of the Chinese law—the horrors of the prisons,
the use of torture and the prevalence of punishment by
flogging.  But such things were the commonplace of Europe
also until the nineteenth century.  What seems to have
struck the sixteenth-century observers as most remarkable
in the operation of the Chinese law was the system of
reviewing all cases in which a death sentence had been

pronounced. As the anonymous says : ' They take all
possible pains to avoid condemning any to death.' This is
hardly in accord with the commonly-held belief that human
life has always been cheaper in China than in Europe.

Another feature which aroused the admiration of our
authors in the sixteenth century, but was not so characteristic of China in the nineteenth, was the excellence of
the roads and bridges. Thus : ' The streets are very well
made and paved with stone, and the highways are all
raised. I say this because they took us from that town
where we had been prisoners for three years, and we went
one hundred and twenty days' journey without going out
of the kingdom, and found all the roads raised and even ;
and several times when we passed rivers and inquired if
most of the roads that ran forward were similar, we were
told that they were, and that it was a four months' journey
to reach the court of the king, and the roads were all alike.'
And again : ' The ways elsewhere are gallantly paved
with four-square stone, except it be where for want of
stone they use to lay brick ; in this voyage we travelled
over certain hills, where the ways were pitched, and in
many places no worse paved than in the plain ground.
This causeth us to think that in all the world there be no
better workmen for buildings than the inhabitants of China.
. . . The streets in Cinceo [Ch'üan-chow] and in all the
rest of the cities we have seen are very fair, so large and
so straight that it is wonderful to behold . . . the breadth
of the street is such that in them fifteen men may ride
commodiously side by side. As they ride they must needs
pass under many high arches of triumph that cross over
the streets, made of timber and carved diversely, covered
with tile of fine clay ; under these arches the mercers do
utter their small wares, and such as list to stand there are
defended from rain and the heat of the sun.' So also
Mendoza : ' The highways throughout all this kingdom are
the best and gallantest paved that ever hath been discovered ;
they are very plain, yea unto the mountains, and they are
cut by force of labour and pickaxes, and maintained with

brick and stone, the which by report of them which hath
seen it is one of the worthiest things that is in all the realm.'

Mendoza gives a vivid description of the palatial resi-
dences of the provincial governors : ' all which, to conclude, are superbious and admirable, and wrought by marvellous art, and are as big as a great village by reason
that they have within them great gardens, water ponds
and woods compassed about. . . .   Their houses commonly
be very gallant and after the manner of Rome, and generally
at the doors and gates of them are planted trees in gallant
order ;  the which maketh a gallant shadow and seemeth
well in the streets.   All these houses are within as white
as milk, in such sort that it seemeth to be burnished paper.
The floors are paved with square stones, very broad and
smooth ;  their ceilings are of an excellent kind of timber,
very well wrought and painted, that it seemeth like damask
and of the colour of gold, that showeth very well ;  every
one of them hath three courts and gardens full of flowers
and herbs for their recreation.   And there is none of them
but hath his fish pool furnished, although it be but small.'

The ordering of society at large seems to have impressed
our authors no less than the magnificence of the high
officials.   ' Everyone is accustomed to have some occupation and to hold some office, even the sons of the officers
and nobles.   All employ their sons, of whatever condition
they may be, setting them to read and write, which they
understand generally.'   ' They have moreover one thing
very good, and that which made us all to marvel at them
being Gentiles ;  namely that there be hospitals in all their
cities, always full of people ;  we never saw any poor body
beg.   We therefore asked the cause of this ;  answered it
was that in every city there is a great circuit wherein be
many houses for poor people, for blind, lame, old folk, not
able to travel for age, nor having any other means to live
. . . besides this they keep in these places swine and hens
whereby the poor be relieved without going a begging.'

We are given a mass of information on every branch of
Chinese social life, on dress and deportment, on manners

and morals, on marriage and funeral customs, on religious rites and current superstitions. We are shown a society of enormous population and great material prosperity, patriarchal in its essence, bureaucratically organized, stable and immobile, expressing itself in a stately ceremoniousness. Perhaps the most revealing picture is one provided by the anonymous account : ' The people of any consequence wear black silk for their dress, because coloured is held dishonourable for clothing ; so much so that no one dares to go before any officer or person of quality without a black dress ; and if he has gone away from home with a coloured cloak and happens to have to speak to any officer, he takes a black cloak from some acquaintance whom he meets, and leaves him his own while he transacts his business. The common people always speak to the nobles cap in hand, and they may not wear black cloaks, but only very short coloured ones.'

As to the diversions of Chinese life, the same author tells of the festivals on the emperor's birthday and at the New Year. ' These feasts last three days ; on all of which they represent scenes by day and night, for they are much addicted to the performance of farces. On these three days the gates of the town are closed, because from much eating and drinking the people are at times beside themselves.' Mendoza describes Chinese dinner-parties and remarks : ' These Chinos are so curious people that in their books are named, besides the cities and towns, the banqueting houses and houses of pleasure, which the gentlemen have for their recreation. . . . Amongst these Chinos, more than amongst any other people of the world, are used banquets and feasts.'

There is a shade of contempt, however, in Pereyra's reference to the mandarin epicures : ' The *Louteas* are an idle generation without all manner of exercises and pastimes except it be eating and drinking. Sometimes they walk abroad in the fields to make the soldiers shoot at pricks with their bows, but their eating passeth ; they will stand eating even when the other do draw to shoot.'

This brings us to the surprising disinclination of the Chinese for the arts of war, a disinclination which appeared to the virile and coercive Europeans of the sixteenth-century expansion to verge upon effeminacy. Our anonymous author declares : ' The people of China are in general neither brave nor skilful nor have they any natural inclination for warlike affairs ; if they maintain themselves it is by the multitude of the people, the strength of the walls and towns, and the provision of ammunition.' Mendoza describes the military system and gives an estimate of the number of troops available (which he puts at between six and seven millions) with the comment : ' All the which, if in valour and valiantness might be equalled unto our nations in Europe, they were sufficient to conquer the whole world. And although they are more in number and equal in policies, yet in their valiantness and courage they are far behind.'

Even more decided is the judgment contained in a letter written in 1584 by a Jesuit, Matteo Ricci, who was later to be the first ambassador of the Church at the court of Peking. Ricci writes : ' The power of China rests rather upon the great number of towns and the multitude of inhabitants than upon the valour of the people. There are more than sixty millions of rated persons inscribed on the royal registers, exclusive of the public functionaries and those people who are too poor to pay taxes. All the neighbouring kingdoms pay tribute to the King of China, except Japan which has freed itself recently ; it is on this account that the Chinese are accustomed to consider their country as the centre of the world and to despise all other nations. They are very much dreaded by all the kings in the vicinity because they can assemble in a moment so considerable a fleet that it frightens them by the number of vessels ; the Chinese are, however, but poor warriors, and the military is one of the four conditions which are considered mean among them. Nearly all the soldiers are malefactors who have been condemned to perpetual slavery in the king's service ; they are only fit to war with thieves. . . . In short, it appears to me the most difficult thing in the world to regard the Chinese as warriors. . . . They spend two hours every morning in combing and plaiting their hair. Running away is no dishonour with them ; they do not know what an insult is ; if they quarrel, they abuse one another like women, seize each other by the hair, and when they are weary of scuffling become friends again as before, without wounds or bloodshed. Moreover it is only the soldiers who are armed ; others are not permitted to have so much as a knife in their houses ; in short, they are formidable only from their numbers.'

This letter was read by one Geronimo Roman, factor of the Philippines at Macao ; he added the following by way of comment : ' The King of China maintains a numerous fleet on this coast, although he is not at war with anyone. . . . These vessels go out a little when it is fine weather, but hasten back at the least wind. They have some small iron guns, but none of bronze ; their powder is bad, and never made use of but in firing salutes ; their arquebuses are so badly made that the ball would not pierce an ordinary cuirass, especially as they do not know how to aim. . . . The soldiers of this country are a disgraceful set. . . . They are mean, spiritless and badly-armed knaves. There is nothing formidable in thousands of such soldiers. Besides, what can the soldiers be in a country where their position is looked upon as dishonourable and occupied by slaves ? Our Indians [i.e. Filipinos] of the Philippines are ten times more courageous. With five thousand Spaniards, at the most, the conquest of this country might be made, or at least of the maritime provinces, which are the most important in the world. With half a dozen galleons and as many galleys one would be master of all the maritime provinces of China, as well as of all that sea and the archipelago which extends from China to the Moluccas.'

The Spanish had overrun without a check Mexico, Peru and the Philippines ; now they had begun to dream of the conquest of China. In 1586 a report with a scheme for such conquest, signed by the Governor of the Philippines, the Archbishop and the superiors of the religious orders, was sent to Philip II from Manila.[1] This report was not quite so extreme in its optimism as Roman's memorandum ; it estimated that the war would need 10,000 or 12,000 men from Spain and an equal number of Filipinos and Japanese mercenaries. The plan had in view the propagation of the Catholic faith with the aid of political ascendency on the model already followed in the Philippines. Mendoza contributed much to the report, and he seems to have felt that his advice as war-maker was not altogether compatible with his Christian missionary purpose, for he says in his book, after his account of the Chinese army and its weaknesses : ' I do not here declare the industry that might (with the favour of God) be used to win and overcome this people, for that the place serveth not for it, and I have given large notice thereof unto whom I am bound. And again, my profession is more to be a means unto peace than to procure any wars ; and if that which is my desire might be done, it is that with the word of God, which is the sword that cutteth the hearts of men, wherewith I hope in the Lord to see it.'

But the proposals of the Manila government were not carried into effect. Heathen China had to wait her turn until after Protestant England for the attentions of Spanish arms, and her turn never came. The ships and men for which Manila asked were not sent to the Pacific but north from Spain to meet their doom in the English Channel, in the North Sea, or on the storm-beaten coasts of the Hebrides and Ireland. The ruin of the Invincible Armada in 1588 was a blow from which the Spanish power never recovered, and though the Spanish-Portuguese naval hegemony in the Far East remained for some time unaffected, Spain was no longer in a position to attempt armed aggression against China. And by the course of events whatever thoughts of a forward policy the high-minded Manila authorities continued to entertain during the next three decades were directed towards Japan rather than towards

[1] Blair and Robertson, *The Philippine Islands*, vol. VI, pp. 13, 197-226.

China. Not that the Spanish considered the Japanese as fighters to be easier prey than the Chinese ; on the contrary, they had as marked a respect for the warlike qualities of the former as they had contempt for those of the latter. But inasmuch as Japan, with no navy able to contend with the Spanish galleons, consisted of a group of islands, it was more vulnerable to Spanish sea power than China. Internally, moreover, it was distracted by feudal factions from the death of Hideyoshi in 1598 to the final triumph of Iyeyasu in 1615, and the considerable number of converts to Christianity, especially in Kyushu, provided an opening for political intrigues of a kind that were not possible in China. The Catholic missionaries, however, had made the tactical error of using violence against their opponents before they were established with sufficient strength in the country as a whole ; after proclaiming that they only entered Japan for peaceful conversion they had initiated persecutions of Buddhism in the fiefs where they had captured the ruling house for their faith. As a result the Christians found themselves viewed with dislike and suspicion when the petty independence of the fiefs was superseded by strong central government and Japan became again a single state.

Tokugawa Iyeyasu, who as *shogun* ruled Japan from 1603 to his death in 1616, seems to have feared an alliance between his enemies of the Osaka faction, the Christians and the Spanish of the Philippines ; he discovered that one of his own most trusted supporters [1] had carried on treacherous intrigues with the aim of bringing about such a coalition. The Spanish had their opportunity for effective intervention in Japanese affairs when war broke out between Iyeyasu and the Osaka faction in 1614, but actually they did nothing, and the opportunity passed. Their inaction may indeed have been prudent, for by this time the Dutch were present in force in the Far East, and

[1] Ōkubo Nagayasu. He acquired rank and wealth under Iyeyasu by opening up and working gold and silver mines, using technical methods learnt from Spanish miners. He was himself a Christian.

would have been ready to aid Iyeyasu by an attack on Manila.

In Luzon itself the Spanish by the beginning of the seventeenth century had become nervous of their security owing to the rapid growth of the Chinese immigrant population. Never very numerous, the Spanish in the Philippines were now greatly embarrassed by the arrival of the Dutch in the China Seas, and feared a sudden rising of the Chinese settlers assisted from the mainland. There was in fact in 1603 a plot among the Chinese at Manila, and the Spanish, aided by the Japanese settlers—of whom there were comparatively few—rid themselves of the danger by a great massacre in which the Chinese community was almost exterminated. Soon after this the Spanish permitted a renewal of Chinese immigration, but would not allow the number of Chinese in Manila to exceed 6,000.

It would be unprofitable to discuss the ' might have been ' of the Spanish plan of 1586 ; it is enough to remark that the Spanish with their experience of easy victory over the Aztecs and Incas probably underestimated the resistance which China could have made to their attack. But the mere fact that a handful of Spaniards maintained themselves permanently in an island so close to China as Luzon and at so vast a distance from Spain is in itself a cause for astonishment. Manila, the colony of a colony, daughter city less of Europe than of America, turning the Pacific Ocean into a Spanish lake, was by its very situation an adventure of consummate audacity. And the passivity alike of China and of Japan in relation to this lonely outpost of dangerous aliens at their very doors is no less striking than the boldness of the Spanish. Hideyoshi indeed threatened to invade Luzon, and would, no doubt, have done so had his energies not been absorbed in the Korean war. Chinese provincial officials gave encouragement to the conspiracy of the Chinese immigrants in Luzon in 1603. In 1630 Matsukura, the persecutor of the Japanese Christians of Kyushu, asked leave from the Yedo court to make an expedition against Manila ; but his request was not granted.

Actually no serious attempt was ever made by either of the two great Far Eastern powers to dislodge the Spanish from Manila.

Nothing shows more clearly than this the contrast between the aggressive navalism emanating originally from the mercantile city republics of Italy and the self-secluding policies inspired by the land-revenue ideology of Chinese civilization. The Ming empire after a brilliant epoch of sea-power reaching to Aden and East Africa had lightly abandoned this most promising maritime ascendency, and in its preoccupation with the Mongolian and Manchurian frontiers had apparently forgotten the very existence of its fleets. In Japan in the sixteenth century there seemed to be every condition favourable to a movement of overseas expansion—a numerous and intensely warlike military class, a breed of seamen feared as far as Java and Sumatra for the daring of their piracies, great opportunities for commercial enterprise and even a genuine free city, the port of Sakai. Yet in the end Japan turned away into an isolation more rigorous than China's, forbidding her subjects to go abroad on pain of death if they returned. In Japan, as in China, a tradition of political ideas too hard and inflexible to adapt itself to changing conditions repressed the emerging tendencies of mercantilism and colonialism.

Mendoza was well aware that the Chinese not long before had been a great power in the Indian Ocean, and he knew also that the need for concentration of strength to meet Tatar attacks had been a reason for abandoning the overseas expansion. But it is clear from his book [1] that he could not quite comprehend so complete a renunciation of sea power by an empire still so strong as China was when he saw it. He affects to regard it as evidence of the political wisdom of the Chinese : ' They without all doubt seem to exceed the Greeks, Carthaginians and Romans, of whom the old ancient histories have signified to us, and also those of later times who for to conquer strange countries did separate themselves so far

[1] Book III, ch. 7.

from their natural, that they lost their own countries at home.'

But here Mendoza appears to be indulging a merely whimsical admiration ; it was certainly not as a good European and a son of Spain in the Philippines that he could extol the virtue of staying at home. It is just possible, indeed, that in a reflective mood he saw that his own nation had overreached itself in foreign conquest and that he envied the Chinese for having withdrawn from such a situation before it was too late. But it is more likely that he was really at a loss to understand the policy of voluntary retreat from maritime dominion and the Ming legislation forbidding Chinese to sail abroad without special imperial licence. He is much more at ease with his theme when he tells us of the relaxation of these laws and incidentally bears witness to the spirit of commercial enterprise latent in the South China ports and now and then escaping from the trammels of the great bureaucracy. ' Now in these days,' he says, ' the governors of the sea ports do dispense with the law that forbiddeth the going out of the kingdom by certain gifts which are given them by merchants to give them secret licence that they may go and traffic in islands bordering there about, as unto the Philippines. . . . The desire of gain hath caused them to travel to Mexico, whither came the year past in anno 1585 three merchants of China with very curious things, and never stayed until they came into Spain and into other kingdoms further off.'

Surely those three Chinese merchants were not less devoted to the quest of wealth than Spaniard or Dutchman ! But they voyaged as truants from their government, not as its privileged emissaries.

Before the middle of the seventeenth century the Ming dynasty had fallen after 276 years of rule. Long before the end the decayed imperial administration had ceased to function, and the disorganization of society was the more ruinous because of the complexity of the mechanism by which it had been controlled. China was devastated by hunger-driven revolts, while a new confederation of the semi-nomad tribes of Manchuria pressed in from the north-east. The transfer of the imperial throne from a Chinese to a Manchu dynasty in 1644 was brought about by the action of a Chinese general Wu San-kuei, who with the best troops in China had been holding the Manchus back from Chihli. Behind his front a rebel army under a certain Li Tzu-ch'êng captured Peking ; the last Ming emperor hanged himself, and Li was installed as founder of a new dynasty. But Wu refused to recognize Li and, when hard pressed by Li's forces, called the Manchus to his aid. Li was defeated, pursued and slain by Wu and his allies, but the Manchus, admitted into China, at once occupied Peking and by degrees made themselves masters of the whole country.

The new regime (the Ch'ing dynasty) repeated the characteristics of the Yüan (Mongol) period. Once more a barbarian emperor held down China with barbarian garrisons, yet adopted the manners and customs of China and left the civil administration to officials of the Chinese scholar class. The principal effect of the Manchu conquest was an accession of military strength to the ' Chinese ' empire. The Manchus provided the country of their adoption with a competent military caste ; they brought as a dowry to China their own land of Manchuria, and during the first century and a half of their dynasty in China annexed to their dominion Mongolia, Tibet, Ili and East Turkestan, and even crossed the Himalayas and compelled Nepal to pay tribute. They did not, on the other hand, bring about any revival of Chinese sea power ; by origin horsemen of inland plains, they had no aptitude for the sea, and in matters of mercantile policy they merely followed Ming precedents.

During the first half of the seventeenth century the power of Spain steadily declined, especially under the strain of the Thirty Years' War, until the garrisons of the Philippines could do no more than barely hold their own. The Portuguese by their ' Sixty Years' Captivity ' shared in the blunders and misfortunes of Spain ; they lost most of their

Asiatic possessions and trade to the English and Dutch, but continued to hold Macao. The Dutch had first come to Indian and Pacific waters after Philip II in 1594 had closed Lisbon against their trade ; before that date they had been content to carry from Lisbon the cargoes which the Portuguese brought back from the Indies. The English were led to seek Asiatic trade at the source by a similar motive of outflanking a middleman monopoly ; the Dutch having in 1599 put up the price of pepper against London from 3s. to 6s. and 8s. per lb., the English East India Company was formed for the purpose of trading directly with India. As a result of these moves there came to be in the Far East in the seventeenth century four European maritime nations, the Portuguese, Spanish, Dutch and English, where in the sixteenth there had been only the first two. Towards the end of the seventeenth century the French also appeared, Colbert's *Compagnie de Chine* being founded in 1698 ; they were followed by Swedish and Danish ships. Finally, in the late eighteenth century, after the War of Independence, the Americans began to take part in the China trade across the Pacific.

In the seventeenth century the English, based mainly in India, were less prominent in Far Eastern commerce than the Dutch, whose power was centred in the Malay Archipelago ; in the eighteenth, however, the English in addition to their expansion in India became the first mercantile power in the China Seas. As a broad generalization it may be said that in the China Seas the sixteenth century was that of the Portuguese and Spanish, the seventeenth that of the Dutch, and the eighteenth that of the English.

In 1602 the Netherlands East India Company was chartered with a capital of 6,600,000 guilders, and in the next year sent out a fleet which laid firmly the foundations of Dutch power in the Malay Archipelago. In 1604 and again in 1607 the Dutch attempted to open up a trade with China at Canton, but on each occasion the intrigues of the Portuguese at Macao defeated their purpose. Then in 1622 Kornelis Rayerszoon with 15 ships and 2,000 men

(900 Dutch and 1,100 Malay and Japanese mercenaries) attacked Macao, but was repulsed by the garrison with heavy loss. This battle fought on Chinese soil between two European nations had a result happy for China ; the retention of Macao by the Portuguese preserved a certain balance of power, whereas the victory of the Dutch might have given them a position of ascendency in South China during the period of chaos in the country about the middle of the century.

Foiled at Canton and Macao, the Dutch made a settlement in the Pescadores Islands and began to trade there with Chinese junks from the mainland. Under pressure from the Fukien authorities they removed themselves from the Pescadores in 1624 and established themselves in Taiwan (Formosa). This island was not then under Chinese rule, being occupied mainly by the savage, aboriginal tribes who still survive in the mountains ; there were, however, settlements of Chinese. At Anping, on the west coast of Taiwan, the Dutch built a strong fort called Zelandia Castel ; here they were nearer to China than were the Spanish at Manila, and the place was also a convenient port of call for the commerce between Dutch Java and Japan. The Dutch more or less ruled Taiwan and traded with Chinese junks until 1662 when they were driven out of the island. This came about as part of the war which the Ming die-hards kept up against the Manchus long after the occupation of Peking by the northern invaders. A faction in the south rallied round the Ming heir, the prince Kwei Wang ; he was driven from Canton in 1650, but an able Ming partisan of mixed Chinese and Japanese parentage, by name Chêng Chêng-kung, better known as Koxinga, successfully maintained himself in Fukien. Desiring to have the island of Taiwan as a base—for he was stronger on the sea than on the land—he crossed over to it in 1661 and attacked the Dutch, who were compelled to withdraw in the next year. Koxinga was now in fact an independent monarch, and he and his son who succeeded him reigned over a kingdom consisting of Taiwan,

Amoy and part of Fukien. But the Manchus were in the end too strong for this relic of the Ming empire. In 1681 they took Amoy and two years later attacked Koxinga's successor in his island stronghold ; he surrendered, and Taiwan was brought under Manchu rule.

The Dutch having been driven out of Taiwan by Koxinga were naturally hostile to his kingdom, and assisted the Manchus in the investment of Amoy. The English, on the other hand, having failed, like the Dutch, to obtain trade at Canton, entered into friendly relations with the Koxingas, sold them arms, and were allowed two factories, one in Taiwan and one at Amoy. In spite of the opposite parts they had played, both nationalities received much the same treatment from the Manchu conquerors after the fall of the Koxinga kingdom ; both were permitted to trade at Amoy, and both were subjected to such tyrannical extortion that the trade there ceased to be worth while. At Amoy, as a consequence of the war, the Manchu military element was predominant at the expense of the Chinese civil administration, and the Manchus, as Morse puts it,[1] ' had not yet learned the methods by which the sheep of trade might be shorn without skinning them outright, and the English traders were skinned with no compensating advantage from trade.'

Wearied by the exactions of the military at Amoy, the English renewed their efforts to open trade at Canton where there was a more orderly administration and, after several vicissitudes, they at length succeeded in 1699 in establishing a regular commercial connection. During the eighteenth century there was European trading at some other places on the coast, but Canton became the principal port for China's foreign trade, and by a decree of the Emperor Ch'ien Lung in 1757 was made the only one. Other nationalities as well as the English participated in the Canton trade once it had been opened up, but the English now took the lead in the China trade. In the

[1] *The Chronicles of the East India Company trading to China*, vol. I, p. 99.

season of 1736 there were trading at Canton 12 ships, of which 5 were English, 3 French, 2 Dutch, 1 Danish and 1 Swedish ; in 1753 there were 27, of which 10 were English, 6 Dutch, 5 French, 3 Swedish, 2 Danish and 1 Prussian.[1]

Apart from the trade in Chinese ports, Chinese products might be bought from junks coming to Manila or Batavia or as re-exports from Tongking or Annam. The total value of the commerce, direct and indirect, between China and Europe tended continually to increase, and with the growth in amount of traffic there was also a greater variety in the commodities traded. The new commerce differed from that of ancient and mediaeval times in the scope of its buying. Some of the Chinese products sought had previously been imported into Europe, such as silk and rhubarb ; others were now introduced into Europe, at any rate in quantity, for the first time, such as porcelain, lacquer wares and tea.

The silk trade became almost as important as it had been in antiquity, in spite of the fact that Europe now produced its own silk. Chinese silks competed in the European market by their cheapness, their special technical qualities and their decorative charm. The trade allowed for a good margin of profit ; the sale-books of the *Compagnie des Indes Orientales* in 1691 show that silks bought in the East for 32,000 livres had been sold for 97,000.[2] Savary writes in his *Dictionnaire Universel* : ' The province of Che-kiang in China is the greatest producer of silk in the world. It is believed to produce as much as all Europe and Asia combined. What is told of the quantities of silk manu-factured there seems scarcely credible. The profits to the purchaser amount to at least 100 per cent.' Not even protective tariffs obtained by the French silk industry could stop the flow into France of expensive Chinese silks to meet the demand of an aristocratic society dazzled by their beauty.

[1] *Op. cit.*, pp. 247, 291.
[2] A. Reichwein, *China and Europe : Intellectual and artistic Contacts in the Eighteenth Century*, p. 37.

Porcelain had first penetrated into Europe from the Moslem world, which imported it from China, in the fifteenth century ; after the opening of the Cape route to the Indies it was brought direct from China by the Portuguese, and was widely demanded. European potters strove to imitate the Chinese ware ; they produced semi-porcelains of the so-called ' soft paste ' type from about 1580, and finally genuine ' hard paste ' porcelain from the first decade of the eighteenth century. Lacquer had a similar history ; lacquered objects imported from China attained a great vogue, and the technique was gradually acquired by European craftsmen until by the eighteenth century Europe had an independent lacquer industry. But neither in porcelain nor in lacquer did the growth of European production eliminate the imports from China ; they had acquired too strong a hold on the market, and, as time went on, the costs and risks of transport continually decreased.

Tea in the eighteenth century could only be obtained from China. The habit of tea-drinking spread to Europe in the second half of the seventeenth century, and Pepys mentions in his diary on September 25, 1666 : ' I did send for a cup of tee, a China drink of which I never had drunk before.' Once it had become fashionable the demand was very great, and by the middle of the eighteenth century the trade in tea was the most important single item of the commerce at Canton and a considerable factor in the world's economy. At the close of the seventeenth century about 20,000 lb. of tea a year, on the average, were being brought into England, mainly from India whither it was carried by Chinese junks ; in the four years 1769–72 the average annual shipments from Canton were 10,619,900 lb. by English ships, and 12,379,000 lb. by French, Dutch, Danish and Swedish ships.[1]

In exchange for these exports China imported mainly not European products, but commodities brought from India and Indonesia by European ships, either purchases

[1] Morse, *op. cit.*, p. 295.

from ports of independent states in those regions or the production of territories under European rule. Such commodities were ivory, pepper, cloves and precious woods. A certain amount of woollen cloth and a few odds and ends were imported from Europe, but there was no great demand for any European goods, and in the eighteenth century there was a favourable balance of trade for China made up with specie. It grew less and less, however, and was at length turned against China by the ever-increasing imports of opium, which came mostly from India. The drug obtained a widespread hold in China in the course of the century, and commanded high prices. The complications arising from the attempts of the Imperial government to prohibit it were to be a main cause of Chinese-European troubles in the next century. Already in the eighteenth some of the European carriers had misgivings about this branch of their trade, and Warren Hastings in 1783 denounced opium as ' a pernicious article of luxury which ought not to be permitted but for the purpose of foreign commerce only.'

The conditions of trade at Canton in the eighteenth century gave rise to a situation of great difficulty which was only resolved in the course of the nineteenth. There were first of all the troubles due to the subjection of Europeans to Chinese law and administrative action without any diplomatic intercourse or formal treaty arrangements with Peking. The Chinese attitude was always that if the foreigners were not satisfied with their position they could go, and they were made to understand that ' while we were out, we might have kept out, but now we are within the king's power, we must be obedient thereto.' [1] Actually the Chinese mandarins had no will to lose the trade from which they derived personally no little profit, but it was with them almost a religious article of faith, finding expression in the language of many edicts, that China was

[1] Morse, *op. cit.*, p. 36. The phrase is actually that of a factor in Tongking, not in China itself, but it applies equally to the Chinese attitude.

economically self-sufficient and could easily dispense with all foreign trade.

Commercially the market was tantalizingly restricted by the formation of monopolies, at first semi-official and later on official in character. On the European side there was plenty of competition ; each nation had its chartered company for carrying on the trade, and these were subject to competition not only from one another but also from independent merchant-ships, most of which were engaged in smuggling oriental goods into European countries in defiance of chartered company privileges and the high duties charged.[1] On the Chinese side, however, there was a constant tendency towards price-manipulating combination, a tendency favoured by the national corner in certain products, by the great insistence of the European demands relative to the Chinese counter-demands, and above all by the venality and absolute power of the imperial bureaucracy.

It was common for the Chinese high officials to enter into a kind of partnership with prominent merchants, who thus received administrative backing for the control of the market. Of these persons an early East India Company report remarks that ' few care to deal with such great Mandarins' Merchants, because their masters for their own advantage do often bear them out in their roguery.' [2] The *Macclesfield*, which came to Canton in 1699, had a bitter experience of these practices, and Morse referring to this voyage says : ' In all Mr. Douglas's trading at Canton, not once did he succeed in having dealings with any merchants other than the four [3] who were " great Mandarins'

---

[1] Notably the ' Ostenders,' English ships sailing nominally in the Austrian service ; they smuggled tea into England from the Austrian Netherlands.

[2] Morse, p. 101.

[3] One represented the Viceroy of the Two Kwang, the second the Tatar-General (Manchu army commander) at Canton, the third the Governor of Kwangtung, while the fourth had been associated with a Chinese vassal prince in the South before the completion of the Manchu conquest, and still possessed great influence.

Merchants " and enjoyed official protection ; the unofficial traders, however much they might wish to share in the trade, " durst not break the way " in opposing the great ones.'

An English fleet arriving at Canton in 1704 found a still more formidable monopolist, ' a new monster sprung up at Canton called an Emperor's merchant, who having given 42,000 taels at Court for his employment is invested with authority to engross the whole trade with the Europeans, and that no China merchant shall presume to interfere with him, unless for a valuable consideration he shall admit him to partnership.' [1] This ' monster ' demanded 5 per cent from the other Canton merchants for a permit to trade with the English, and exacted considerable sums, though his activities were curtailed by the hostility of the *Hoppo*, the Imperial Commissioner of Customs.

The *Hoppo* himself was also wont to make use of his official powers to do a profitable business in the market. A typical instance of such action is given by Morse : [2] ' He [the *Hoppo*] made a profitable bargain in forcing a sale of cloth to himself at half the price at which it had been sold nine months before. The bargain was even more advantageous than appears ; he was approaching the end of his term of office—in later times, and presumably then, three years—and on his return to Peking he would sell in a better market than Canton, in a climate better suited for woollen cloth, and in a market not accessible to foreign traders ; and he would carry his cloth there without the taxation which ordinary Chinese traders must pay.'

As the trade grew the conflicting interests of the various officials produced a measure of free competition, but in 1720 the leading Canton merchants formed a guild for the control of prices. The English East India Company appealed to the Viceroy, threatening to discontinue the trade unless the guild were dissolved, and they were successful in their application, but the danger continued to loom

[1] Morse, p. 137.      [2] *Op. cit.*, p. 100.

on the horizon, and in 1725 the Court of Directors of the Company wrote instructing their supercargoes : ' We hope they will not make another attempt that way ; but if they have already or should do, while you are there, you must also strenuously oppose it in the best manner you can : let the Merchants and, if necessary, the Hoppo and Mandarins know you are under positive orders not to be tied to buy of any particular people.'

In 1771 the English obtained the dissolution of another Chinese monopoly combination by the expenditure of 100,000 taels in bribes. But the factors favouring monopoly were in the end too strong. The constant disputes with foreigners and the tendency of the Chinese imperial court to put the blame on the Kwangtung provincial authorities made the latter afraid to have any direct dealings with the European traders. In their desire to shift the burden of responsibility they at last came to authorize the establishment of a merchant association which in return for a lucrative monopoly might be charged with the settlement of all questions arising out of the foreign trade. Thus was formed the famous Co-hong, the officially designated group of merchants which was the sole intermediary in relations between China and the European maritime powers in the last period before the ' Opium War ' of 1839. Behind this screen the officials themselves retired and were able to view events with lofty unconcern, while at the same time keeping a very real grip on the conduct of affairs. It was a device whereby the mandarins escaped from a situation that became ever more embarrassing, and maintained intact the theory that all foreign trade in Chinese ports was by favour and conferred no rights. They refused to consider complaints and demands addressed to them by foreigners.

The attitude of the bureaucracy was made clear in 1742, when Commodore Anson had an interview with the Viceroy of the Two Kwang [1] : ' he pointed out the vexatious impositions to which the British merchants were subjected

[1] *China, an Outline, etc.*, by Peter Auber, London, 1834, p. 165.

in their trade, and hoped that the Viceroy would give orders that the same should not hereafter occur. To this no direct reply was given. After some time had elapsed, the interpreter stated that he did not believe any reply would be given. The audience closed by the Viceroy wishing the Commodore a prosperous voyage to Europe.'

The theory finds perfect expression in the decree of the Viceroy ordering Lord Napier to leave Canton in 1834 : ' The Celestial Empire appoints civil officials to govern the people and military ones to terrify evil doers. The petty affairs of commerce are to be settled by the merchants themselves ; the officials have nothing to hear on the subject.'

In the history of European-Chinese commerce before 1800 it is neither monopolism nor official venality which distinguishes the Chinese ; neither was peculiar to China, and much of the indignation of the Europeans at the troubles of their commerce in China was nothing but the pot calling the kettle black. The contrast really lay in the radical weakness of the Chinese mercantile class as compared with the European. The great chartered companies of Europe had monopoly rights and state backing ; they sinned against the light of free trade no less than the Chinese guilds, but they stood for the self-organization and autonomy of the merchant class, not the mere rapacity of government officials. In China the merchant was powerless against official-dom ; politically he was nothing ; there was no tradition of city-state commercialism to teach him his potential strength. In Europe the *bourgeois* was rising to be master of the state ; in China he was but the servile agent of the mandarins. Morse admirably sums up the situation when he says [1] : ' It may be taken as a rule through the Far East that the governing powers claimed a monopoly of all transactions in which they saw any profit to themselves. The merchants were nowhere in evidence.'

As in fact all the conditions of trade at Canton were determined by the mandarins, the Europeans found intoler-

[1] *Op. cit.*, p. 99.

able the principle that they were beneath the notice of that
exalted order, and before the end of the eighteenth century
England made a great effort to open direct diplomatic
relations with Peking and obtain a treaty regulating the
trade.[1] In 1792 Lord Macartney was appointed ambassador to China and sent out with instructions to press
for the opening of ports other than Canton and for a
depot in Peking as well as for redress of the grievances of
the traders. On arriving in China he was escorted to
Peking under banners marked 'tribute-bearers,' and then
on to Jehol, where the Emperor Ch'ien Lung was residing ;
he was received with courtesy, but his requests were refused.

England sent another embassy under Lord Amherst in
1816, but obtained nothing except a baton of delegated
authority for King George III. The issue was not destined
to be decided but by war. There could be no agreement
otherwise between the international law of sovereign states
evolved by Post-Reformation Europe and the Chinese
assumption of world-suzerainty.

The Chinese imperial court was never more arrogant
nor more secure in its own imagination than in the early
years of the nineteenth century. But the hour of coercion
was drawing near and there was to be no escape. Europe,
like a gigantic crab, held China between two pincers, one
by sea from the south and the other by land from the
north.

We have observed the approach to China of the European
maritime nations ; it only remains to consider the comple-
mentary movement of the Russians across Siberia, the other
European pincer. The advance of the Russians into the
Far East had been much later than that of the maritime
powers, and it may be said that it was only at a still later
date that they became Europeans at all, for Russia had
to be 'westernized' by Peter the Great at the beginning
of the eighteenth century. The bands of half-savage

---

[1] No European nation had so far made a treaty with China except
the Russians. Dutch 'tribute-bearing' missions, however, had visited
Peking and had their presents graciously accepted.

Cossacks, gold-prospectors and fur-traders who carried the dominion of Muscovy to the Pacific hardly represented any sort of civilization ; they had little to distinguish them from the wild Kazaks and Kalmuks of the steppes. Nevertheless they moved from west to east, from Europe into Asia, and not in the reverse direction as had every great folk movement north of the Caspian for 2,000 years ; and, in spite of their mobility and restless habits, they stood for a sedentary agricultural nation and not for nomadic pastoralism. For the first time they bridged the land gap between Europe and the Far East with an empire that was not essentially nomadic.

The Russians of Novgorod had penetrated across the Urals into Siberia as early as the eleventh century, but these incursions left no trace, and the real conquest began with the Cossack Yermak in 1580, some thirty years after the Russians now united under the rule of Moscow had overcome the Tatar khanates of Kazan and Astrakhan, the succession states of the Golden Horde on the Volga. The Russians moved east in high latitudes, avoiding the still formidable power of the nomad Kalmuks in Central Asia ; Siberia was a land of forest and marsh which the tribes of nomad pastoral economy had not cared to occupy, and it was thinly inhabited by hunting and fishing tribes, Ostiaks, Tunguses, Yakuts and others. In 1637 the Russians founded the fort of Yakutsk on the Lena, and two years later they reached the Sea of Okhotsk. Their subsequent attempt to settle on the Amur brought them into violent conflict with the Manchu-Chinese, for the Manchus regarded the whole basin of the Amur as their territory. In the fighting which followed the Manchus were victorious, and in 1689 the Russians concluded the Treaty of Nerchinsk whereby they abandoned their settlement at Albazin and withdrew from the Amur, nor did they again advance their frontier to that river until 1855.

The Treaty of Nerchinsk also provided for Russo-Chinese commercial relations. In 1721 another treaty was concluded at Peking ; it allowed a Russian diplomatic mission to reside in Peking, a unique privilege for foreigners. The Treaty of Kiakhta in 1727 fixed frontiers and made further arrangements for trade. In 1733 a Chinese embassy was sent to Russia, and relations continued to be more or less friendly throughout the eighteenth century. The trade which grew up was carried on by caravan, chiefly through Urga and Kiakhta, and its chief commodity was tea, for which the Russians gave gold and furs. They had first received tea in the early seventeenth century from the Kalmuks, and soon they became greater tea-drinkers than even the English.

In Central Asia the Russians received in 1730 the submission of the Little and Middle Hordes of the Kazaks, and at the end of the eighteenth century that of the Great Horde (the furthest of the three to the east). Meanwhile the Manchu-Chinese had subdued Mongolia, Dzungaria and East Turkestan. Thus the whole steppe and desert belt of Asia—with the exception of West Turkestan (Khiva, Bokhara, Ferghana, the Turkomans and the Kara Kirghiz), which was conquered by Russia in the nineteenth century —was partitioned by 1800 between Petersburg and Peking, and the age-long rampancy of tribal nomadism was at an end.

The collapse of the power of the nomads with so slight a resistance, after they had again and again turned the course of history with their military prowess, is to be attributed not to any degeneracy of the nomads themselves but to the evolution of the art of war beyond their capacity for adaptation. The Tatars in the seventeenth and eighteenth centuries had lost none of the qualities which had made so terrible the armies of Attila and Baian, of Jenghiz Khan and Tamerlane. But the increasing use in war of artillery and musketry was fatal to a power which depended on cavalry and had not the economic resources for the new equipment. The change of weapons cancelled the advantages of extreme mobility and perfect horsemanship which the nomads derived from their way of living ; in the new age they suddenly appeared few and feeble as

compared with the great sedentary populations to whom
they had once been so formidable.

The contrast between the willingness of the Chinese to
make treaties with the Russians and their refusal to have
any dealings with the maritime European powers may be
explained by the need for fixing land frontiers and by the
expediency, from the Chinese point of view, of an agreement with Russia as a check on the turbulence of the
Central Asian tribes. With the maritime nations there
was, of course, no question of arranging a frontier ; the
sea itself was such, and no purpose could be served by
admitting foreigners from that quarter to treaty rights.
And even with the Russians there was no real diplomatic
intercourse in the manner of European states. For the
Chinese the Russians were, after all, only the barbarians
who had succeeded the Kalmuks as the chief power in
Central Asia, a power moreover on which they themselves
(or rather the Manchus) had inflicted defeat. It should
not be forgotten that in the first war between China and
a European nation it was China that won.

# CHAPTER IX

## The Rococo Style

A STUDY of the relations between the arts of Europe and of China in the eighteenth century follows naturally on an account of commercial intercourse, inasmuch as the exports to Europe of Chinese painted silks, porcelain and lacquer furniture constituted the most important factor in those relations. The intellectual contacts of the same period, on the other hand, were made chiefly through the Jesuit missions in China, and are therefore most conveniently considered in connection with missionary enterprise ; for the Jesuits were the only Europeans who really penetrated into China and also became acquainted with Chinese literature and thought, and they not only brought European religion and secular learning to the notice of the Chinese, but further by their written accounts and by translations from the Chinese made Europe familiar with the philosophy of the empire they strove to convert. In addition to all this, it is true, they were also brokers of exchanges in the arts, but the part they played in this respect was subsidiary to their activity as interpreters of thought, and less important than the material commerce in decorative wares for the æsthetic movement which now calls for our attention, the development of the Rococo style in Europe.

Long before the opening of the all-sea route between Europe and China artistic influences had passed between the two by indirect transmission. From the time of Alexander's conquests to the third century A.D. Hellenistic art had had a strong influence in North India, and the art that developed there was carried to China by

Buddhism.[1] Again, in the mediaeval period, there was a great export of Chinese silk textiles, pottery and porcelain to the capitals of the Islamic world ; these certainly influenced Moslem art, which in turn affected mediaeval Europe.[2] As we have already seen, Chinese painted silks were brought to Europe in the early fourteenth century, but it is difficult to say in what quantity or whether they had any influence. In general it may be stated that all passage of influence between Europe and China before the sixteenth century was through intermediaries, and such influences must be excluded from the scope of this book, because of the extreme complexity of the problems involved which demand highly specialized treatment. Indirect trade is a fairly simple matter because the ware traded remains recognizable through however many hands it passes, but indirect artistic influence is one of the most subtle and baffling of historical phenomena, since the artistic trait transmitted is nearly always modified by the intermediary in such a way that it is almost impossible to distinguish it in the next borrowing.

The Rococo style's borrowing from China, however, was direct, and up to a point it is generally admitted by art historians. The outstanding fact of this epoch is that the balance of influences is greatly in favour of China. Chinese art is affected by European contact, but on the whole tradition is too strong for the exotic manner to gain an entry. In France, on the other hand, a new style full of Chinese traits arises at the beginning of the eighteenth century, and for a brief period dominates taste in most European countries.

The European influence, such as it was, on the Chinese art of the Ch'ing dynasty, was an outcome of the Jesuit missions.[3] The Jesuits in addition to the medical, mathe-

[1] See A. W. Lawrence, *Later Greek Sculpture*, Sir Aurel Stein, *Ruins of desert Cathay* and *Serindia*, esp. vols. I and IV, and A. Foucher, *The beginnings of Buddhist Art.*

[2] See D. Talbot Rice, *Byzantine Glazed Pottery*, pp. 86–7 and Ebersolt, *Les arts somptuaires de Byzance*, pp. 10, 11, 148.

[3] The art of cloisonné enamel was termed ' Frankish ' in China, and was probably introduced from the East Roman empire in the Mongol period.

matical and mechanical accomplishments by which they commended themselves at the Court of Peking, were in some cases proficient as architects and painters, and it was part of their policy to interest the court as far as possible in everything European and to impress the self-satisfied Chinese with the excellence of European achievement in all the arts and sciences.   They brought to China French and Italian pictures and engravings, Sèvres porcelain [1] and other artistic products of Europe, as a result of which European styles and effects came to have a certain vogue. Engraving was the European art most admired, and in this sphere the Jesuits made themselves indispensable.   In painting there was for a time a regular European school. At the request of the Emperor K'ang Hsi the Jesuits sent to China two of their best artists, Frs. Gherardini and Belleville, who arrived in Peking in 1699.   They had several pupils whom they trained in European methods, notably a certain Chiao Ping-chêng.   A painter who learnt something from this school was Chen Nan-ping, who in 1731 settled in Nagasaki and gave an impetus to the growth of the Japanese naturalist school which has Okio for its chief representative.   Under Ch'ien Lung Frs. Attiret and Castiglione were court painters, and made portraits of the Emperor and various dignitaries ; Castiglione not only worked in the European manner but also learned to paint in the Chinese style under the name of Lang Shih-ning. As architects likewise the Jesuits made their mark.   A church built in Peking in European style had been dedicated in 1703, and the Chinese were made familiar through prints with European palaces.   In the middle of the century Ch'ien Lung commissioned the Jesuits to build him a new palace in the Imperial grounds ; it was constructed in a mixed Chinese-European style, and the interiors were decorated with frescoes by Castiglione.   This was the famous palace of Yüan-ming-yüan destroyed by the British in the war of 1860.

It further seems likely that it was from Europe that

---

[1] The Chinese potters imitated the Sèvres blue.

colour-printing was introduced into China. Colour-prints first occur there about 1625, and as colour-prints had been produced in Germany and Italy in the preceding century, a European derivation is indicated. It was neither in Europe nor in China, however, that the colour-print was destined to have its golden age, but in Japan, where it seems to have been introduced from China early in the eighteenth century. And the derivation from Europe can have been one of craft only, for the earliest Chinese colour-prints show no trace of European influence in design.

The sum total of European influence on Chinese art in the seventeenth and eighteenth centuries is comparatively small.[1] It was marginal, not central. The European school was not more prominent than that which imported Persian forms after Ch'ien Lung's conquests in Turkestan, or than the architecture of Tibetan derivation which balanced the French exoticism of the Yüan-ming-yüan with a copy of the Lhasa Potala at Jehol. And untouched by all these imported styles the art of pure Chinese tradition continued to hold the first place in the esteem of the scholar class. As G. Soulié de Morant observes in his summing up on the eighteenth century in *A History of Chinese Art* : ' Relations with the West, though growing steadily, had very little influence. . . . Its art had not that attraction for China which Chinese art had for Europe.'

The influence of Chinese art in Europe was a tide that swiftly flowed and swiftly ebbed, but at its flood it was sufficient to bring the fantastic argosy of the Rococo style to the inner harbour of European taste. Not that the Chinese traits of the Rococo are to be taken as representative of Chinese art as a whole. The Rococo designers took from China just what appealed to them, and that was only one side of the Chinese tradition ; much of the art of T'ang and

---

[1] The porcelain and lacquer work turned out in China for the European market according to patterns and specifications provided by merchants for adaptation to European taste cannot be classed under the head of art influence, since there was no Chinese market for such wares before the nineteenth century.

Sung they would not have appreciated even if they had been acquainted with it, which they were not. They were indifferent to the grandeur and stateliness of which the Chinese genius was capable ; they sought only to pluck the flowers of its more whimsical and gracious mood. They created a China of their own fancy, a fairyland conjured up from silk and porcelain and lacquer, exquisite and unsubstantial, giving to the motives of Chinese art a fresh imaginative value just because there was nothing known to which they could be related.

The painted silks and embroideries, the porcelain, the lacquered cabinets and screens, which made the courtly society of Europe familiar with Chinese forms and principles of design, were at first imported not for their value as fine art so much as for the qualities of their material technique. The Chinese silk industry commanded a range of subtle effects which the European could not yet equal, while no hard-paste porcelain or satisfactory lacquer was produced in Europe before the eighteenth century. It was therefore the beauty of the materials themselves, specialities of China, that made the demand for Chinese imports ; the forms of the decoration were regarded as merely quaint and curious, or even as detracting from the quality of the object. But in time both the forms and the world represented in painted scenes began to take hold on the imagination of European buyers ; they brought acquaintance not only with the manner and atmosphere of Chinese painting, but also, through pictorial representation, with Chinese architecture and gardens.

But the accumulation in Europe of Chinese ornamental stuffs and wares was only one condition of the Rococo style. That style could not have arisen without a movement of events which caused a loosening of the tradition of taste in France, the chief arbiter of elegance for Europe by the end of the seventeenth century. Up to about 1700 Europe, or at least Catholic Europe, had been dominated by the Baroque manner in art. This style, with all its extravagances and variations, was fundamentally Roman ; it had been originally developed at Rome, and it sought to revive the majesty and magnificence of the ancient empire. It was the art of the Counter-Reformation and of the New Monarchy which had followed the Renaissance. It was an art of pride and power ; it aimed at being at once grand and sumptuous. It often allowed itself a great exuberance of capricious ornament, yet its chief characteristic was massiveness. In its more severe form it was well suited to the dignity and pomp of *le Roi Soleil*. But by the beginning of the eighteenth century both the Counter-Reformation and the New Monarchy had lost their power to capture the imagination. The fervent conviction of the former had exhausted itself, and the latter, at least for France, had failed to fulfil the high hopes that had been set on it. Scepticism in religion had become deep and widespread ; the Enlightenment was beginning to undermine the foundations of belief. The French monarchy had stripped the nobles of political power, and bound them to itself by a leadership that was to become the hegemony of Europe, but instead of such supremacy came a succession of disasters which made the end of the reign of Louis XIV a miserable anticlimax to its glorious beginning. With the pricking of the great royal bubble of the seventeenth century, the French aristocracy was left socially privileged but politically powerless as a class, isolated from the people, disenchanted both of Church and State, an unadapted survival from an era of feudal, land-revenue economy, yet with all this steeped in a fine artistic culture and esteemed throughout Europe as the pattern of elegant living.

In such a situation of affairs the Rococo style was born. The Classical-Baroque tradition suddenly weakened ; its heavy dignity came to appear stupid and tiresome, and its grandiloquence ceased to impress. It is an age of scepticism and disillusionment, but we have still our revenues and domestic peace and order ; there is as yet no fear of a revolution—nor any hope of one. The times are out of joint, but we were not born to put them right, nor does it matter very much whether they are put right or not. We have our art ; let us then make for ourselves a new world with as little as possible of the grand manner, a world of light, airy fantasy, of delicacy and grace and gaiety and freedom of the imagination.

If Peking was more or less impervious to the attractions of European art, it was because nothing had yet happened to disturb the inner poise of the Confucian scholar or to undermine the ramparts of tradition ; the mandarins were at once Church, State and ' Society,' and their world was complete and self-sufficient. In France, with the uncertainty and restlessness of mind which followed the deflation of the Baroque pride, there was opportunity for the intrusion of the exotic. The Chinese suggestions provided the chief inspiration of the new style, a style which over a large field of the arts departed entirely from the main lines of European tradition.

The first signs of the Rococo spirit appear soon after the death of the art dictator Le Brun in 1690, but to the time of his death Louis XIV strongly disapproved of the new tendencies, and the Rococo artists had to remain, as it were, an opposition faction. Yet as Reichwein [1] points out, ' there is a certain symbolical significance in the fact that the first New Year's Day of the eighteenth century was celebrated at the French court with Chinese festivities.' With Louis XIV's death in 1715 the Rococo burst forth full-grown, and ruled French taste for four decades ; then in 1755 the archæological discoveries at Pompeii started a revival of classicism, which continually gained strength until it finally overcame the Rococo about 1780. The renewed ascendency of the European antique was no mere vagary of fashion, but reflected the passing of the mental phase which had created the Rococo style. The Rococo was the art of an interval of levity and relaxation between two eras of strenuous belief ; it corresponded to the earlier, more witty, negative and destructive period of the Enlightenment. After the middle of the century we come to a new

[1] A. Reichwein, *China and Europe : intellectual and artistic contacts in the eighteenth century*, p. 22.

seriousness and stir of reforming enthusiasm which reacts on the feeling for style, and leads by gradations from the butterfly fantasies of the Rococo to the Empire style and to David, painter of the heroisms of republican virtue.

The Rococo style spread from France to England about the middle of the eighteenth century and found a notable exponent in Chippendale. It cannot be said that the Rococo ever took root in England as it did on the Continent ; it was not of natural growth in English soil. England, however, received a current of direct Chinese influence apart from that transmitted through the French Rococo ; Chambers, who had actually visited China, developed what came to be known in Europe as the ' Chinese-English ' garden.[1] In Central Europe the ' French Grotesque,' as the Rococo was called, had a great vogue, and in architecture had greater effect than in France itself.

Chippendale in his *Director* classifies the ' tastes ' in which he worked as French (i.e. Louis XV, the Rococo), Chinese and Gothic. His ideas as to what forms were Chinese or Gothic were often quite arbitrary, and there was necessarily an overlapping of Chinese and French, since so much Chinese influence had already entered into the Rococo. But the grouping of styles—and Chippendale sometimes tried to combine all three in a single piece of furniture— shows the fundamental tendency of the movement. It was a romanticism, a departure from the classical, and it anticipated the analogous movement in literature. The conjunction of Chinese and Gothic is especially significant ; towards the end of the century the epithet ' Chinese-Gothic ' was often used. There had been as yet no real study of Gothic ; Wren had called it Saracenic and now it was put into a category with Chinese ; what was clear, however, was that all these styles offended against the canons of the great Roman-academic tradition.

---

[1] For the Chinese-Rococo influence in England cf. W. and J. Halfpenny, *New designs for Chinese Temples* (1752) ; T. Chippendale, *The Gentleman and Cabinet-Maker's Director* (1754 ; 1762), and W. Chambers, *Designs of Chinese Buildings* (1757) and *Essay on Oriental Gardening* (1772).

The age of Louis XIV had marked the limits of permissible taste with a high wall, and had declared all other art of no account. Art must be, according to Molière :

Assaisonné du sel de nos grâces antiques,
Et non du fade goût des ornements gothiques,
Ces monstres odieux des siècles ignorants,
Que de la barbarie ont produits les torrents
Quand leur cours, inondant presque toute la terre,
Fit à la politesse une mortelle guerre,
Et, de la grande Rome abattant les remparts,
Vint, avec son empire, étouffer les Beaux-Arts.

A standard of art criticism which despised the Gothic cathedrals could hardly have been expected to see beauty in the more alien tradition of China. And a sweeping condemnation of Chinese art is just what we find in the letters of Louis Le Comte,[1] the Jesuit missionary, who left France in 1685. Mendoza, writing a century before, had shown a keen appreciation of the qualities of Chinese architecture and decoration ; the taste of sixteenth-century Spain, so deeply affected by the Moresque inheritance, tended to be sympathetic towards the arts of Asia. But Le Comte, although there are many things in China that evoke his admiration, cannot bring himself to a favourable judgment in the realm of the fine arts. Of the imperial palace in Peking he says [2] : ' When you come to the Emperor's lodgings, there indeed the porticoes supported by stately pillars, the white marble steps by which you ascend to the inward halls, the gilt roofs, the carved work, varnish, gilding and painting they are adorned with, the floors made of marble or porcelain, but chiefly the great number of different pieces of architecture of which they consist, dazzle the beholder's eye, and truly look great, becoming the majesty of so great a monarch. But still, the imperfect notion the Chinese have of all kinds of arts, is betrayed by the unpardonable faults they are guilty of. The apart-

[1] *Memoirs and observations . . . made in a late Journey through the Empire of China*, tr. from Paris ed., 1699.
[2] *Op. cit.*, p. 59 (Letter to the Cardinal of Furstemberg).

ments are ill contrived, the ornaments irregular, there wants that uniformity in which consists the beauty and conveniency of our palaces. In a word, there is, as it were, deformity in the whole, which renders it very unpleasing to foreigners, and must needs offend anyone that has the least notion of true architecture. Some relations, however, cry it up as art's masterpiece ; the reason is because the missionaries who wrote them had never seen any thing beyond it, or else long use has accustomed them to it ; for it is observable that, let us dislike a thing never so, time will at length make it supportable.'

Elsewhere Le Comte writes [1] : ' Their houses are neat and decent, but not fine. They seem still more negligent as to their gardens. . . . The Chinese, who so little apply themselves to order their gardens, and give them real ornaments, do yet delight in them, and are at some cost about them ; they make grottos in them, raise pretty little artificial eminences, transport thither by pieces whole rocks, which they heap one upon another, without any further design than to imitate Nature.'

Of Chinese painting [2] : ' Besides these varnished [lacquered] cabinets and vessels of porcelain, the Chinese likewise adorn their apartments with pictures. They do not excel in this art, because they are not curious in perspective, notwithstanding they diligently apply themselves to painting.'

Against these comments of Le Comte may be set a judgment in similar vein from the other side, a criticism by Tsou I-kuei of the painting of the Jesuits : ' Our students will be able to make use of some small part of these methods, which are, however, quite lacking in a personal touch. Although these works bear witness to skill in drawing and conscientiousness in work, they cannot be regarded as true painting.' But Tsou I-kuei had more justification for his strictures than Le Comte, for none of the Jesuit missionary painters seem to have been more than mediocre, whereas

[1] Op. cit., pp. 157, 159 (letter to the Duchesse de Bouillon).
[2] Op. cit., p. 156.

Le Comte must have seen masterpieces of Chinese art during his residence in Peking.

The narrow, formula-bound attitude of Le Comte is again the normal outlook of Europeans with regard to Far Eastern art in the nineteenth century. But between the insensibility of the seventeenth and the insensibility of the nineteenth there was a period when there was a most lively appreciation and enjoyment of Chinese forms by Europeans. For the qualities of irregularity and asymmetry, which had seemed to Le Comte to be but disorder and deformity, were just the qualities of the Rococo style itself, and Le Comte would no doubt have been as pained by the art of Meissonier as he was by the imperial palace at Peking.

On this same palace another Jesuit, Fr. Attiret,[1] writing in 1747, passes a verdict quite opposite to that of Le Comte and typical of the change in taste in the time between the two judgments. According to Attiret : ' Everything in the place is great and truly beautiful, as regards both the design and the execution. . . . In the great variety and multiplicity which the Chinese give to their buildings I admire the fertility of their genius. Indeed, I am tempted to believe that in comparison with them we are poor and sterile.'

Variety and multiplicity were indeed of the intention of the Rococo decorative style. Its design at its best was complex and exuberant, while yet retaining a subtle unity and balance ; it delighted above all in free curves in the Chinese manner, in richly ornamented curved movements breaking up straight lines, or in rectilinear compositions of irregular rhythm like Chinese lattice-work. Its profusion differed from that of the Baroque in that it avoided all appearance of massiveness and rigidity ; it favoured light, springing forms, which have certain analogies to those of Flamboyant Gothic, but are akin more to plant life than to

[1] *Lettres édifiantes et curieuses*, Paris, 1843, III, p. 791. The contrast between the judgments of Le Comte and Attiret on the same palace is pointed out by Reichwein, *op. cit.*, p. 56.

flame. It sought to modify all right-angled corners with curves and to diffuse its decoration in continuous growth without stiffness or emphasis. It set store by lustre and brilliance of surface effect, fresh and bright, but not strong, colour, delicacy and elegance of draughtsmanship, caprice and playfulness of imagination. It was perfectly suited to express the spirit of French aristocratic life in the time of Louis XV ; it provided an admirable setting for fan-language and the minuet.

The architecture of major buildings was hardly at all affected by the Rococo style ; in them the Classical tradition continued to hold sway. But in minor buildings and especially in the country retreats and summer-houses,—for which this age had a great affection and to which it tended to devote more care than to edifices of more serious purpose —the Rococo had full scope for its creations, and borrowed forms from both Chinese pavilions and Turkish kiosks. Many-storied pagodas in direct imitation of the Chinese were also erected. Lightness of construction, concave roofs, fantastic finials, bells hung from the eaves, verandahs, curiously shaped windows and elaborate lattice-work are characteristic features of Rococo architecture. Owing to the complete change in taste of the succeeding period and the flimsy nature of most Rococo structures, very few have survived ; notable examples remaining are the Palace of Pillnitz on the Elbe, the Japanese Palace at Dresden, the Japanese Pavilion at Sans-Souci, and in England a pavilion in the grounds of Shugborough in Staffordshire.

It was, however, in interior decoration and furniture that the Rococo reaped its most abundant harvest. In this field Juste-Aurèle Meissonier gave the finest expression to its spirit. To quote from O. Brackett's *Thomas Chippendale* [1] : ' It cannot be denied that in essence the rococo style in its most unbalanced phase was borrowed from Chinese ornament, the studied contempt of symmetry and disregard of straight lines being essentially opposed to the

[1] O. Brackett, *Thomas Chippendale, a Study of his Life, Work and Influence* (1924).

laws of construction which are an inherited tradition in Europe. More than any other artist of the period Meissonier seems to have been responsible for this passion for brilliant irregularities which for a time captured the imagination of the French nation.'

The extremes to which Meissonier carried the style could not fail to produce a violent reaction later on, a reaction which put all Chinese art under the ban of its disapproval. One of the reasons for the rapid exhaustion of the Rococo impulse was the exoticism of its inspiration ; Meissonier and his followers worked with a method difficult and dangerous to use without a thorough grasp of its fundamental æsthetic principles. Thus the movement soon ran to ridiculous excesses, especially in Germany and Italy. At its most successful Rococo ornament can bear comparison with any European period, but no other before the nineteenth century shows also such disastrous failures. So the tide soon began to ebb and classicism returned to curb the riot of fantasy. Yet the Louis XVI style in interior decoration and furniture was no mere reversion to the Louis XIV ; a persistence of Rococo tendency is seen in its general lightness of effect and still more in its colour sense and its use of porcelain plaques.

It was in the Rococo interiors that the porcelain, lacquer and silks imported from the Far East first found themselves at home, and indeed the endeavour to give an adequate reception to these guests was one of the main factors in developing the style. Houses had ' Chinese rooms ' in which everything was Chinese, and whatever was lacking in the real thing was made up with imitations. Thus Chippendale designed a Chinese bedstead for a room with Chinese wall-papers, mirrors and chairs.[1]

' Porcelain,' says Reichwein,[2] ' was regarded as a gift from the Chinese world, and it was only natural that the Chinese manner of painting should be taken as a model.' The same author quotes some French lines which reveal

[1] Brackett, op. cit., Plate 24.
[2] Op. cit., p. 29.

vividly the feeling which was evoked by fine porcelain in the early eighteenth century [1] :

Allons à cette porcelaine,
Sa beauté m'invite, m'entraine.
Elle vient du monde nouveau,
L'on ne peut rien voir de plus beau.
Qu'elle a d'attraits, qu'elle est fine !
Elle est native de la Chine.

It was in Saxony that genuine porcelain ware was first produced in Europe, and the Saxon Rococo under Augustus the Strong was carried away by the intoxication of the material ; walls and ceilings were panelled with porcelain, and even tables and chairs were made of it. The peculiar qualities of porcelain used in abundance gave a distinctive character to Rococo interiors, and reacted strongly on the whole sense of form and colour.

For porcelain, however, there was already a powerful European ceramic tradition to compete with the Chinese influence in decoration ; it was otherwise in lacquer, where the close study of Far Eastern models for the development of the technique made orientalism of design almost absolute. The special association of lacquer with *chinoiserie* is shown by the fact that lacquered objects continued to display Chinese motives and style after the Rococo manner had been banished from furniture in general. Some European lacquer of the eighteenth century is only with some difficulty distinguished from its Chinese originals. Robert Martin, who made lacquered furniture for Madame de Pompadour, copied both Chinese and Japanese [2] designs with great technical skill, and his accomplishment led Voltaire to speak in *Les Tu et les Vous* of

les cabinets où Martin
A surpassé l'art de la Chine.

---

[1] *Embarras de la Foire de Beaucaire en vers burlesque* (1716).

[2] Japanese lacquer and other artistic wares were imported by the Dutch, who had a monopoly of European trade with Japan. Chinese and Japanese objects were often confused in the eighteenth century, but the country of the original is usually apparent in European copies.

Chinese silks and European imitations of them, and Chinese cotton stuffs wrongly called ' Indian ' were extensively used for panels, hangings and covers. Another fashion was that for Chinese painted screens and wall-papers. Wall-papers had been produced in Europe since the sixteenth century, but the imported Chinese were the first large-scale ones, and the general use and production of this form of decoration in Europe dates only from the eighteenth century. One European school devoted itself to copying Chinese designs to compete with the originals, and produced the so-called Anglo-Chinese and French-Chinese wall-papers. At first flower and bird motives had been preferred in the Chinese papers, but during the eighteenth century there was a growing demand for landscape compositions and subjects such as the cultivation of tea or the making of porcelain. Single Chinese wall-papers usually measured about twelve feet by four, and they were generally made in sets, forming series of related scenes with which a whole room could be papered.

The Chinese-English garden was yet another emanation of the Rococo. It was closely connected with the Rococo summer-houses and pavilions already mentioned ; it developed specially in England through the work of the architect Chambers, who had been to China in his youth in the service of the Swedish East India Company and later visited it a second time for study. Just after the middle of the century Chambers designed a Chinese garden for the Duke of Kent at Kew, and this became the model of the Chinese-English style, which spread at once to France and Germany and was the chief feature of the last phase of the Rococo, now losing its hold on furniture and interiors.[1] The Chinese-English garden was indeed the side of the Rococo which had most in common with the Romantic cult of the succeeding period, albeit the purists of romanticism would have none of it. It cannot be maintained that

---

[1] See W. Chambers, *Designs of Chinese Buildings* (1757) and *Essay on Oriental Gardening* (1772) ; *Le Jardin Anglo-Chinois* (1770–87) ; C. S. E. Hirschfeld, *Theorie der Gartenkunst* (Leipzig, 1779–85).

Chambers or the writers such as Père Attiret who admiringly
described the gardens of China for the European public
had penetrated far into the classic art of Chinese gardening
with its profound symbolism and æsthetic of landscape.[1]
But they appreciated its more obvious charms, and they
developed a style in Europe which was sharply separated
both from the line-and-rule, geometrical, formal gardens of
the Louis XIV era and from the park-like ' natural ' gardens
which had so far represented the instinctive reaction against
the former, especially in England.    The style formed by
Chambers was all asymmetry and irregularity with hillocks
and winding streams, yet with this wildness it had an
artificiality all its own—of fanciful bridges, grottos, miniature
pagodas, kiosks and so on.    Here, as in Rococo furniture, it
was the extravagances of an imperfectly understood, borrowed æsthetic which led to an early exhaustion of the
movement.

In painting the Rococo had Watteau as the great interpreter of its mood.    He gave expression to its sense of
relaxation and imaginative freedom, its delicacy and
intimacy of sentiment, its gaiety and its undertones of gentle
melancholy, its ultramundane aspiration, not for the other
world of religion but for a fairyland of pastoral idyll and
masquerade.    And for this Watteau's spirit found its proper
technique, which gave to his pictures their peculiar, dream-
like emotional atmosphere.

Watteau learnt many of the secrets of his art from Rubens
and the Venetians, but there were some things which this
painter of *chinoiseries* derived neither from any European
model nor merely from his own genius.    Reichwein [2]
admirably indicates the Far Eastern affinities of Watteau in
a comment on the *Embarkation for Cythera* :  ' Anyone who
has studied closely Chinese landscapes of the Sung period

---

[1] Chinese gardens were described by Du Halde (*Déscription* . . .
*de l'empire de Chine*, Paris 1735) and in Attiret's letter of 1747 (*Lettres
édifiantes et curieuses des Missions étrangères*, XXVII, Paris, 1749).    An
English translation of Du Halde appeared in 1741.

[2] *Op. cit.*, p. 48.

is immediately struck by their affinity with the landscape background which Watteau has painted here. He was unable to make it unite with the human actors in the scene. His blue distant landscape maintains a separate life of its own. The fantastic forms of his mountains he had never seen with his own eyes ; the Flemings had not shown them to him ; but they closely resemble the Chinese forms. The darker tone of the contours is Chinese, and so is the curious manner of indicating clouds. The use of monochrome colouring for background landscapes, such as Watteau loves, is one of the most prominent characteristics of Chinese landscape painting . . . the men of that age were enraptured by the atmosphere, and by the unusual, somewhat bizarre forms of the Chinese paintings. They found again in them the delicate tones which they had first met and loved in the porcelain, the brilliance which had charmed them in the silks of China.'

Eighteenth-century Europe knew the manner of Chinese landscape from lacquer and wall-papers and decorated objects generally, but both the buyers and producers of these things aimed at the superficial ornamental effect, and it was hardly through these ordinary commodities of commerce that the deeper inspiration of Chinese landscape art could be communicated. But at the time when everything Chinese was in fashion and indiscriminately admired, there must have been borne in on the flood a few specimens, probably copies of old masterpieces such as were made in China in great numbers, of the classic landscape of the Southern School, or of the more modern ' Literary Man's Painting,' styles of ink monochrome, which to an artist of genius already made familiar with Chinese forms would have unlocked the gate of a new world of vision. Such works may have reached Europe either as regular hanging pictures or as screen and fan paintings ; it is hard now to trace particular varieties of objects brought from China, as items often of personal buying rather than general import. But there is every probability, if not, as far I know, full proof that ink sketches adequate to convey the tradition of the great Chinese landscape painters reached Europe and would have been available along with other Chinese works of art for inspection by European artists. There are of course those who will in this case be satisfied with nothing less than precise, documentary evidence ; the less exacting will be content to observe that certain traits formerly peculiar to the art of China begin to appear in European painting at a time when there was a fashionable craze for everything Chinese and a vast import of Chinese art objects.

The Chinese flavour in Watteau is associated with Rococo feeling ; later in the century we meet with a Chinese affinity in a painter no less great but of a very different temper. The work of John Cozens is allied with the Romantic movement, a movement which was in many ways antagonistic to the Rococo, yet shared its opposition to Classical and ' Augustan ' conventions.[1] Romanticism gave birth to the cult of wild nature and solitude, a mysticism of pantheistic tendency such as had been prevalent in China in the great age of its landscape art, but had not hitherto emerged in Europe. John (and his father Alexander in his later work [2]) first gave adequate expression in painting to the spirit represented in poetry by Collins and Wordsworth. ' Cozens,' said Constable, ' is all poetry.' He was indeed the greatest interpreter to the eye of the new feeling for landscape which was to enlarge the æsthetic sensibility of Europe.

Of Watteau we at least know that he constantly painted *chinoiseries* and must therefore have been interested in Chinese works of art. We have no evidence for any such general interest in Cozens, but then we know hardly anything of

[1] Although Cozens does not in any way belong to the Rococo he grew up while it and its *chinoiserie* were still in vogue ; his father Alexander was still more a contemporary of it. It was the Rococo world which gave them whatever Chinese suggestions they took up. The Romantic Movement at its height had no taste for *chinoiserie*.

[2] Alexander Cozens, the ' blotmaster-general ' of Bath, did work very like that of his son in his later years ; in his freest vein Binyon says that he ' reminds one curiously of Chinese monochrome sketches.' Perhaps it was really Alexander who led the way in the new field.

his life ; even the dates of his birth and death are uncertain, though we do know that he travelled widely. A single good ink-sketch of the old Chinese tradition would have been enough to deflect a man of Cozens's temperament into new realms of experiment ; as primarily an artist of water-colour and as a true poet of landscape he could not but have been susceptible to one had he seen it. At a time when the normal method of English water-colour was based on pen-drawing, Cozens drew with the brush in Chinese ink, and his technique in this alone allies him to the Chinese. But much more, the result of his art in its spacing, its exquisite tonality, its intense feeling for mountain solitudes, its extraordinary directness and simplicity of expression, is far more akin to Chinese landscape of the great age than is any other European landscape of earlier date. Two modern critics [1] say of his work : ' To the analytic eye his drawings are baffling and bewildering in the extreme ; it is impossible to find a trace of cleverness or conscious artifice in them. They make you feel that you are looking at the work of a somnambulist or of one who has painted in a trance. They are, I believe, the most incorporeal paintings which have been produced in the Western world, for the paint and the execution seem to count for so little and the personal inspiration for so much.' This is just the sort of language that criticism uses in appraising the great landscape masters of Sung and Ashikaga. [2]

Though Cozens had hardly any success in his lifetime his subsequent influence was very great. Constable, whose own art was of a different kind, called him ' the greatest genius that ever touched landscape ' ; Turner declared that he had learnt more from Cozens' *Landscape with Hannibal on his march across the Alps, showing his army the fertile plains of Italy* (exhibited at the Royal Academy in 1776 and since lost) than from any other picture. Mr. C. E. Hughes [3]

[1] J. Finberg and E. A. Taylor, *The Development of British landscape painting in water colour* (Special Winter Number, Studio, 1917–18).

[2] Cf. Laurence Binyon, *Painting in the Far East*, pp. 152–5, 178–81.

[3] *Early English Water Colours* (1913).

writes : ' In his hands water colour took its place for the first time in English art as a perfectly complete and independent medium of expression. . . . The influence of his noble achievements was decisive on English landscape art.'

From the abundance of the Chinese models spread before the eyes of Europe in the eighteenth century we thus find that each artist chose whatever was suited to his own purposes. Meissonier chose the more eccentric and fantastic features of Chinese ornament, Watteau forms which would give a setting to his sentimental, theatrical Rococo conceptions, while Cozens, unless his genius was purely original, derived inspiration from the great tradition of monochrome landscape that descended from the age of Sung.

I have in this chapter spoken of the Rococo style rather than of the Rococo period because of the great contradictions that confront any endeavour to arrive at the European *Zeitgeist* in the eighteenth century. The distinctive Rococo manner was of the visual arts only, and the severest classicism ruled in French literature while Meissonier was violating every canon of European tradition in his visual decoration. At the end of the century in England, on the other hand, the Romantic is in the ascendent both in poetry and in painting, but architecture and furniture are in the grip of a neo-classicism, and this schism of the arts becomes yet more apparent in the nineteenth century when we see a succession of great writers, poets and painters over against the complete *débâcle* of architecture and furniture. The distinctness of the several arts as well as their interconnection has to be borne in mind when we generalize about the culture of an age.

It was, I believe, in painting, that the most ultimately important exchange of influences took place during the eighteenth century between Europe and the Far East. The Far Eastern note which we seem to detect in Watteau and Cozens has its complement in the European affinities of Okio and the Shijo school in Japan. And, whether or not we attribute all these similarities to direct influence, the fact remains that Japanese painting enlarged its borders in the direction of European conventions just about the time that European art was extending its range into provinces hitherto cultivated only by the Far Eastern tradition.

# CHAPTER X

## *The Jesuits in Peking*

THE relations of the Catholic Church with China from the sixteenth to the eighteenth centuries [1] have a history quite separate from that of the political and commercial relations of European states. In their non-political and non-commercial capacity the Catholic missionaries succeeded not only in penetrating into the interior of China but also in establishing themselves permanently at the Court of Peking itself, thus becoming the main channel for news and information in both directions between China and the outside world. These relations of religious propaganda were entirely one-sided ; no Chinese missionaries of any kind went to Europe to balance the activity of the Catholic Church for the conversion of China. The former proselytizing ardour of Buddhism had exhausted itself, and the intense conviction of the Confucian scholars that they alone were enlightened did not carry with it any impulse to preach wisdom to outer barbarians. As it turned out, however, China's passivity in this sphere was more influential than Europe's propaganda, for the intellectual stress and disintegration of traditional beliefs in eighteenth-century Europe caused certain Chinese ideas made known by the Catholic missionaries to have a greater effect on Europe than did the missionaries' religion on China.

Christian missions in China in the period between the arrival of the Portuguese and the year 1800 were exclusively Catholic. The Nestorian communities seem by the beginning of the sixteenth century to have completely disappeared

[1] The standard work is K. S. Latourette, *A History of Christian Missions in China* (London, 1929).

both from China itself and from Central Asia, nor was there any further propaganda from the Nestorian centres in Western Asia. The small Catholic nuclei formed in China under the Mongols had also disappeared, so that there was no Christianity at all left in China when Xavier tried to enter in 1552. The Protestant missions, on the other hand, did not begin until the nineteenth century, the first Protestant missionary to reside in China being Robert Morrison who arrived in 1807. The Russian Orthodox Church was allowed in the eighteenth century to have priests in Peking to minister to Russian traders and the descendants of a small force of Russian prisoners who had been incorporated in the Manchu army after the Albazin war ; but they did no mission work among the Chinese. The field was thus left to the Catholics.

The Portuguese-Spanish overseas expansion in the six-teenth century was very closely allied with the propaganda of Catholic Christianity. It had grown out of a holy war against Moorish Islam, and by the agreements which gave Papal recognition of monopolies in newly discovered lands the Catholic kingdoms were bound to promote the con-version of the natives. The wars of Albuquerque had all the character of crusades, and after the capture of Malacca a Portuguese embassy was sent to Pope Leo X with rich presents from the spoils of the East and an elephant which knelt three times before His Holiness. Later, when Legazpi sailed from Mexico to the Luzon Islands political annexation and religious conversion were both included in his com-mission, and in the first approach of the Spanish to China the endeavour to secure permission for religious propaganda was united with the aim of opening up commercial and political relations. In Japan during the period of decen-tralization the missionaries were able to prevent Portuguese merchants from visiting any principality which would not tolerate the preaching of Christianity, thus using commercial boycott as a wedge to break open locked doors. Well supported by the laity of the conquering Spanish and Portuguese, the Church had great hopes of compensating

for the Reformation in Europe by winning Asia and the
Americas for the Faith ; the Counter-Reformation was
not only to drive back Protestant heresy but also to wage
war against Islam and to storm the hitherto untouched
strongholds of paganism.

China as the greatest non-Christian and non-Islamic
empire, a country known to contain an enormous population,
was naturally a magnet for the proselytizing ambition of
the Counter-Reformation. But to obtain an opening was
no easy matter. The use of lay economic discrimination,
which proved so effective with Japanese feudal states, was
out of the question in China, which was a single, vast unit.
All attempts to open up diplomatic intercourse, through
which recognition might be obtained for missions, failed,
and while the converts in Japan grew to numbers of five
figures China remained inaccessible. Beyond the normal
difficulties confronting missionary enterprise in a strange
country there were in China two most formidable obstacles :
one the laws forbidding foreigners to enter the country
without special licence, and the other the *Law against
Heresies*.

The great difficulty of getting into China at all was a
fatal bar to any unlicensed and clandestine propaganda.
Even with the utmost apostolic fervour the missionaries
had to deal with a situation quite different from that which
had faced primitive Christianity in the Roman empire.
The religion then had been propagated from within the
empire ; it had had no frontiers to cross. The success of
Christianity in the Roman world as compared with its
failure in Persia must be largely attributed to its original
relation to political frontiers. In China in the sixteenth
century it must first find a way through the frontier wall
before it could begin to build up a Christian community.
Divergence of physical type as well as ignorance of language and customs made it impossible for European missionaries to enter China in disguise. Without special
permission from the Government there was nothing to be
gained by reckless attempts at entry. Such attempts were

made, however, even in defiance of secular authority in the Catholic dominions. A Franciscan, Pedro de Alfaro, in 1579, disobeying the Governor of the Philippines who still hoped that normal diplomatic relations might be opened up with China, sailed from Manila to Canton in a small boat with three other Franciscans, four Spanish soldiers, four natives of the Philippines, and one Chinese Christian from the Philippines to act as interpreter. Having eluded the Kwangtung coast defence flotilla and entered the port of Canton, they were brought before a magistrate, to whom Alfaro wished to state their religious mission, but the more cautious interpreter explained that they had not intended to come to China, but had been shipwrecked. They were allowed to remain for a while in Canton, and as they were destitute, were assisted from public funds, but they were not allowed to preach ; after a time they were sent to Foochow to be questioned by the Viceroy, and were courteously received, but afterwards they were ordered to leave the country and given passports for Macao or Manila. Despite this failure another party of Franciscans tried a similar descent on China in 1581, and were likewise arrested and deported.

Such fiascos showed clearly enough that if Christianity were to make headway in China it must be through obtaining some kind of official licence. But to gain permission for the propagation of a new heresy in a land already too much given over to religious novelties for the liking of its rulers needed more than the asking. The *Law against Heresies*, under which Christianity automatically came, had been enacted in 1511 ; it was to remain in the civil code throughout our period. It was a law which affirmed the right of the state to persecute at its discretion any non-Confucian form of belief ; actually it was directed against certain secret sects regarded as politically dangerous, notably the White Lotus (*Pai-lien*), an offshoot of Sukhavati Buddhism which had a widespread organization among the masses and had been implicated in sedition. But apart from movements which showed a definite anti-governmental tendency, Confucian orthodoxy was now much narrower, more exclusive and more strongly entrenched than it had ever been before.

The old practice of China in matters of religion had been very similar to that of pagan Rome. Except for certain reigns when Buddhism and Taoism had received zealous patronage, Confucianism (*Ju Chiao* or ' Scholars' Doctrine ') had been the religion of the state (or states), but it had not made itself the one and only religion of society. Indeed, except for certain ceremonies, its profession could have little meaning outside the ranks of the scholar class, for it was essentially the religion of an intellectual élite. For the unlearned vulgar it allowed Buddhism, Taoism and other forms of religion suited to their under-standing, and even Confucian scholars might dabble in such beliefs provided always that there was nothing in them judged by State authority to be either politically dangerous or morally pernicious. Thus was possible for many eclectic-ally-minded Chinese the union of the *San Chiao* or ' Three Doctrines ' (Confucianism, Taoism and Buddhism), a syn-cretism which, along with the flourishing of the two latter religions separately from the Confucianism of the state, has led some admirers of China too hastily to conclude that the idea of religious persecution has always been a stranger to the Chinese. The fact is, however, not that there has been thoroughgoing toleration, as modern liberal-ism understands it, but that there has been a middle category of what may be called licensed heresy between Confucian orthodoxy and proscribed heresy. No such middle category was recognized in Christian Europe ; men were either within the Church or outside it, and as the Church existed for the eternal salvation of souls, to be outside it was dam-nation. Churchmanship, moreover, involved acceptance of a clear-cut system of theological dogma. Confucianism, on the other hand, was primarily a theory of the moral and political order of society, and before about A.D. 1100 it had only the slightest metaphysical teaching. The Confucian, therefore, was disposed to tolerate whatever did not threaten the system of society according to Confucian principles ; from this point of view Taoism and Buddhism with their rituals, abstruse metaphysical notions, and mystical experiences were at worst a harmless diversion, while their sound moral teachings were good for ' the small people.' But wherever such licensed heresy impinged adversely on the Confucian ethical-political order it became proscribed heresy, and was liable to ruthless persecution.

In the twelfth century Confucianism had been expanded by a kind of scholasticism so as to become a more complete and systematic doctrine than it had been hitherto, and this change, to which was added the strong nationalist feeling evoked by the foreign innovations under the Mongols, led to a marked increase of Confucian intolerance. Under the Ming Confucianism became an all-powerful orthodoxy keenly aware of the dangers of false doctrine to society. The interpretation of the classics was held to have been fixed beyond dispute, and the line between truth and error was sharply drawn ; Buddhism and Taoism remained, but their organizations were subject to close official supervision and interference, while the White Lotus was violently persecuted. The outlook for the propagation of a new and uncompromisingly dogmatic religion by foreigners was not promising.

Whatever intolerance, however, confronted Catholicism in China, it was hardly reasonable for Catholics to complain. The very fact that they did ultimately succeed in obtaining a limited toleration in the seventeenth century is proof that China was more liberal than Catholic Europe at that time in the matter of religion ; it is certain that no non-Christian missions would then have been admitted to Spain or Italy or any part of Europe. While the Catholic missionaries in the Far East were seeking toleration for their propaganda in China Alva was striving to drown in blood the Protestantism of the Netherlands, and the *auto-da-fé* was consuming the victims whom the Holy Office ' relaxed ' to the secular arm. When in 1692 the French Jesuits obtained from the Emperor K'ang Hsi an edict granting liberty of Christian worship, the Huguenots had only a few years previously been driven from France after the infamous persecution of the *Dragonnades*. Until far into the nineteenth century the Catholic Church did not cease to proclaim that it was the duty of Catholic secular authorities to extirpate heresy within their borders. On what principle therefore her missionaries claimed toleration for themselves is not clear, but it seems from their writings that they regarded every attempt to obstruct their proselytism as a malicious outrage.

It may be noted in passing that, whereas Catholicism held to a position of greater intolerance than Confucianism, Protestant states, after abandoning legal processes for heresy, took up an attitude very similar to the Chinese. In England the writ *de haeretico comburendo* was not abolished until 1677 (the last burnings under it were in 1612) ; under the law of blasphemy which remained [1] a Chief Justice held (*Tayler's Case*, 1675) that ' the allegation that religion is a cheat tends to the dissolution of all government, and such kind of wicked and blasphemous words are not only an offence against God and religion but a crime against the law, State and Government. . . . Christian religion is part of the law itself.' In *Woolston's Case* (1728) the Common Law doctrine was further expounded : ' We do not,' said Lord Raymond, ' meddle with any difference of opinion, we interfere only where the very root of Christianity is itself struck at.' Finally in *R. v. Boulter* in 1908 Justice Phillimore expressed the doctrine in a form better suited to the twentieth century : ' A man,' he declared, ' is free to speak and to teach what he pleases as to religious matters, though not as to morals '—a not insignificant exception for any religion with its own ethical teaching ! These English legal decisions reveal a line of thought closely resembling the Chinese state attitude.

To return from this digression on the subject of comparative intolerance, we find that at the end of the sixteenth century Catholic missionaries had not yet succeeded in

[1] See H. L. L. Bellot, art. *Blasphemy* in *Encyclopædia Britannica* (14th ed.).

preaching the Gospel in China. There had been several approaches, however, in addition to the rash attempts of the Franciscans already mentioned. The first had been made by the great St. Francis Xavier himself. Xavier had gone to Japan in 1549, but he found there that the chief method employed in argument against his preaching was reference to Chinese classical authority, and he therefore came to the conclusion that Christianity must attack China, which converted, Japan would follow. He complains that the absence of Chinese authority for the existence of a personal Creator was a great stumbling-block to his Japanese hearers : ' If there were really one First Cause of all things, then surely the Chinese would not have been ignorant of it. For the Japanese defer to the Chinese as being first in wisdom and knowledge in all things, whether pertaining to religion or to civil administration.' So on his return to Goa in 1551 Xavier formed a plan of opening up China to mission work. ' If,' he wrote in a letter, ' the Chinese adopt the Christian religion, the Japanese will abandon the religions they have received from China.' Permission to preach the Gospel was to be sought along with a trade agreement by a new Portuguese embassy, which was sent out by the Viceroy of Goa under Xavier's friend, Diego de Pereira. But by one of the anarchic acts characteristic of Portuguese overseas governors in the sixteenth century Pereira was stopped at Malacca by the commandant, Alvaro de Ataide, and Xavier had to go on alone to the little island of Shang-ch'üan south of Canton, at that time the only place in China where the Portuguese had a trading settlement, for Macao had not yet been granted them. From Shang-ch'üan he found it impossible to cross over to the mainland, and he fell ill and died on the island (1552).

After several further attempts to enter China had been baffled the Jesuit Visitor of the Indies, Alessandro Valignani, determined to prepare for a more serious assault by obtaining for selected members of the Order a thorough training in the Chinese language at Macao, where the Portuguese had their settlement from 1557. Here on the very edge of China new tactics were devised, but for a long time no opening showed itself, and according to a mission historian ' Father Valignani, looking one day out of a window of the College of Macao towards the continent [1] . . . called out with a loud voice and the most intimate affection of his heart, speaking to China, " O Rock, Rock, when wilt thou open, Rock ? " '

It was Matteo Ricci who was to find a way. He had studied mathematics and astronomy in Rome and was an able linguist. He came to Macao in 1582 and in the following year he and another Jesuit, Ruggerius, obtained permission to reside at Chao-ch'ing near Canton ; there they wore the garb of Buddhist monks and devoted their time, not to preaching, but to winning the respect and friendly interest of Chinese scholars and officials by their scientific and mathematical attainments, only introducing Christian propaganda after they had made their way into favour. The new tactics were at once successful. There were indeed so many difficulties yet to be overcome that the missionaries still clung to the idea of an embassy to China from some Catholic kingdom to obtain a treaty of toleration for missions, and Ruggerius returned to Europe in 1588 for the purpose of arranging one—but he met with no success and died at Salerno in 1607, while the progress of Ricci soon rendered such political support superfluous. [2] In 1594 he exchanged his Buddhist monk's garb for the dress of a scholar, which he found improved his status ; he made friends with several high officials, and at last in 1601 he was fully accepted and allowed to reside and preach in Peking. He was also given a house and a stipend from the imperial treasury. With his ' curly beard, blue

[1] Macao is situated on a peninsula.

[2] Ricci at one time seems to have toyed with the idea of a Spanish conquest of China, or at least that was the construction which Geronimo Roman put on his letter of 1584 setting forth the military weakness of China. Later Ricci perceived that the best hope for the missions lay in a complete detachment from European State power and diplomacy.

eyes and voice like a great bell,' [1] with his remarkable
learning in the Chinese classics, with his scientific attainments and mechanical ingenuity, and above all with his
perfect tact and urbanity Ricci made a profound impression
in the highest circles of the capital.   His converts included
two members of the Hanlin Academy and an imperial
prince. [2]

Ricci combined great zeal with an unerring sense of
the practicable.   He saw on just what terms it was possible
to propagate Christianity in China.   He saw that in a
vast non-Christian empire, where the Faith could neither
be supported by force of arms nor guaranteed by treaties,
its spread depended on two conditions, first that the missionaries should in some secular way make themselves useful
to the Chinese Government, and second that they should
abstain as far as possible from attacking those ceremonies in
honour of Confucius and of ancestors which the Confucians
regarded as essential to the order of State and Family.

For the fulfilment of the first condition Ricci himself
pointed the way, and it was followed by his successors.
A high standard of secular education and accomplishment
more than anything else distinguished the Jesuits from the
older Catholic orders ;  within the limits that their religion
imposed they were true children of the Renaissance.   It
was as scholars and courtiers and men of the world that
they made their way, in the Far East as in the kingdoms
of Europe.   To the scholar mandarins, whose esteem
Europeans as traders could never gain, the Jesuits represented not unworthily the intellect of Europe, and compelled their hosts to recognize the existence of an admirable,
if not equal, civilization outside their own.   Merely as
highly educated men, whose learning was established by
their proficiency in Chinese literature as well as by their
own specialities, the leading Jesuits made themselves accept-
able to a society of *literati* accustomed to honour high
scholarship and still retaining a degree of intellectual

[1] Quoted from a Chinese record by Latourette, *op. cit.*, p. 98.
[2] *Op. cit.*, p. 96.

curiosity. Yet this regard would hardly have enabled the Jesuits to keep their hold in spite of hostile intrigues and political changes, had they not been able to turn their talents to more practical uses.

For the determination of the calendar, which was of superlative importance for the ceremonial side of Chinese government and was a province of the Board of Astronomy, the Chinese already employed foreign technical experts. The Islamic world still possessed a prestige in astronomy and mathematics derived from the Hellenistic-Arab science which had flourished in Baghdad and Samarkand in the early Middle Age,[1] and Moslem mathematicians were in charge of the calendar. Ricci, seeing the great importance attached to their profession, persuaded the Society of Jesus to send out an expert astronomer, Fr. Sabbatino de Ursis, who arrived in Peking in 1606. In 1611, after the Moslem experts had made a serious error in forecasting an eclipse, the reform of the calendar was entrusted to the Jesuits by an imperial decree. Henceforth the calendar became the key position for the Jesuit strategy in China. From 1616 to 1629 the Christians from various causes were out of favour, and the control of the calendar was taken away from them, but from 1629 to 1664 it was restored to them, and managed with great ability by the astronomers Terrentius and Schall. The latter was raised by Shun Chih, the first Manchu emperor, to be Vice-President of the Board of Astronomy ; a Jesuit thus became a high official of the Chinese bureaucracy. From 1664 to 1669 the Jesuits were again thrown out by a court cabal, but in 1669 the Emperor K'ang Hsi applied the appropriate Chinese test of competitive examination to Verbiest, Schall's successor as Jesuit astronomical specialist, and to the Moslem champion ; Verbiest emerged victorious, and the Bureau of Astronomy remained a Christian stronghold until 1838.

---

[1] The Chinese themselves did some work of distinction in mathematics in the twelfth and thirteenth centuries. See D. E. Smith, *History of Mathematics*, vol. I (Boston, Mass., 1923).

In several other ways the Jesuits were able to render secular services to the court and government of China. One was in medicine ; several of the Jesuits were very competent physicians and made use of recent discoveries in European medical science. Another sphere of Jesuit activity was in diplomacy. As we have seen, the one European country with which the Chinese empire had been unable to avoid diplomatic relations was Russia ; but dealings with Russia were extremely difficult owing to the lack of interpreters for negotiation. By their ability to draft proposals and agreements in Latin the Jesuits performed the function of diplomatic middlemen in the settlements between China and Russia after the war on the Amur. Last but not least, the Jesuits served their adopted country as gun-founders, and that with admirable impartiality as between parties, for they cast cannon for the Ming against the Manchu before 1644, and afterwards for the new dynasty against the Ming partisans in South China. It may seem a little strange that the evangelists of Christianity should be thus prominent in the making of weapons, but it must be remembered that the missionaries of the seventeenth century had not, like those of the nineteenth, the guns of European armed forces to secure for them toleration in China, and enable them to give all their time to works of peace.

Whatever licence the Jesuits obtained to preach their religion in China was a tribute to their secular accomplishments and a reward for their secular services. This was made clear by the edict of K'ang Hsi in 1692, which gave to the Christian missionaries the same privileges that were enjoyed by Tibetan lamas. The edict declared that the new religion had shown no tendency towards sedition, and that its priests had rendered valuable services to the State in revising the calendar, in conducting diplomacy and in casting cannon.

The Jesuits might rely on their reputation for usefulness to keep open that door into China which Ricci had opened and even to obtain for them permission to preach. But if Christianity was to make any real headway in China, a further adaptation to circumstances was necessary, and one which involved more delicate points of conscience than casting cannon. Unless the new religion were to invite persecution, it must make some accommodation with that reverence for Confucius and for ancestors which was considered by the mandarins as essential to the moral and political order of Chinese society—or as an English Common Law judge would have put it, ' part of the law itself.' If they refrained from attacking the ceremonies which belonged to this side of Confucianism, the missionaries might be free to propagate their teachings on the nature of God, on the destiny of the soul and on the sacraments of the Church, and Christianity could take its place in China on the same terms as Taoism and Buddhism. Ricci believed that such an accommodation could be made without any derogation to the Holy Catholic Faith. He held that the honours paid to Confucius and ancestors had only a civil significance and were not acts of religious worship, so that a Chinese Christian could participate in them without disloyalty to his religion.

On these and on several minor points Ricci initiated a policy of concession to Confucian customs and beliefs. He himself was so thoroughly steeped in Chinese literature and thought that in many ways he acquired an almost Chinese outlook difficult for his European co-religionists to understand. In all his dealings with the Chinese *literati* he showed the same subtlety of mind and exquisite tact. In drawing a map of the world he was careful to put China in the middle. He was a master of the arts of conciliation, and if anyone could have established the Church in China at that time, it was Ricci. But there was no second Ricci. The policy of concessions which he adopted was maintained more or less by the Jesuits for nearly a century after his death, but even the Jesuits were divided among themselves as to its wisdom, and the tendency was to make the Church more intransigent. By the Franciscans and Dominicans the Ricci policy was bitterly opposed. These orders owed their admission to the Chinese mission field entirely to the pioneering of the Jesuits, and were far inferior to the latter in their knowledge of Chinese language and literature, yet they were intensely jealous of their benefactors and lost no opportunity of speaking against them at the Vatican. They accused the Jesuits of conforming to pagan practices, and their agitation led at length to the great rites controversy which ruined whatever chance there was of a general spread of Christianity in China.

The crisis of the rites controversy did not come until 1706, but there were anticipations of it from Ricci's death in 1610, for Longobardi, his successor at the head of the China mission, was opposed to many of the practices which he had approved. The more uncompromising note thus sounded by the new religion was no doubt one of the causes of the two outbursts of persecution which it had to endure in the course of the seventeenth century, persecutions which in any case showed the insecurity of the Church in China and the need for walking warily. The missionaries had always enemies—ultra-orthodox Confucians who hated all heresies and especially foreign ones, Chinese polymaths who were jealous of the intellectual distinction of the Jesuits, and the Moslem mathematicians who had been turned off the Board of Astronomy to make way for the Christians. So when in the second decade of the seventeenth century a fresh rebellion fomented by the White Lotus sect caused a temporary panic in Peking, the Christians were accused of holding secret doctrines similar to those of the White Lotus, and an edict suppressing Christianity was obtained. Some of the missionaries were arrested and deported ; others went into hiding with Chinese friends until the ban was raised a few years later. In 1664 the Regency which governed during the minority of K'ang Hsi again proscribed Christianity and sought to expel the missionaries ; this persecution was terminated by K'ang Hsi himself, when in 1669 he dismissed the regents and began his own rule. It is to be observed that in neither of these persecutions were any missionaries put to death, though some died from the rigours of imprisonment.[1]

It is hardly possible to determine accurately the numbers of the Christian community in China in the seventeenth century, but it certainly reached six figures. Accounts vary widely in their estimates ; one for 1664, just before the second period of persecution, gives 110,000, another 255,000. Probably the lower figure is nearer the mark. It was perhaps a quarter of a million at the end of the century. As long as the Jesuits were in favour at court, missions flourished in the provinces, and the Church grew rapidly, especially during the time of civil wars between 1640 and 1660. By K'ang Hsi's edict of 1692 the future seemed assured. But only fourteen years later the crisis of the rites controversy involved the Church in a setback from which it never recovered.

Up to 1704 the conflict between the advocates and opponents of the policy of concession, which had become in fact one between the Jesuit and Dominican orders, had not called forth any really definite pronouncement by the Papacy, though tentative decrees on the matter had been issued in 1645 and 1669. But the Dominicans continued to press their case, while the majority of the Chinese converts had been given to understand that the ceremonies under dispute were not incompatible with Christianity. Then in 1693 Maigrot of the French *Missions Etrangerès*, as Vicar Apostolic in Fukien, made a sweeping condemnation of all compromises with Confucianism, and removed two Jesuits for ignoring his orders. The issue thus brought to a head was referred to Rome, and in 1704 Pope Clement XI decided against the practices which had been allowed by the Jesuits. A certain Maillard de Tournon was sent out as Papal Legate to secure obedience to the decree among the missionaries and their converts, and to inform

[1] The Dominican Capillas was martyred in Fukien in 1648. But this was a persecution by provincial authorities in time of civil war. The proximity of Fukien to the Philippines made the Spanish missions in that province specially suspect.

the Emperor of the Papal decision.   On arriving in Peking
in December, 1705, Tournon met with bitter hostility from
the Jesuits.   He went on to Jehol to have an audience
with the Emperor, accompanied by the brusque and fanatical
Maigrot.   The discussion turned largely on the meaning
of certain Chinese words ;   whether *t'ien* could be taken
to mean God, and whether the epithet *shêng* as applied to
Confucius meant ' holy.'   The Jesuits had appealed to
K'ang Hsi for a ruling as to the significance of these and
other terms in Chinese philosophy, and his decision had
been favourable to their interpretation.   But Maigrot flatly
contradicted the Emperor as to the meanings, and the
latter showed the indignation to be expected from an
absolute monarch not allowed to know his own language.
He dismissed the Legate, and banished Maigrot from the
country, then issued an edict ordering all missionaries either
to admit the practices allowed by Ricci or to leave China.
The Legate at Nanking issued a counter-edict forbidding
the said practices under pain of interdict and excommunica-
tion.   Most of the missionaries provisionally obeyed the
Emperor, and appealed to Rome for some modification of
the Papal decision ;   the Legate meanwhile was escorted
by the Chinese to Macao, where the Bishop refused to
recognize his authority, and kept him virtually a prisoner
in the Portuguese settlement until his death there in 1710.

The Pope rejected the appeal of the Jesuits, and finding
that his former decree was not being obeyed in China,
issued the bull *Ex illa die* in 1715, and sent a new Legate
to China to see that it was proclaimed and to explain its
purport to the Emperor.   This Legate, Mezzabarba, was
more tactful than Tournon had been, but K'ang Hsi was
extremely displeased by the wording of the bull.   The
Jesuits were now compelled to submit to the decision of
Rome, though they continued to find ways of evading it
until such points as still remained doubtful were finally
settled by the bull *Ex quo singulari* of 1742.   Rome had set
her face decisively against any compromise with Chinese
customs.

The conflict over the rites imposed a fatal check on the growth of the Church in China. Christianity was henceforth committed to an assault on fundamental institutions of Chinese society. It was now much harder to make converts, and the hostility to the new religion among the *literati* was greatly increased. The wrangling and intrigue which had marked the course of the controversy had greatly lowered the dignity of the Church in the eyes of non-Christians. Most important of all, the controversy had brought into prominence the Papal supremacy, a feature which had been kept discreetly in the background by the Jesuits. K'ang Hsi's eyes were opened to the fact that at least 100,000 of his subjects were now taking orders from abroad. The conflict between the Papal Legate and the Emperor of China was only a new version of the oft-repeated struggle between the international authority of Rome and a sovereign state. But China was not a Christian country at all, and K'ang Hsi very reasonably remarked that he did not understand why the Pope should expect to have his bulls enforced in China when he had been unable to impose the bull *Unigenitus* on Catholic France.

The rites controversy, however, did not lead to any systematic endeavour to eliminate the Church from China. The Government made up its mind that Christianity must not be allowed to spread further ; on the other hand the Chinese Christians were not yet sufficiently numerous to be a real menace, while the Jesuits were much too useful to be driven away. K'ang Hsi had indeed some new work for them to do in a projected mapping of the empire. The result of this state of affairs was that a curious policy of semi-persecution was pursued by the Chinese Government during the eighteenth century. A series of formidable edicts against Christianity were issued, and there were spectacular arrests and deportations of missionaries, and occasional outbursts of real persecution with martyrdoms in the provinces, especially in Fukien where the Spanish Dominican and Franciscan missions were very unpopular with the provincial authorities. But all the time the

Catholics were firmly established in Peking with some of their priests employed at Court and three or four churches open in the city. The edicts were indeed intended more as deterrents against fresh adhesions to the Church than as measures for its destruction, and there was no serious effort to extirpate Christianity as it had been extirpated in Japan in the previous century. Nevertheless the capricious, harassing tactics of the officialdom made it virtually impossible for the Church to increase, and as the years passed its numbers began to fall off. To official disfavour in China were added unfortunate events in Europe. The Society of Jesus was dissolved by the Papacy in 1773, and though its work was carried on by the Lazarists, the Jesuit organization could not be replaced. Then in 1789 and the years following the turmoil in France, and in Europe generally, depleted the finances and personnel of the missions. Even so, Macartney was told by Fr. Raux in 1798 that there were then 5,000 Christians in Peking and about 150,000 in all China. But this figure, even if correct, was almost certainly short of the total in about 1700, in spite of the natural increase of Christian families.[1]

The net result of Catholic missions at the end of the eighteenth century was by no means insignificant, but it was disappointing in comparison to the hopes that had at one time been entertained. There was a Christian community scattered throughout China and strong enough to hold its own against mandarin disapproval and spasmodic persecution. But it numbered only a minute fraction of the total population of China, and its membership was almost entirely among the poor. On the scholar class and on Chinese culture as a whole the missions had made hardly any impression. There had been a few converts in high places, but none of any great distinction. The secular, scientific learning of the Jesuits had aroused considerable interest in court circles without leading to any appreciable

[1] The population of China appears to have doubled in the eighteenth century. But the statistical records must be taken with great reserve.

change in Chinese habits of thought. The contact probably stimulated a heterodox school which applied new critical methods to the study of the Confucian classics during the eighteenth century.[1] But this school had to remain in the wilderness, and dwindled away, while the old orthodox tradition continued all-powerful in the official world. Elements of European mathematics were adopted, but no original work was now done in this field [2]; nor was there any awakening in the natural sciences. There was no movement towards revision of ethical and political ideas. There was indeed far less liveliness of intellectual life than there had been in the T'ang and Sung periods. In so far as China reacted at all to the Catholic missionary penetration it was on the whole towards a greater conservatism and rigidity of thought and custom. China in the nineteenth century faced a changing world with a united front of inherited conviction and a mental outlook unmodified since the time of Mendoza, or rather since the twelfth century. It was not until the 'eighties and 'nineties of the nineteenth that a new ferment of ideas began to make itself felt among the educated.

In comparing Chinese with European thought during the seventeenth and eighteenth centuries it is not sufficient merely to contrast the immobility and imperviousness of the one with the immense vigour and fertility of the other ; account must also be taken of the extraordinary social and political success of Chinese culture under the conditions it had so far had to meet. It would of course be absurd to regard the intellectual activity of Europe in this period as a mere product of social disharmonies, but they were a powerful stimulating factor. Success in social organization, no less than intellectual incompetence, ensures the ascend-

[1] See Latourette, *op. cit.*, p. 196. Of modern Chinese scholars Liang Ch'i-ch'ao credits the missions with an influence on this school ; Hu Shih denies it.

[2] In mathematics, as in painting, the Japanese were more ready to experiment with ideas borrowed from Europe. An original method of the differential calculus was worked out in Japan from hints coming through the Dutch. See D. E. Smith, *History of Mathematics*, vol. I.

ency of a pedantic orthodoxy in thought ; breakdowns of
the social mechanism with a people of advanced intellectual
technique inevitably discredit orthodoxy and lead to ques-
tioning of fundamental beliefs. In China the traditional
system was so successful in practice that there was little
disposition to tamper with its theoretical presuppositions.
Let us consider briefly what it had achieved. Since the
thirteenth century, save for two brief intervals of civil
war, China had been politically unified. Peking was the
capital of an empire that extended from the Himalayas
to the Sea of Okhotsk. The empire from 1644 had been
Manchu and not native Chinese, but the Manchus had
been assimilated to such a degree that the distinction was
of slight significance. The Manchus had identified themselves with China far more than had the Mongols, and
had not introduced colonies of unassimilable aliens as their
auxiliaries. The population of China according to census
returns was in 1762 over 200 million, and though there
must be a certain amount of doubt about such figures, the
available evidence indicates that the estimate was not far
out. The leading European states could show no comparable masses of population ; statistics at about the same
date give less than 18 million for France and under 7 million
for England and Wales. And the huge population of China
was not only under one sovereignty, but also under a
uniform system of law. Still more significant, it lived by
a social order which occasioned the minimum of class
conflict. Chinese society admitted only two great classes :
below, the producers—peasants and artisans, and above,
the rulers—a bureaucracy of salaried officials recruited by
public competitive examination in the Confucian classics
and in literary composition based thereon.

In such a society neither landed property nor commercial
capital was able to gain power and privilege. At the apex
of the pyramid there was dynastic royalty, but outside the
imperial house there was no order of hereditary nobility.
The tendencies towards caste and feudalism inherent in a
land-revenue society were held in check by the open

examination system, reinforced by the rule that no official might hold a post in his native province. The Manchus formed a military caste but their organization was not feudal ; they were quartered in the cities as paid garrisons, and their generals were professional soldiers for whom an appropriate form of examination was introduced in imitation of the civilian system. There was no class of great landed proprietors ; law and custom were adverse to the formation of large estates, and there were no fiscal immunities.

The mercantile interest had neither politically powerful organizations nor a tradition of independence. Trade might be a road to great wealth, but it had neither social dignity nor a voice in public policy. As we have seen in our survey of the foreign trade at Canton, the merchant was at the mercy of the bureaucracy. For the old Chinese theory he was merely an agent in distribution, and as such, of less consequence than the producer.

In the state religion there was no dualism of State and Church, no system whereby a creed with its own organized clergy distinct from the state was yet accepted as orthodox by the state and given a share in state power. The Confucian scholar-officials were at once both Church and State. The scholar class was not indeed quite identical with the bureaucracy, for a successful examinee might live in retirement and devote himself to study without holding public office. But Confucianism had no organization or priesthood separate from the civil administration ; it was not so much the state religion as the state itself. The Buddhist and Taoist priesthoods were merely tolerated, and had no voice in affairs of state.

Thus we have a society which in a manner without parallel identified social privilege, state service and intellectual cultivation, a society which had no dualism of Church and State and no privileged or politically powerful class outside the bureaucracy. This society possessed great internal unity and stability. It is not by any means suggested that it enjoyed a Utopia. The system was one of autocracy and subordination ; insane pedantry and incompetence, callous cruelty and rapacity, and above all, venality, too often marked the ways of the bureaucracy. In an intensively cultivated land of primitive transport and exchange a large part of the population lived ever on the edge of starvation, and there was always a strong undercurrent of discontent finding expression in the growth of half-religious, half-political secret societies, in brigandage and in occasional savage revolts of overtaxed peasantry. Yet it is true to say that there was no great class struggle in Chinese society, because there was no great privilege of property ; the officialdom was the state itself, which could not be abolished, but only renovated at intervals by putting a new and capable dynasty on the throne in place of an old and effete one.

Soon this Confucian system was to be confronted with problems with which it was quite unfitted to cope. On the stage of the nineteenth century it would provide a forlorn and pitiable spectacle ; in a little while it would have endured too long, and would be an object of contempt to the rest of the world and to a new generation of Chinese. But in the days of K'ang Hsi and Ch'ien Lung it as yet showed no signs of a breakdown ; it commanded universal acceptance in theory, and its prestige was such as to make the Chinese mind virtually impervious to the influence of European thought. While in contemporary France there grew up a school which saw in this same system the model of political perfection, and proposed in Europe ' inoculer l'ésprit chinois.'

In the eighteenth century the literary public in France was quite familiar with the outlines of the Chinese social system ; it was even said that China had been made better known in France than were some parts of Europe itself.[1] The missions were the principal channel of information. The missionaries, a large proportion of whom were French from the last quarter of the seventeenth century, wrote extensively on China, partly to arouse interest and gain

[1] *Relation du banissement des Jésuites de la Chine*, 1769.

support for their work, partly as a service to science and scholarship. Men often of great intellectual power and highly educated, long resident in China and learned in Chinese literature, many of them employed at the Chinese Court, the missionaries, and especially the Jesuits, acquired a knowledge of China and its culture which would not have been possible to any mere traveller or trader. All this knowledge they communicated to the European public in books which were widely read. And to their own accounts of things Chinese they added translations from Chinese literature. In 1662 appeared *Sapientia Sinica*, a translation of the *Ta-hsüeh*, in 1673 *Chum-yum, Sinarum scientia politico-moralis*, a rendering of the *Chung-yung*. Other translations followed, and the European reader was able to obtain some idea of Chinese thought at first-hand.

The Jesuit authors state with perfect clarity the essentials of the Chinese system. Thus Le Comte, in a letter to the Cardinal D'Estrees *On the policy and government of the Chinese*, writes [1] : ' Nobility is never hereditary, neither is there any distinction between the qualities of people, saving what the offices which they execute make ; so that excepting the family of Confucius, the whole kingdom is divided into magistracy and commonalty. There are no lands but what are held by socage tenure, not even those lands which are destined for the *bonzes* or which belong to the temples of the idols. So that their gods, as well as men, are subjected to the state, and are obliged by taxes and contributions to acknowledge the Emperor's supremacy. When a viceroy or governor of a province is dead, his children, as well as others, have their fortunes to make, and if they inherit not their father's virtue and ingenuity, his name which they bear, be it never so famous, gives them no quality at all.'

In order to appreciate the force of such passages for a French reader it is only necessary to consider what was the normal social structure of European states at the beginning of the eighteenth century. It was characterized by

[1] *Memoirs*, p. 282.

the existence of privileged orders of nobility and clergy distinct from the civil administration of the Crown and by important fiscal immunities of landed property. This situation was the result of a compromise, a compromise that had not made for social cohesion and stability. In most European countries at the end of the Middle Age the Crown had gained power at the expense of the feudal aristocracy and of the international Catholic Church. The struggle had ended not in the destruction of the older forces, but in an accommodation whereby the Church and the nobility lost nearly all their political powers but retained most of their social and economic privileges.

The position of landed aristocracy in the eighteenth century varied in different European countries. In England, owing to the parliamentary constitution, it was really a ' ruling class,' though it had to share power up to a point with the mercantile interest. In Poland it was also a ruling class, but in the mediaeval and feudal sense, for the Polish *pans* were still able to levy private war with their retainers. In Russia the Government was formally an autocracy, but the imperial guards, a force recruited from the nobility, disposed of the throne. In France, however, as also in Spain, Austria and the larger German states, the typical compromise had been reached, and a socially privileged but politically powerless nobility co-existed with a centralized absolute monarchy. As Professor F. C. Montague says [1] : ' The French nobles as a class were without political power. . . . For centuries the Crown with its lawyers and officials had been sapping the power of the *noblesse*, and had at length reduced it to political nullity. The nobles had lost all voice in making laws and levying taxes when the States-General ceased to meet. The bureaucracy had carefully stripped them of administrative power in their respective neighbourhoods. . . . The French noble had no opportunity of combining with his fellows or of offering himself as a leader to the commons.' But the nobles were exempt from the bulk of the direct

[1] *Cambridge Modern History*, vol. VIII, ch. II, p. 57.

taxes, a few of them possessed immense wealth, and all had rights which were oppressive to the peasantry and offensive to the *bourgeois*. They retained as one of their privileges their old feudal jurisdictions in petty cases with the result that ' writers of repute have reckoned in France on the eve of the Revolution at least three hundred and sixty distinct bodies of law, in force sometimes throughout a whole province, sometimes in a much smaller area.' [1]

The Church since the Reformation had ceased to be the deposer of kings, and had become generally the docile auxiliary of the state. In Protestant countries separate churches had been established, in Catholic ones the international organization remained, but Crown patronage was stronger in each state than ultramontane pretensions. In return for its subservience the Church retained great privileges ; in France the Crown was pledged to extirpate heresy, and the clergy disposed of revenues equal to about half those of the state from tithes and landed property with tax exemptions. One consequence of the system under the compromise was that the open career in the Church was greatly reduced, and lucrative ecclesiastical office came to be monopolized by the noble caste ; ' all the archbishoprics, all but five of the bishoprics, all the commendatory abbeys, the commanderies of the Knights of Malta, and the noble Chapters of men and women, were reserved for persons of gentle birth, who received in this way a large proportion of the enormous ecclesiastical revenue.' [2]

Opposite in interest to these privileged orders was a class which, though unprivileged, had traditions of political power, and was being made ever more important by the course of economic development. The *bourgeois* like the feudal noble and the bishop had had his day of power in the loose-knit society of the Middle Age ; he had been lord in the free cities and communes. The centralization of the French monarchy had extinguished the liberties of the towns just as it had subdued the feudal chivalry and nationalized the Church. Socially the *bourgeois* suffered

---

[1] F. C. Montague, *op. cit.*, p. 49.  [2] *Op. cit.*, p. 55.

more by the process than did the noble or the cleric ; he was swallowed up in a great community of predominantly rural economy, and relegated to an inferior status ill-suited to the old civic pride. He could indeed purchase offices which conferred nobility, but the lot of the *parvenu* in the aristocratic order was not a pleasant one, and the *bourgeoisie* as a class chafed at a system which with all the expansion of commerce and increase of mercantile wealth left it less dignity and initiative than it had possessed in the thirteenth century. It had certainly gained new openings in commerce from the centralized monarchy, and these had long reconciled it to its social and political disabilities, but in the eighteenth century disastrous wars lost French trade and colonies, and made it the enemy of the Bourbon monarchy and of the privileged orders. It had no means of controlling State policy, but it was strong enough and self-willed enough to be dangerous. It had been more successful in the race for the profits of European colonialism than had the Spanish, but less successful than the English, and envy of the English prosperity turned to admiration of the institutions under which that prosperity had been achieved. The victories of England in war disproved the assertion that only autocracy could be efficient ; the French *bourgeois* saw his English rival sharing in political power through parliamentary representation, operating through joint-stock companies far less subject to government control than the French, and generally free from the innumerable petty restrictions and vexatious local taxes with which officialdom, feudal survivals and an antiquated guild system combined to harass and obstruct French trade. When finally the French State from its financial rake's progress was threatened with bankruptcy, the French social system with its fiscal immunities was felt to be intolerable, and the temper of the *bourgeoisie* became revolutionary.

With a society so complex and internally discordant as that of eighteenth-century France there could be no one all-powerful social philosophy. The warfare of interests was reflected in the realm of ideas, and provoked sceptical inquiry into first principles. The constitutional struggles of the previous century in England had already produced a great literature of controversy in political theory, culminating in Locke, whose work became the starting-point for the French Enlightenment. Not only politics, but also religion was involved, for the problem of the relations of Church and State could not be treated without consideration of religious dogmas. The progress of natural science and the great triumph of Newton had given a new confidence in the power of human reason ; the rationalism of the scientist was brought out from the study into the *salon* and from the *salon* into the market-place, and everything was subjected to criticism.

In eighteenth-century France there grew up two distinct schools of thought with proposals for social change. They may be distinguished as the liberals and the neo-monarchists. The former included all who believed in popular sovereignty and parliamentary institutions, whether they favoured a constitutional monarchy of the English type or a republic. The neo-monarchists consisted of those who wished to sweep away noble and clerical privilege, and yet distrusted parliamentarism and democracy ; they were the advocates of 'enlightened despotism.' They hoped to make the French monarchy itself the instrument of reform ; they desired it to renew its former warfare against the nobles and the Church, and to save itself by jettisoning the social anomalies with which it was associated, by making an end of the fiscal immunities and the survivals of feudalism.

Each of these reform parties had its own models and authorities to quote in controversy. The liberals appealed either to the present success of parliamentarist England or to the Roman tradition. The neo-monarchists found their exemplar and vindication in China. The reason for their cult of China is really very simple. They appealed to Asia because there was nothing in the past of Europe on which they could take their stand. The whole past and present of Europe was infected with the political tendencies which they disliked. If they went back to the Middle Age they found there feudalism and clericalism and free cities ; if they went to the Classical Age they were everywhere confronted by republics. How could they even appeal unto Cæsar when Cæsar had been a leader of the Roman democrats, and Rome had never to the end abandoned the doctrine that sovereignty belonged to the Roman people and was only delegated to the emperors by election ? The tradition of Rome indeed provided no secure foundation for the apologetic of monarchy, and soon the republicans captured it almost entirely for their own use. But in the Far East was an empire as old as Rome, yet alive in the present, as populous as the whole of Europe, free from privileges of caste nobility and Church, ruled by heaven-bestowed royalty through a bureaucracy of scholar-officials. Here was the model for the neo-monarchists, and an example to quote. Against the priesthood that held the keys of heaven and hell, against the *noblesse de l'épée*, and against the republican heroes of Livy and Plutarch the neo-monarchists arrayed Confucius and the silk-gowned mandarins. For the enthusiasts of the China cult distance only lent enchantment to the view. ' China,' wrote Poivre in 1769,[1] ' offers an enchanting picture of what the whole world might become, if the laws of that empire were to become the laws of all nations. Go to Peking ! Gaze upon the mightiest of mortals ; he is the true and perfect image of Heaven.'

It was admitted that in the mathematical and natural sciences China was far behind Europe. But it was held that the Chinese had attained a peculiar eminence in *scientia politicomoralis*. ' They have,' said Voltaire,[2] ' perfected moral science, and that is the first of the sciences.' Translations of Confucius were widely read, and the normal feeling of the French Enlightenment for the Chinese sage is expressed in lines quoted by Voltaire :

[1] *Voyages d'un Philosophe*, p. 148.
[2] *Oeuvres complètes*, Gotha, 1785, XVI, 85.

De la seule raison salutaire interprète,
Sans éblouir le monde, éclairant les esprits,
Il ne parla qu'en sage, et jamais en prophète ;
Cependant on le crût, et même en son pays.

' *Jamais en prophète* ' might be taken as the motto of the Enlightenment. The eighteenth-century French ' philosophers ', whether liberals or neo-monarchists in politics, were nearly all deists, believers in a common-sense ' natural religion ' without miracle, revelation or sacrament, a religion which would provide a basis for morality without giving an opening for clericalism and priestcraft. Precedents for deism were to be found in the pre-Christian age of Europe, and the movement was largely influenced by the Stoic tradition. But nowhere in European pagan antiquity had a philosophy of this type been formally adopted by the state as Confucianism had been in China. In China the deists believed that they saw ' the religion of the philosopher ' as the national cult.

The Jesuits had freely admitted the excellence of Chinese ethical doctrine ; it did not disturb them, for it was their position that the existence of God and moral obligation could be established by reason, but that revealed dogma was necessary for salvation. Le Comte writes in a letter to the Archbishop of Rheims,[1] after quoting from the Confucian classics : ' By this scantling of Confucius his philosophy you may judge, my Lord, that reason is of all times and of all places. Seneca hath spoken nothing better, and had I the leisure, as I have the design, to make an entire collection of the maxims of our philosopher, peradventure no requisite would be wanting to give him a place amongst our sages of antiquity.'

In the generation after Le Comte Reichwein declares [2] that ' the headquarters of Catholic theology, the University of Paris, was the centre of the enthusiasm for China.' Leibnitz likewise combined Christian faith with an intense admiration for Confucian China, and even went so far as

---

[1] *Memoirs*, p. 210.  [2] Reichwein, *op. cit.*, p. 85.

to suggest that ' Chinese missionaries should be sent to us
to teach us the aim and practice of natural theology, as we
send missionaries to them to instruct them in revealed
theology.' But Wolff was expelled from Halle for an
address *De Sinarum philosophia practica* in which praise of
Confucius seemed to verge on the negation of Christianity.
And Voltaire and the deists boldly turned against the
Church the admiration of China which the Catholic missionaries had fostered, and used the example of China to
prove that France might be virtuous and well-governed
without a clergy holding one-fifth of her land.

The thinkers of the Enlightenment were preoccupied, not
with the destiny of the soul, but with secular ethics, and they
believed they saw in China a society founded on the highest
moral principles. They tended to account a virtue even
that which earlier European observers had regarded as the
most serious defect in the character of the Chinese—their
lack of martial courage. Before the eighteenth century the
Chinese weakness in arms had forfeited the respect of even
the most sympathetic Europeans. Ricci remarks contemptu-
ously that ' running away is no dishonour with them ; they
do not know what an insult is.' Le Comte [1] declares that
the Chinese army is ' numerous, well looked after, duly
paid and exactly disciplined . . . yet soon broke, and by
the least thing in the world put into disorder. The occasion
of this I apprehend to be, because in the education of their
youth they never instil into them principles of honour and
bravery, as we do as soon as ever they are big enough to
know what weapons are. The Chinese are always talking
to their children of gravity, policy, law and government ;
they always set books and letters in their view, but never a
sword into their hands. . . . The Chinese policy hinders
hereby a great many domestic feuds and disturbances, but
at the same time it does expose its subjects hereby to the
insults of foreigners, which is ten times worse.'

The traditions, indeed, both of ancient and mediaeval
Europe laid stress on the military virtues ; the city-states,

[1] *Memoirs,* p. 306.

which depended for their defence on citizen armies, and the feudal aristocracies, which were founded on military service, alike attached the greatest importance to valour in arms as a moral quality. In the seventeenth century France had been intoxicated with military power and glory. But with the failure of the attempt to dominate Europe there was a revulsion of feeling against militarism in France, and we have to wait for the Revolution and Napoleon to bring back the cult of *la gloire*. The prevailing temper in the eighteenth century is civilian, cosmopolitan, unpatriotic and pacific. People ceased to take seriously the dynastic wars fought with small professional armies ; the day of the ' nation in arms ' and the great patriotic hatreds was not yet. The export of fashion-dolls from Paris to Vienna went on without interruption through the War of the Spanish Succession.[1] In this age the Chinese lack of martial prowess did not seem so reprehensible ; on the contrary it was interpreted as a sign of superior culture, and stress was laid on the fact that the Chinese had absorbed all the warlike barbarians that had conquered them.

This was the point of view maintained by Voltaire against Rousseau. Rousseau heralds the return of patriotic passion ; for him a man's highest virtue is his willingness to die for his country in war. Attacking the fashionable cult of China he writes : ' If the sciences really purified morals, if they really taught men to shed their blood for the fatherland, if they inspired courage, then the people of China would assuredly be wise, free and invincible. . . . If neither the ability of its ministers nor the alleged wisdom of its laws nor even the numberless multitude of its inhabitants have been able to protect this realm against subjection by ignorant and rude barbarians [i.e. the Manchus], of what service have been all its wise men ? ' Voltaire sought to rebut these attacks ; he claimed that civilization must always prevail ultimately by its moral superiority over a barbarous militarism.

Voltaire indeed roundly asserted [2] that ' the organization

[1] Reichwein, *op. cit.*, p. 75.    [2] *Oeuvres complètes*, XXXVIII, 492.

of their [the Chinese] empire is in truth the best that the world has ever seen.' A similar opinion was expressed in *Le despotisme de la Chine* (1767) by Quesnay, the leader of the philosophic sect known as the *Économistes* or *Physiocrates* and the most notable theorist of the neo-monarchist school.

Quesnay (1694–1774—he was born in the same year as Voltaire) was an advocate of enlightened despotism, and his aim was to expound the content of the adjective. For him enlightenment in a ruler consisted in recognizing the principles of the ' natural order ' and making legislation conform thereto. When the king has reformed legislation he should then ' do nothing, but let the laws rule ' ; this is the *wu wei* of the Chinese ideal monarch.

The ' natural order,' according to Quesnay,[1] is ' the supreme rule of all human lawgiving, of all political, economic and social action.' He conceives it chiefly in terms of the economic life, and works out a system which borrows much from European social contract doctrines but much also from classical Chinese theory. All wealth consists ultimately of materials derived from land (by agriculture, mining, lumbering, etc.) ; real wealth is the ' net product,' the balance of the total output of such materials over the cost of production. The manufacturer and the merchant in this theory are ' useful,' but ' sterile ' ; they depend on the supply of raw materials, to which they do not add, but transform, transport or sell them. The revenues of the State, like all other incomes, must really come out of the ' net product ' ; hence the most simple and just method of taxation is a single *impôt territorial* laid on the producing capacity of land. The care of the State should be devoted to encouraging primary production and increasing the ' net product,' and manufactures and commerce should be left to adjust themselves according to demand. The efforts of government to control trade by monopolies and to stimulate manufactures by protection do not create wealth, but only interfere with the natural processes of distribution ; they are violations of the ' natural order.'

[1] *Oeuvres économiques et philosophiques*, ed. Oncken, p. 375.

Most of Quesnay's economic reasoning was fallacious, but in his time and country it had great force from the way in which it lent itself to contemporary social tendencies. By his theory of taxation Quesnay struck at the fiscal immunities of landed property. Further by his doctrine of free trade he won for his enlightened despotism a following among the *bourgeois* who had come to dislike bureaucratic interference in industry and commerce almost as much as they did noble and clerical privilege. Quesnay indeed gave the first systematic exposition of free trade doctrine, and his teaching of government non-interference in economic distribution was one of the most powerful factors in thought preparing the way for the French Revolution.

What is remarkable is that this free trade doctrine so welcome to the rising *bourgeois* class and so revolutionary in its tendency, was for Quesnay the corollary of an economic theory appropriate to conditions almost prehistoric as far as Europe is concerned. The doctrine that land is the source of all wealth belongs to the ideology of pure land-revenue economy untouched by city-state commercialism ; it is approximately correct for the early riverine cultures where civilized life grows up on the surplus of agriculture. It is in fact ancient Chinese doctrine, and there can be little doubt that it was chiefly because of his admiration for Chinese philosophy that Quesnay, a scholar and a theorist and not a man of affairs,[1] came to elaborate a theory which was really quite out of place in the world of already complex capitalist-commercial economy in which he lived. The philosophy of *laissez-faire* destined to become the creed of the *bourgeois* radicals was deduced from a theory which denied that commerce increased wealth ; Quesnay's free trade was an inference in the light of modern conditions from primitive economic thinking which hardly gave any account of trade at all.

The doctrine of the net product did not really provide a satisfactory basis for the full free trade philosophy, since

[1] Quesnay was by profession a court surgeon and physician ; he was thus in contact with politics, but not at all involved in them.

its logical implication was that all middleman profits
between the primary producer and the consumer should
be reduced as far as possible, the trader being only an agent
of exchange to be paid out of the net product.  Hence there
was a strong case for government intervention to prevent
speculation and profiteering in the interest of the community, and such intervention was a commonplace of
Chinese legislation ; indeed, nowhere was trade actually
more restricted by bureaucratic regulations than in China.
The Physiocrats agreed up to a point with the view that only
a minimum share of the net product should go to the trader.
But they were less concerned with the measures a government
might take to limit speculation than with the legislation of
mercantilism, the legacy of Colbert.

It is necessary to distinguish two kinds of government
interference with trade, springing from quite different
motives though often fused together in a single piece of
legislation.  The first has as its aim the limitation of trade
profits in the supposed interest of the community ; its
extreme form is socialism.  The other kind is the use of
state power to promote national industry and commerce
by means of navigation acts, monopolies, protective tariffs
and so on.  The latter type of state intervention is fundamentally different from the first in that its object is not to
repress the mercantile class, but rather to serve its interests,
the state receiving its reward in the shape of increased
revenue and national power.  Mercantilism was indeed a
partnership between the state and the mercantile class
which was for a while very useful to both parties.  But when
capitalism came of age, the partnership became irksome to
the traders and manufacturers, and they conceived their
interest to lie in its dissolution.  The *bourgeois* found that the
state was making more use of him than he could make of
the state, and the contention that the paternal regulation
was for his own good only gave him a pretext for revolt,
since he claimed to know his own interest better than a
government official could know it for him.  The phrase
which became the motto of the *bourgeois* was uttered by a

manufacturer when Colbert asked what he could do for industry ; ' *Laissez-nous faire* ' was the reply.

Free trade theory was therefore in the beginning directed against the mercantilist legislation which sought to promote trade expansion, but had in practice become inconvenient to the majority of the *bourgeois*. Soon the theory was extended to apply to all checks on capitalist enterprise. This development involved the abandonment of the net product doctrine, and that step was taken by Adam Smith. He was influenced by the Physiocrats, but was a stranger to the Chinese studies which influenced *them* ; he is thoroughly European in his mental outlook.

Apart from their contributions to the theory of free trade the Physiocrats are historically important for their part in the history of education. They led the way in the eighteenth century in demanding that education should be secularized and that it should be made universal. Universal state education was to become an ideal of the liberals, and to be carried into practice in the nineteenth century. But the liberals' theory of education differed from that of the Physiocrats. The former regarded it as a right of the individual, ' the right of every child to be properly trained for life ' ; the latter conceived it primarily as an interest of the state, which required for its well-being that its subjects should be instructed in approved social doctrine, and that the best available talent should be brought out and enlisted in the public service. This was in accordance with the Physiocrats' idea of enlightened despotism, and it had obvious reference to the Chinese model which they had always in view. In China education was essentially related to the state in a way without parallel in Europe under the *ancien régime*. The system of public competitive examination gave an open career through local graduation up to the Hanlin Academy, and made an education centred on social theory the sole key to civil office. Quesnay, like all the Sinophils of his time, was a great admirer of this system, and desired something like it for Europe ; he held that the public welfare depended on the study of the ' natural order,' i.e. of the right constitution of human society,[1] and that it was the first duty of a ruler to promote education in this. But, he declares, ' with the exception of China,[2] the necessity of this institution, which is the foundation of government, has been ignored by all kingdoms.'

For a year and a half (1774–6) French neo-monarchism was put to the test of practice with Turgot, disciple of the Physiocrats, as comptroller-general, and the experiment proved that nothing could be done on those lines. Turgot must rank as one of the great men of the eighteenth century ; he was intelligent, able and sincere, but the forces of opposition he aroused were too strong for him. The court life of the Bourbons was too much entangled with the aristocracy and the Church for a minister to attack the privileged orders, and the reform was to come, not through the monarchy, but through the States-General. With the Revolution enlightened despotism on the Chinese model ceased to be an idea for practical politics. Royalty was now welded with aristocracy and clericalism in a solid conservative *bloc* opposed to the new *bourgeois* ascendency which was republican and democratic. Neither side had any use for Chinese political theory.

Because of the almost complete extinction of the cult of China after 1789 the great majority of European historians have failed to do justice to the influence of Chinese ideas in eighteenth-century Europe. They have dismissed the cult as a mere freak of fashion, or as a Utopian fantasy assuming the name of China but having no relation to the real China or its culture. Such an estimate entirely overlooks the facilities which the eighteenth century had for a knowledge

[1] The theory of the natural order was itself of European descent, being mainly derived from the Stoics and Roman jurists, but in the eighteenth century it was modified by Chinese conceptions. Cf. the opening lines of the *Chung-yung* : ' The endowment of Heaven is nature ; accordance with nature is right way (*tao*) ; cultivation of right way is education.'

[2] Quesnay undoubtedly had an exaggerated idea of the actual extent of education in China. But he was right as regards the importance attached to such education in Chinese political theory.

of China. Besides the immense quantity of Chinese art objects of which we have spoken in considering the Rococo style, there were current a number of astonishingly accurate descriptions of China and its institutions, and tolerable translations of the most important works of Chinese philosophical literature. In spite of the advances which specialized sinological scholarship made in the nineteenth century, it is true to say that the ordinary educated public was better informed about China in the eighteenth.

The eclipse of Chinese cultural prestige after 1789 is not hard to explain quite apart from the fact that the new social alignment in Europe made Chinese ideas irrelevant politically. For one thing China itself in the nineteenth century was not what it had been in the eighteenth ; the Ch'ing dynasty was in decay, population was overflowing, the administrative mechanism was getting out of order, Chinese art had fallen into decadence. There were no longer Jesuit courtier scholars in Peking, and as the mandarinate grew more and more suspicious and hostile towards foreign penetration, whether religious or commercial, so the opinions of China spread by missionaries and traders grew more and more unfavourable.[1] But China's decline and aggravated troubles over missions and trade were only minor factors in the change of view. The great cause was the prodigious progress of European civilization, which now began to move on a plane altogether above that of the Chinese. The industrial revolution and the era of steam gave to Europeans a sense of superior power and efficiency such as they had never had before. And not only in natural science, commerce and invention, but likewise in that moral science which Voltaire thought the Chinese had perfected the European now felt himself to be pre-eminent. The Englishman especially, who was the chief representative of Europe in relations with China during the nineteenth century, had ascended by 1850 to a moral elevation which would have

[1] The traders' reports on China had from the beginning been generally unfavourable ; compare quotations in Morse, *The East India Company trading to China*, vol. I.

been incredible to his great-grandfather. It could no longer be said in English politics that 'every man has his price,' and the Englishman might now be shocked at the venality of the mandarins. The Regency was past, and with Queen Victoria on the throne he might shake his head over the evils of oriental licentiousness. Slavery had been abolished in the British dominions in 1833, and he could now speak freely of the disregard for the sacredness of human personality shown by Asiatics. His Parliament in 1818, after four rejections of the bill, had abolished the sentence of death for stealing goods worth five shillings from a shop, and soon it was possible to talk about the lack of humane feeling among non-Christian peoples. In 1814, after one rejection of the bill, his Parliament had consented to abolish disembowelling alive as part of the statutory penalty for treason, and henceforth the Englishman could express his disgust at the atrocities of the Chinese penal code. With so much moral progress it is no wonder that England and Europe as a whole ceased to entertain the admiration for Chinese rationality and virtue which had been prevalent in the eighteenth century.

Nevertheless the course of events in recent times has vindicated in a measure the Sinophilism of Voltaire and Quesnay. For the last sixty years the British civil service has been recruited on the principle of open competitive examination, and since 1882 the 'merit' has been gaining against the 'spoils' system in the United States. It has come to be recognized that the offices of the permanent administration cannot be abandoned to democratic partisan patronage any more than to mere royal favouritism or caste privilege, but that the vast complexity of the modern state requires the most rigorous selection according to intellectual qualifications. And the events of the last two decades have compelled admission that the sovereign peoples may not be able to maintain civilization unless they can think more constructively than hitherto on social and inter-national questions. To make the political animal able to bear the stress of civilized life in the age of machine power—

that is the task of the twentieth century, and the recognition of it marks the end of the belief once common that man needs only better machines and better salesmanship in order to reach the millennium.    Education of the electorate for the solution of the menacing evils of the body politic has become the most imperative need of the time, and the problem is no easy one.    Fascism and Communism have chosen the old way of uniformity of thought and the persecution of heresy ;   each trains its youth in its own social doctrine secluded from rival opinions.    The countries of free speech have a harder task, yet one which promises a greater success if failure can be avoided ;   they must give a moral and political education to the young where every moral and political issue is the subject of acute controversy.

The study of social man is to be again the central science. Not through any devaluation of the other sciences, but because the other sciences ultimately depend for their value on the maintenance of civilized life, which is the activity of men in a society.    No knowledge of the stars or of plants or of electricity avails a humanity that does not know itself ; without the intelligence that can harness human passions the science that discovers the effects of diphenylchlorarsine on the human body is but an instrument of suffering and death.    But what is this if not to admit the principle to which the Chinese have held more steadfastly than any other people, the principle that the study and understanding of social man should be the premier subject of education and the indispensable preparation for political responsibility ?

# INDEX